I0822984

PRAISE FOR

WHERE THE EARTH MEETS THE SKY

"*Where the Earth Meets the Sky* is an elegant and insightful memoir set in seemingly bleak and featureless Antarctica but made rich and textured through the sharp eyes of Louise K. Blight. There is serious work being done here—a study of penguins, a study of humans—but also humour, curiosity, and reverence for every creature who spends their days and lives trying to make sense of this beguiling corner of the world."

—Harley Rustad, author of *Lost in the Valley of Death: A Story of Obsession and Danger in the Himalayas*

"Louise K. Blight paints a vivid portrait of a harsh and unforgiving landscape in *Where the Earth Meets the Sky*, succeeding in making the inhospitable seem inviting. Surrounded only by penguins—and a few lovable curmudgeons—Blight weaves a captivating memoir of a field season spent on the White Continent. Full of scientific curiosity, and equal parts illuminating prose and wry humour, *Where the Earth Meets the Sky* is a wonderful addition to Antarctica's rich literary history, told from the unique perspective of a wildlife biologist. . . . A heart-tugging requiem for Antarctica's imperiled penguins."

—Gloria Dickie, author of *Eight Bears: Mythic Past and Imperiled Future*

"Stunning. Part love story for the wildest place on Earth, part meditation on what we've lost, Louise K. Blight combines a scientist's clarity and rigour with an artist's appreciation of landscape and language to create a hauntingly beautiful depiction of her season studying Adélie penguins at a remote Antarctic field station. *Where the Earth Meets the Sky* gives us brilliantly rendered sketches of people, place, and penguins; fascinating, funny, insightful—and occasionally bizarre—details of an isolated, stripped-down life and its effect on those who live it; an ultimately positive personal trajectory; and a powerful testimony to the vital importance of the Ross Sea as the most intact marine ecosystem on Earth."

—Kate Rawles, author of *The Life Cycle: 8,000 Miles in the Andes by Bamboo Bike*

"Louise K. Blight presents an intriguing theatre of emotions, a fascinating world of highs and lows where ice, humans, and birds interact. At the centre of this evocative book is a small team of dedicated scientists and their support crew surviving in the cold, snowy, windswept wastes, while studying these amazing and lovable birds. But it is the small community of academics and support crew, isolated at the end of the world, which provides a fascinating mix of harmony and conflict. The wonder, beauty, and tragedy of nature meet human love, fear, and dispute. A fascinating story of the family life of penguins and those who study them."

—Brian Hall, author of *High Risk: Climbing to Extinction*

"*Where the Earth Meets the Sky* vividly chronicles the experience of working in Antarctica in a moment of profound change, capturing not just Blight's delight in the penguins she studies, but also the strange isolation and intense closeness of life in the most remote place on Earth and the transformative power of the landscape. Deeply felt and expansive, it is a reminder that science is, at its heart, a deeply human endeavour."

—James Bradley, author of *Deep Water: The World in the Ocean*

"There is so much to praise about Louise K. Blight's multi-layered account of her season as a researcher on Ross Island, but for me there are two standouts: her lyrical portrayals of Antarctica's ever-changing skies, landscapes, ice, and weather; and how she brings us deeply into the world of Adélie penguins, and her interactions with them. Her description of skiing back to camp alongside curious penguins tobogganing on their bellies will never leave me."

—Maria Coffey, author of *Where the Mountain Casts Its Shadow* and *Instead*

WHERE THE EARTH MEETS THE SKY

WHERE THE EARTH MEETS THE SKY

A STORY OF PENGUINS, PEOPLE, AND PLACE IN ANTARCTICA

LOUISE K. BLIGHT

PEGASUS BOOKS
NEW YORK LONDON

WHERE THE EARTH MEETS THE SKY

Pegasus Books, Ltd.
148 West 37th Street, 12th Floor
New York, NY 10018

First Pegasus Books cloth edition April 2026

Design by Talia Abramson
Typeset by Daniella Zanchetta and Six Red Marbles
Original map design by Alexandra King. Reproduction by Talia Abramson
Interior photos courtesy of the author

Library of Congress Cataloging-in-Publication Data is available.

ISBN: 979-8-89710-060-6

10 9 8 7 6 5 4 3 2 1

Printed in the United States of America
Distributed by Simon & Schuster
www.pegasusbooks.com

For the birds.

One day recently, while I was in Atlantic City doing some writing, the elevator man in my hotel remarked to me, "It must be mighty quiet down there around the South Pole."

"Yes," I replied, "it is. That's why I like it."

—LINCOLN ELLSWORTH, *MY FLIGHT ACROSS ANTARCTICA*, 1936

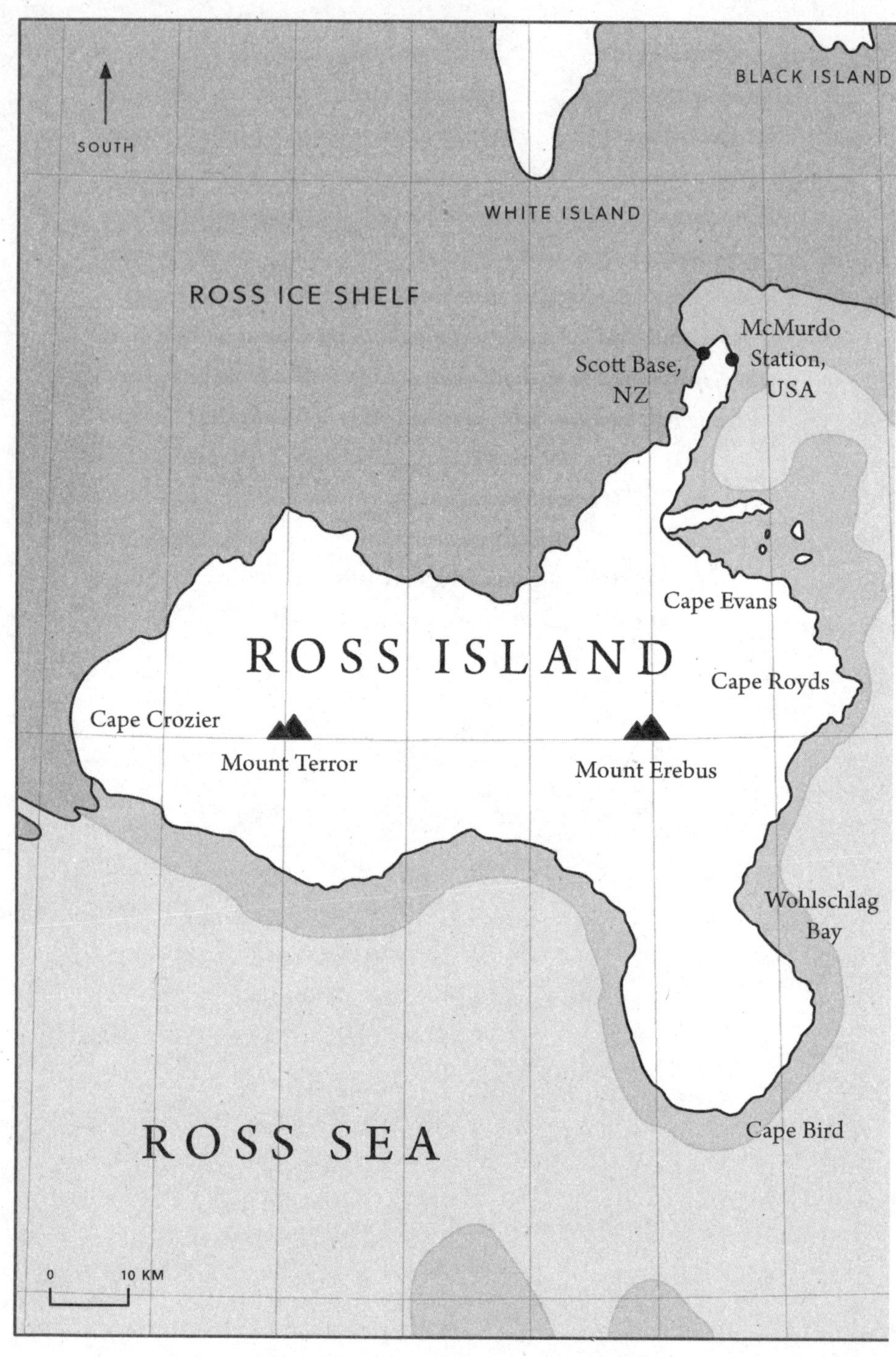
SOUTH
BLACK ISLAND
WHITE ISLAND
ROSS ICE SHELF
McMurdo Station, USA
Scott Base, NZ
Cape Evans
ROSS ISLAND
Cape Royds
Cape Crozier
Mount Terror
Mount Erebus
Wohlschlag Bay
Cape Bird
ROSS SEA
0
10 KM

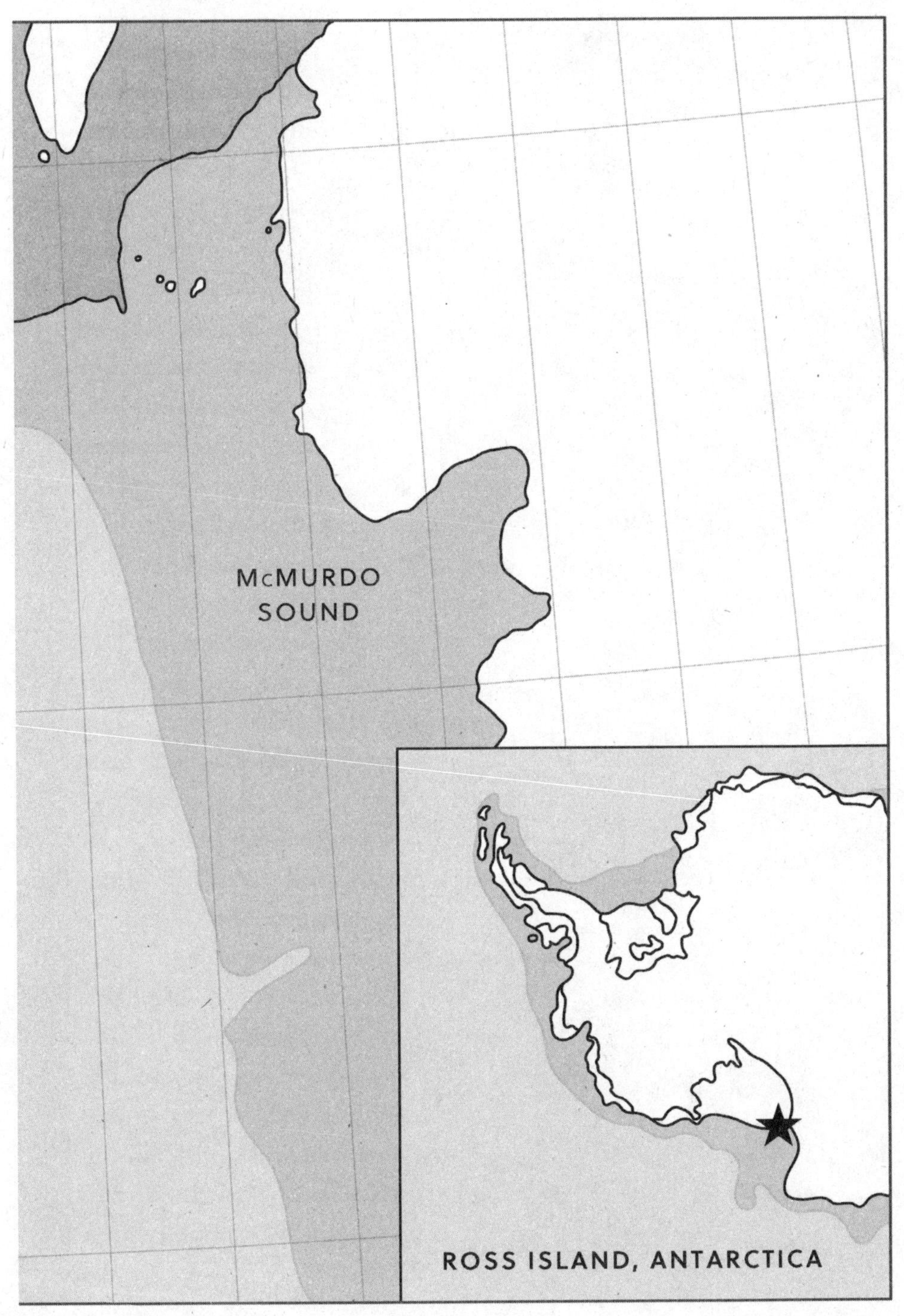
McMURDO
SOUND
ROSS ISLAND, ANTARCTICA

AUTHOR'S NOTE

IN EARLY 2024, after a second season of record-low Antarctic sea ice, news outlets around the world reported mass breeding failure at 20 percent of the world's emperor penguin colonies, following early fast ice break-out in December and January. Emperors need fast ice—ice that is frozen fast to the shoreline or an overland ice shelf—to lay their eggs and raise their young. But when the ice breaks up before the chicks have fully grown their adult plumage, many are forced to enter the sea too early, where they will either freeze to death, or drown.

However, 2023 saw fewer breeding failures than 2022. Some of the emperor penguin colonies that had failed subsequently re-formed on more stable ice or large icebergs, where the birds were safe to breed the following season. Do such adaptations provide hope that penguins may be able to adjust to a changing Antarctic, at least over the short term?

When I first travelled to work there as a young ecologist, Antarctica felt so far away that it seemed untouchable. Its very existence appeared to be a mystery to most people, at least in the northern hemisphere. "Oh, you're going to the South Pole!" they would exclaim, as if the entire continent could be reduced to a point on a map. I heard this response as much from the well-travelled airline employees checking me in at flight counters as I did from family and friends. However, with the advance of the twenty-first century, Antarctica has begun to intrude into our headlines. With its collapsing ice shelves, melting ice sheets, and record-high temperatures, the place has become emblematic of a changing planet. But the reality is that humanity has been altering Antarctica since the ships of sealers and whalers first plied its icebound waters. What has changed so suddenly is the scope and the reach of human impact. This is a story of an Antarctica on the cusp of that change.

In the summer of 2003, after travelling to Antarctica as a tour guide more times than I could count, I was offered the opportunity to live on the frozen continent working as a field assistant to one of the world's most renowned penguin scientists. I would be situated for an entire field season at Ross Island, one of the most remote research sites on the planet, and the place from which British explorer Robert Falcon Scott had begun his race for the South Pole. My previous Antarctic trips had all been stints aboard luxury cruise ships, where my roles included naturalist, Zodiac driver, and visiting scientist; and while these ships sailed about as far from civilization as is possible on the face of the earth, on board we were never far from being handed a glass of champagne in a warm and well-appointed lounge. Understandably, the comfort and safety of the passengers was always the focus of those trips; science there took a back seat.

In contrast, the work on Ross Island offered the chance to live with just one other person in a rudimentary hut far from even the basic amenities offered by the nearest research station, and to spend each day doing nothing other than studying penguins, and surviving. There was to be no finery, no comfort, and precious little warmth; but there would be plenty of time to live among wild birds, coming face to face with them each day in their own world. Simply being with them as they went about their lives. At the time it sounded like a dream come true, and in many ways it was—although I never dreamed how much the experience would consume my soul while I was there, and how it would haunt me for years to come. In fact, this experience never left me: the spare beauty of Antarctica—that hypnotic, monochromatic land of rock and ice—and the trusting nature of its animal inhabitants, who have not evolved a fear of people, had such a transformative effect that the feeling of it still remains in my bones. That particular place and time showed me more than any previous wilderness or fieldwork episode just how much there is to gain from listening to the natural world.

In a sense this experience was nothing revelatory. It was more of a return to some ancient and wiser way—after all, a longing to be one with creation is a yearning as old as humankind. The British essayist John Berger pointed out that before the "rupture"[1] that severed Western society from the rest of nature, non-human animals were everywhere with humans, at the centre of our lives. To be held in the gaze of a wild animal remains a primordial thrill, one that takes us back to a place beyond remembering. There is a profound sweetness in opening oneself to the natural world: We feel it when sitting on a quiet seashore, or at sunset while watching a flock of birds skim the unbroken surface of an evening pond, or while contemplating a dawn sky lightening beyond the ridge of a distant mountain. But such moments of oneness with the earth are ever harder to find on our increasingly crowded planet, and the loss of this fundamental relationship pervades our society now, a deep but almost forgotten grief. We are wounded by the loss of our connection with wild beings and wild places without quite knowing what it is that we have lost.

The Canadian landscape artist E. J. Hughes said that he painted as a form of worship, because the world is so wonderful. In the same vein, I wanted to write this book as a way of bearing witness to the world's beauty. And as a way of bearing witness to what we are losing from it. This is a story of falling in love with a wild place—and of what can be learned from penguins, other wild creatures, and the coldest, most isolated place on Earth. That we as humans are not central to life, but are mere specks carried along by its flow: important, but no more so than anything else. And that nature is indifferent to all human suffering—and yet, paradoxically, it holds the key to our healing from it.

PROLOGUE

*In a white world there are many words to describe the whiteness. Fast ice, brash ice, nilas, bergy bits, growlers, pack ice, ground blizzard, pancake ice, grease ice, sastrugi, graupel . . .**

THE ANTARCTIC WIND hammers my tent. Despite being thousands of kilometres from the sounds of civilization I have gone to bed wearing earplugs, as I have every night since I've been here. Even on a calm evening the tent is a noisy place to sleep, with the cold air that constantly flows down from the Polar Plateau flapping and snapping the nylon around me with a sound like luffing sails in a squally breeze.

It is easy to see why a century ago the men from Antarctica's Heroic Age of Exploration wrote about hearing voices in the wind outside their shelters. I, too, have heard them—people calling out, footfalls, animal noises. On more fanciful nights, I ask myself whether these could be the ghostly sounds of the explorers who died here in an

---

* See Glossary

earlier era. But my companion David and I are the only people alive for many kilometres in this wilderness, and in Antarctica there are no foxes or bears.

Hours ago, a storm took hold, blasting in from the south over the continent with endlessly blowing snow. After turning in I lie restless inside my sleeping bag, trying to think of a metaphor for the noise, and finally drift into a troubled doze with the thought that it is like sleeping in a tent that has been erected on the back of a flatbed truck driving full speed down the freeway, in a hailstorm.

By early morning the winds have risen to hurricane force, and in my tortured half-awake state it seems like a giant bellows is squeezing in and out around me. The tent collapses inward until it touches my face, then blows out to the point where an exploding mess of flying poles and shredded nylon seems inevitable, then collapses inward again, repeating the motion like some giant creature breathing, until I give up on any more rest. I pull on extra layers of clothes over the wool and fleece I wear in my sleeping bag and go into the hut to start the day. The sun is up, of course, not having set for weeks now. On quiet days the calls of the penguins drift up from the nearby colony, but this morning all I can hear is the frenetic flapping of the tent, and the shriek of the frigid wind.

1

THERE EXISTS WHAT is known as a boomerang point on the flight from Christchurch, New Zealand, to McMurdo Station, Antarctica. It is literally the point of no return. Up on the flight deck of the C-141—a bare-bones military transport that looks like a 747 with any trace of comfort stripped away—the Air Force pilots constantly monitor weather satellite data with this in mind. In reality, it's the point at which the aircraft still has sufficient fuel to return home if the weather suddenly goes to hell at our destination, but to me it feels like the sort of tipping point that exists in a children's fantasy book, where the fates and the angles of the heavens align and the characters are able to slip into a parallel reality. Pass the boomerang point, and you enter Antarctica; fall short and miss it, and you're jerked back to the Real World with the sense that a state of grace has slipped through your fingers.

I am on my way to live in Antarctica for three months. I depart Canada in early November, leaving behind an intimation of winter in the air, and head toward springtime in the southern hemisphere. As a wildlife biologist I have already been lucky enough to travel many times to the frozen continent, but on previous trips I had been based on the small tourist vessels known in the trade as "expedition" cruise ships. There I worked on board as a naturalist or visiting scientist, battling seasickness while giving lectures on whales, penguins, and climate change, and censusing the seals and seabirds at the sites we visited along the Antarctic Peninsula, that skinny handle-shaped protuberance that stretches up to South America from the Antarctic continent proper. These trips helped pay my way through an undergraduate degree and an MSc in seabird ecology and provided satisfying enough work, but they mostly involved dealing with passengers and their questions: How long do penguins live? How deep do they dive? Do they bury their dead?

When I found out that I would actually be going to live in Antarctica to work on a long-term penguin study, it felt as if I'd just been told I was going to the moon. I walked around feeling lightheaded for days. It had been my childhood dream to become a biologist studying animals in faraway lands: As a girl growing up in a small town, I took notes on songbirds in summer and watched the seaducks flock in their thousands in winter, nursed a range of injured fauna—snakes and lizards, wasps and crows—back to health, and imagined a career in isolated and inhospitable places pursuing a deeper understanding of the other beings with whom we share our world. After finishing my undergraduate degree I lived in remote field camps to study seabirds on Canada's west coast, and I did a stint as a field assistant on a howler monkey project in the muggy and mosquito-infested rainforests of Belize. Despite these exposures to extremes of both beauty and adventure, they somehow never felt like what I'd had in mind as a child. The locations were remote, but not remote enough; the studies were interesting, but didn't profoundly change my understanding of the world; and, as my skills grew, I was often in charge of field logistics and boat operations, so I dealt as much with people and paperwork as I did with animals and data.

But this trip would be different. This time, three years after my latest cruise ship voyage, I would be going to Antarctica to study the world's southernmost penguins at their colonies on Ross Island, a place remote even by Antarctic standards, and one that would be blissfully free of humans. It would be the research questions of the project—*What drives the demographics of Adélie penguin populations?*—rather than those of the tourists—*Does this island go all the way down to the bottom of the sea?*—that would define our days.

Antarctica is a continent of extremes. It is the highest, driest, windiest, and coldest place on Earth, and the most inaccessible. Ross Island is as many as nine hours away via military transport flight from New Zealand, with research teams passing through the sprawling US base of McMurdo Station—situated on Ross Island's southern shore—and deploying from there into the deep field. I am to be spending the southern hemisphere's summer field season in a remote camp near the Adélie penguin colony at Cape Royds: Approximately thirty-five kilometres from McMurdo, Royds is about a twenty-minute helicopter ride or a long trek by snowmobile over the fast ice covering the ocean. Situated at Ross Island's westernmost point, Cape Royds is the place Ernest Shackleton chose for the base of his 1907–09 Nimrod Expedition, his unsuccessful attempt to be the first person to reach the South Pole. Towering above the cape is Mount Erebus, Ross Island's tallest peak and the world's southernmost active volcano. And the entire island is embedded into the edge of the Ross Ice Shelf—an immense glacial sheet the size of Spain, or two and a half Great Britains—that flows off the Antarctic continent and covers half the Ross Sea with a frozen cap several hundred metres thick.

If Ross Island is home to the world's southernmost penguins, it is also the location of some of the world's southernmost humans. Each year at its summertime peak, McMurdo Station houses over a thousand people: scientists and engineers working on research projects like sea ice studies and NASA missions, and non-scientists such as firefighters, physicians, dishwashers, heavy equipment operators, field safety trainers, administrators, and the dozens of other personnel required to run an isolated community centred around scientific research. McMurdo also supports the outlying US field camps, and serves as the waystation for people and supplies making their way to Amundsen-Scott South Pole Station (or "Pole" to the locals). Scott Base, the compact New Zealand facility that sits three kilometres to the west of McMurdo, houses eighty or more residents—or ten in winter—working in a similar diversity of roles. And although I was going to Antarctica to study penguins at their remote colonies, I was to find myself as fascinated by the continent's strange and quirky human subculture as I was by the penguins themselves. At McMurdo, I would learn that the isolation, extreme weather, and mediocre pay create a unique society that combines the banal, the bizarre, and the unexpected: Think US military infrastructure meets Burning Man.

"Men go out into the void spaces of the world for various reasons," wrote Shackleton at the start of his epic autobiography, *The Heart of the Antarctic*. "Some are actuated simply by a love of adventure, some have the keen thirst for scientific knowledge, and others again are drawn away from the trodden paths by the 'lure of little voices,' the mysterious fascination of the unknown."[2] Ever since humans set their eyes on the perennially frozen continent, the concept of Antarctica has attracted adventurers, iconoclasts, and loners—and the modern day is no exception.

I will be working on a research project that has its roots in Antarctic history, spending a season on an enterprise that in some form or another has been underway for more than fifty years. The lead scientist, David Ainley, has been working on Adélie penguins since studying them for his PhD in the late 1960s. David himself began his career with the great Bill Sladen, the man best known for his work with Canadian naturalist and inventor Bill Lishman training orphaned geese to migrate by following ultralight aircraft, popularized in the Hollywood film *Fly Away Home*. But Sladen was also a pioneering penguin biologist, and his group was one of those that spearheaded penguin research at Ross Island back in the 1960s.

"William J. L. Sladen, Expert on Penguin Libidos, Is Dead at 96" read the headline for his obituary in *The New York Times* in 2017.[3] Sladen's first trip to Antarctica was in 1948, as medical officer and biologist for an expedition led by the British explorer Vivian Fuchs (later Sir Vivian Fuchs, leader with Sir Edmund Hillary of the first overland Antarctic crossing in 1957–58). Soon after their ship dropped them off a fire destroyed their hut and supplies, killing two of his companions. The other members of the expedition were dogsledding far afield, and Sladen survived alone for more than two weeks by living in his observation tent at the nearby penguin colony, and eating members of his study population. He used his medical background to derive as much information as possible about the physiology of the Adélie penguins he ate and lived alongside—their sex, level of maturity, and more. That experience led to him switching from medicine to ornithology, more specifically to animal behaviour, where he was the first scientist to collect information from penguins individually marked with metal bands. He is also credited with being the person who first moved our understanding of these birds toward a modern scientific one instead of the quaintly anthropomorphic accounts of Edwardian naturalists—penguins as comical little men in dinner jackets—that prevailed in the Heroic Age of Antarctic Exploration. Nonetheless, it was the Heroic Age that defined the modern idea of Antarctic inquiry, despite lasting a mere twenty-five years. It began in 1897 with the Belgian Antarctic Expedition, the first group to overwinter south of the Antarctic Circle, and ended with the Shackleton-Rowett Expedition in 1922, which finished early with Shackleton's death from a heart attack at the island of South Georgia, a decade and a half after the Nimrod Expedition that saw him based at Cape Royds.

Now, with David as one of its leaders, penguin science has moved into the modern world of satellite tags (and, more recently, drones and automated underwater gliders). This particular four-year segment of the project is studying how the demography of the region's Adélie penguins is being affected by the world's largest-ever iceberg, named B-15 and literally the size of Jamaica. For the last couple of years a large portion of this berg—called B-15A—has been wedged against Ross Island and is currently responsible for restricting the ice movement patterns of half the Ross Sea. Its impact is geological in scope and life-changing for the tens of thousands of breeding penguins now rushing to mate and then rear their young. The breeding season here is short, restricted to the few weeks in summer when the sun remains above the horizon twenty-four hours a day and the sea ice retreats. The giant berg has meant that local ice break-out is late, and access to open water for foraging and travel is limited. Despite this, the penguins' egg-laying and incubation must take place in November and December as it always does, followed by chick-rearing and fledging from mid-December to February. Our field season will coincide with this portion of the birds' annual cycle, and the presence of the midnight sun.

On the flight down to New Zealand I run into David and two other team members at Los Angeles International Airport, picking them out from the lineup at security by their field clothing, unkempt hair, and mounds of gear. In research terms, David is our study's principal investigator, or PI. Like Bill Sladen, he's a legend in the world of penguin research, revered for his endless stream of publications and the ground-breaking ideas he has consistently generated over a lengthy career; he is probably the biggest thinker in his field in half a century.

He looks the part of an academic genius—a tall man with bushy eyebrows and a thick shock of grey hair. Unusually for a researcher, he has also become known to the Antarctic-loving public since he penetrated the wall between science and the rest of society by appearing in Lloyd Fales's *Wild Kingdom* documentary "Return to Penguin City" and in Werner Herzog's Oscar-nominated *Encounters at the End of the World*. He has a reputation among seabird scientists for being hard to talk to, something that has mildly concerned me since being told pre-deployment that he and I will be alone at our Cape Royds field camp. Previous brushes with isolation have taught me how communication can break down in remote places, causing a descent into a tortured and wretched world. Working in the deep field is a make-it-or-break-it thing for human relationships. By the time the season ends you're either firm friends for life—a bond born of profound mutual respect forged in the fires of some interpersonal hell—or you despise each other with a burning hatred forged in that same place. It's the isolation, of course, but it's more than that. It's something about relying on another person for your survival.

But David seems friendly enough when we greet each other in the security line-up, shy and taciturn, with no sign of the snarky superiority of a lot of leading academics. I recognize in him a fellow nerd, albeit one perhaps further along the spectrum than I am. His voice is hesitant and slightly hoarse, as though he doesn't use it very much. "I don't have the gift of the jabber," he tells me much later, in what I'll come to recognize as his pithy style of communication.

Grant Ballard, second-in-command and a long-term associate of David's research program, is tall, dark-haired, and thin, with a warm smile. Viola Toniolo, Grant's partner, looks Italian—dark and expressive eyes, olive skin, lithe physique—and it turns out that she immigrated to New York from Milan in her early teens. We will be working from three study sites on Ross Island—the penguin colonies at Cape Royds, Cape Bird, and Cape Crozier. Grant and Viola are to be based at Crozier, the most distant of the three from McMurdo and isolated by the fierce weather systems that roll straight off the ice shelf and prevent any chance of an incoming helicopter for days at a time. When I meet the two of them, they are fiddling with a small Pelican case loaded with the fearsome-looking syringes used for injecting ID tags just beneath the skin of the study penguins. The large hollow needles are a few centimetres long, three or four millimetres in diameter, and have a sharp and steeply bevelled tip.

"Are they actually going to let those through as carry-on?" I ask disbelievingly. "They look like some sort of weapon."

"I expect so," says Grant with a grin. "Last time we just told them they're research equipment and it wasn't a problem."

Katie Dugger, David's co-PI from Oregon State University, is supposed to be joining us on this flight but she's nowhere to be seen and eventually we assume she's either missed her connection or headed out a day early. Rachael Orben, from Pennsylvania and another assistant on this project, has missed her connections due to weather delays, and has been rerouted via Sydney. These are the people with whom I'll be spending the next three months, and happily the ones I've met don't seem crazy or unkind.

Antarctica is unique in being the only continental landmass never to have been inhabited by an Indigenous population of people. Humans are a late arrival here, with the first only setting foot on the continent in the 1800s. This is in stark contrast to the Arctic, which has been inhabited by people for thousands of years. The true Antarctic natives are the non-humans, lesser terrestrial life forms such as springtails, mosses, and lichens, which survive the punishing winters through extreme strategies like supercooling, drying, and freezing; for example, in the McMurdo Dry Valleys—an ice-free area of about 4,800 square kilometres that is one of the most extreme deserts on the planet, and situated just across McMurdo Sound from Cape Royds—soil-dwelling nematodes can desiccate and survive in a state of suspended animation (called anhydrobiosis) for decades. Then there are the ocean dwellers: marine mammals, fishes, and birds. These get through the coldest part of the year by spending it in the relative warmth of the ocean, possessing blood-borne antifreeze proteins, or migrating north to leave the Southern Ocean entirely. The coastal seas teem with these animals, and in spring the seals and penguins come ashore by the millions to breed. This is a world where natural rhythms hold sway.

Hand in hand with my childhood dream of becoming a wildlife biologist went a conviction that nature needed people to be its voice. Growing up, I was drawn to books about extinct or endangered species with evocative names: passenger pigeon, Tasmanian tiger, blue whale, Eskimo curlew, Labrador duck. As a teenager I was inspired by the barren Arctic vistas described by Farley Mowat in his Canadian classics and by my father, who travelled the North while working as an engineer for the Canadian Coast Guard, and wrote me letters about the wildlife there. But as I started to study biology in university, I turned toward the mysteries of the Antarctic. I saw it as an unspoiled reminder of what the natural world used to be, and perhaps could be again: a place to study ecological baselines, with penguins as canaries and Antarctica as coalmine. The whole continent offered a place that seemed scarcely touched by society's impacts, a beacon of hope and possibility for a humanity increasingly concerned about biodiversity loss and climate change.

But without knowing it at the time, I was also drawn to Antarctica's indifference. At the age of thirty-five, my sister had died of cancer: a long and pain-filled demise, a grim and drugged slide toward death. For two years she shrivelled before her family's eyes, including those of her two young sons. She had been beautiful, but toward the end an image of her standing naked in her bedroom was burned into my mind as a metaphor for the horror of it all, her buttocks turned by the ravages of disease into loose flesh sagging from bone, the body of a woman in her eighties. A decade earlier, my beloved father had succumbed to leukemia in his mid-fifties. In the wake of this earlier loss, my sister's death mostly just left me numb, the sorrow too deep to release all at once; I feared it might overwhelm me. And so I mourned my sister in increments. Sometimes I cried uncontrollably on hearing a kind word or a moving story; more often, I was shut down entirely. After four years of grieving the unfairness of her death, I craved a place where human suffering felt insignificant. I wanted to lose my sorrows in a place whose vast immensity had stripped better souls than mine.

And travelling came naturally to me. By the time I reached the age of four my parents and sister and I had lived in three places in Scotland and England then suddenly emigrated to Canada, leaving behind grandparents, cousins, aunts, uncles, and all the rest of the extended family. My father's job as an engineer took us first to a small community on the wooded shores of west Montreal, then to California, to a new house built at the interface of the desert and the Los Angeles sprawl, and then back to Canada again. We had lived in eight communities in four countries by the time I turned eleven. Wandering toward new horizons was in my blood.

From my seat in the C-141, I hear an announcement that we aren't going to boomerang, and a palpable feeling of relief settles over the cabin. I'm invited up to the cockpit by one of the flight crew to see the frozen continent emerging on the horizon. The cockpit is entered by a doorway one deck above us, via a metal ladder bolted to the bulkhead forward of our passenger cabin. Ahead of us lies Victoria Land, the first region of Antarctica landed upon by Captain (later Sir) James Clark Ross in 1841, on a four-year voyage of discovery that explored the sea that was later to bear his name. I watch as a craggy white landscape begins to unfold below, and then return to my seat to doze. Aft of the two or three dozen passengers is an open cargo area, where a small mountain of supplies is strapped to the floor under a massive tarpaulin—mail, food, and equipment for McMurdo Station and Scott Base.

Finally, we descend over Ross Island and the wheeled aircraft roughly touches down on the frozen ocean—the McMurdo Ice Runway (airport code NZIR), its ice up to three metres thick—then bumpily taxis to a standstill, a disorienting experience from the windowless space of the passenger zone. We gather our belongings and then line up in the cavernous, gloomy belly of the plane, waiting to disembark. The door of the aircraft cracks open and the light floods in, and at first all that I can see outside is a brilliant whiteness. Frigid air rushes in through the doorway, gnawing at the exposed parts of my face. My time on the Antarctic Peninsula—a place some call Antarctica's banana belt for its comparatively mild weather—has barely prepared me for this. A voice, unintelligible with static and Kiwi vowels, comes over the speaker from where it is mounted up on the bulkhead below the cockpit, and the flight crew, trim in their Air Force uniforms, begin directing us toward the stairs and down onto the sea ice runway.

At the military airbase in Christchurch, we had all been made to change into our regulation Extreme Cold Weather gear, or ECW: big blue puffy polar boots that lace up to the knees, with soles ten centimetres thick; insulated windproof coveralls; oversized red parkas with a faux-fur fringe around the face and a white nametag with black lettering Velcroed onto our chests. Back in New Zealand someone had said the name tags were all the better to identify each other under our glacier glasses and all that ECW, but I suspect that really we have to wear them so they can identify our bodies if anyone steps outside into a whiteout, or gets unlucky with a crevasse before we get to our field safety training. On the flight, parkas doubled as pillows and necks of undershirts gaped open. Now, as we press together on the plane's gangway, our excessive clothing is welcome, even necessary.

We disembark down the ramp onto the sea ice, frozen McMurdo Sound beneath our feet. Once off the plane we mill about like a flock of young penguins, disoriented by the newness. My first impression was right. Everything is brilliantly white. To be sure, there are McMurdo Station personnel in matching red parkas; a few people from New Zealand's Scott Base in earthier tones, there to pick up the handful of Kiwis on board; and a collection of bizarre orange vehicles with big wheels or massive tracks, clearly ready for whatever weather extremes the continent can throw at us. A colourfully flagged route leads from the sea ice runway toward McMurdo, with its utilitarian collection of drab buildings crouched just a few hundred metres up the slope, and black electrical cables snake back down toward us to feed the aircraft operations. But apart from these insignificant objects we are in a vast monochromatic frozen world. Smooth sea ice underfoot, the surface of a frozen ocean. Hummocky fast ice, lumpy against the nearby shore. A thin layer of snow dusting the ground around the buildings of McMurdo. A luminous sky of high cloud hiding the twenty-four-hour-a-day sun. And surrounding us, glaciated mountains and the continental ice sheet stretch to the horizon. For a moment I feel we've been transported via a time warp to the ice caps of Mars, trapped on the surface of an inhospitable planet.

We are herded toward a massive six-wheeled people-mover that is waiting nearby, with "Ivan the Terra Bus" lettered on its sides.* Most of us bumble along, unaccustomed to feeling the icy surface beneath our feet, encased in their unfamiliar field-issue boots with the double-thick soles. Everyone's parka hood is pulled tight against a bitter wind from the south, blinkering our vision and causing us to bump into each other as we slowly turn our heads to see this new world through a narrow red field of view. The shapeless red girl in line in front of me is distinctive because she's carrying a plastic lunchbox in the shape of a sandwich in her gloved hand. Perhaps sensing me checking out the lunchbox, she turns around.

"Hi, my name's Sandwich," she says, introducing herself from within her hood.

"Hi," I say. "I recognized your lunchbox. I saw you in the departure lounge in LA. What are you going to be doing here?"

"Working in the Galley," she replies. "You?"

"Working on the penguin project at Cape Royds," I say.

"Oh great!" she says. "I know Grant and Viola. Not my first year here."

I'm reminded of the saying in Antarctica: The first time you go for the adventure, the second time you go for the money, and the third time you go because you no longer fit in with the rest of the world.

From the superheated interior of the Terra Bus there is nothing to see through the windows, encrusted as they are with sheets of frozen condensation, and some of us get off again to linger outside, gawking,

---

* After thirty years of service, Ivan was retired to New Zealand at the end of the 2024–25 summer.

until we are yelled at to get back on board for the short trip to the station. I breathe a hole in the window ice to look at the scenery and futilely scan the frozen ocean for signs of penguins or seals. At this time of year, however, the edge of the sea ice is at least thirty kilometres to the north and the nearest penguins are likely no closer than Cape Royds, so a sighting is unlikely until we move out to the field. Here at Antarctica's largest logistics hub we are mostly too far south even for these birds. Though everybody in the world who hasn't been here equates Antarctica with penguins, for most of the people stationed at McMurdo these are creatures that are rumoured to exist out where they don't get to go, except very rarely, on a so-called boondoggle.

In fact, it begins to dawn on me that even here in Antarctica our group is considered to be supremely lucky to be going into the field to study these birds. I find out later that the occasional appearance of a lost Adélie out on the sea ice runway will prompt a massive downing of tools at McMurdo and a rush to the site for photo-documentation of this element of the "real" Antarctica. Of course such penguin envy excludes the deep nerds of the more obscure branches of polar science, those here to study nematodes or glaciers or phytoplankton or muons. None of these scientists are much impressed by the banal higher life forms represented by marine birds. One of my companions on the Terra Bus is a biomedical researcher who is here to study the effects of extreme cold and lack of daylight on human physiology. She barely seems to know that penguins are in the animal kingdom.

To be fair, she's not alone in her confusion about their taxonomy, for with their flightless behaviour and phenomenal swimming and diving ability it is natural to wonder if penguins are more fish than fowl. In the year 1620, the French commodore Augustin de Beaulieu said of the African penguin that "they have nothing of the taste of flesh, and I take them to be feathered fish."[4] But with their combination of feathers, beaks, warm-bloodedness, and egg-laying, penguins are decidedly in the same taxonomic class as ostriches and hummingbirds, and like other families of birds, they come in a variety of colours and sizes. The emperor and king penguins—both by far the largest of the penguin species—have a pinkish lower bill, and an attractive flush of yellow and orange on their head and neck feathers. Crested penguins, such as the macaroni, royal, and rockhopper, have fat, bright orange beaks and foppish yellow plumes atop their heads. The smallest species of penguin, which is variously known as little, blue, or fairy, is as diminutive as its names suggest, and with dorsal plumage that's an attractive blue-grey in colour.

On Ross Island, the focal penguin for our research will be the Adélie, a basic knee-high, black-and-white variation on the penguin theme. Adélie penguins were named in the 1800s after the wife of French explorer Jules Sébastien César Dumont d'Urville, Adèle, and were the first member of the penguin family to receive widespread public attention. The ubiquity of this species in the Ross Sea meant that the expeditions of Scott, Shackleton, and other Antarctic heroes of the early twentieth century exposed Adélies to positive press early on. In 1936, in his classic book *The Oceanic Birds of South America*, the great seabird biologist Robert Cushman Murphy wrote that "with singular unanimity, explorers have likened the Adélie penguin to a smart and fussy little man in evening clothes."[5]

Adélie penguin breeding distribution follows the coastline of the Antarctic continent, with our study site at Cape Royds described in the literature as the species' most southerly nesting location in the world—although in recent years a few breeding pairs have sometimes taken up residence at neighbouring Cape Barne, a few kilometres farther south still. Cape Royds has been occupied by Adélies for about one thousand years, from the time that this tiny point of land became free of the West Antarctic Ice Sheet. Ross Island, in its entirety a mere 2,500 square kilometres, is home to about 8 percent of the world's

Adélie penguins—with the vast majority breeding on its eastern shore at the giant Cape Crozier colony, which is home to literally hundreds of thousands of Adélies at the height of the breeding season. Anticipation at being in their midst is building in me; I would much rather be in the field in their penguin city than here at McMurdo, an isolated but very human village.

The bus pulls up the slope leading off the sea ice toward a collection of utilitarian prefabricated huts and barracks-like dormitories, hunched together against a backdrop of volcanic grit. The scene is reminiscent of a remote and dirty Arctic mining camp, or a High Arctic village circa 1980. "Ugly" is the first word that comes to mind to describe it, an assault on the continent's purity.

Our vehicle stops at the entrance to the main building, 155, where the driver tells us we'll be assigned a room before receiving an orientation session. As I step off the bus a cheerful woman bundled in thermal National Science Foundation garb passes me a printed handout that reads "Welcome to McMurdo," as if I'm entering some bizarre polar holiday camp. Everything here seems slightly off-kilter or larger than life, a bit like something out of Alice's Wonderland—from landing in a military plane on the frozen ocean to the fact that I've already glimpsed one of the locals wearing a coloured party wig. Even the infrastructure is arcane. Where at home one might find a garbage can and a blue box for recycling, for example, here each building holds entire waste stations composed of a bewildering array of containers.

One of the first things I learn at the orientation is that McMurdo's waste management system requires separation into more than twenty streams of trash for shipping back off-continent, where about three-quarters of the items are reportedly recycled. I soon find it's the norm to see a puzzled resident standing in front of one of these stations reading the many waste stream descriptions while some article of garbage hangs forgotten from their fingers. Avoiding this sort of behaviour is one of the many things that distinguishes an old hand from a fingee—an FNG or fucking new guy, army slang dating back to Vietnam. McMurdo (Mactown to the locals, or just "town" to the field crews) is rife with such anachronistic jargon from the days when the station was run by the US Navy: The cafeteria is the Galley, the station's shop is also known as the Ship's Store, and if we work late we can go for midrats, the term for the midnight rations cooked for the night shift crews.

We're toured around Building 155 and I'm drawn to the hustle and bustle of the station store, the notices for yoga sessions and cross-country ski lessons posted on sundry bulletin boards, and the photographic studies of workers from previous seasons, courtesy of a participant in the National Science Foundation's Antarctic Artists and Writers Program. McMurdo's recreation department dispenses everything from cross-country skis and board games to high heels, feather boas, and penguin costumes—these are important party ingredients in a place where people have to make their own entertainment. There are two bank machines (somehow run from afar by Wells Fargo) and a bowling alley, and over at Scott Base there's a well-used rugby pitch on the adjacent ice shelf (the Kiwis always win). Next door to Building 155 is the coffee shop and wine bar, in a cozy, wood-panelled Quonset hut that's the oldest building in town, originally erected in 1959. Apart from espresso and liquor, the Coffee House has herb tea, board games, and mellow music. Also around the station are two more bars, a computer lab, science labs, a bouldering gym, and a library. McMurdo feels consummately self-contained in its extreme isolation, like a ship stuck just above the fast ice of the frozen sea. This is the place that will be our base until we head into the field, and our point of contact with the rest of the world for the two and a half months after that.

At the end of our station tour I'm led to my room—an impersonal cave-like dorm—to unpack. I sit on my bed, contemplating the blackout curtains drawn back to let in the sun, and realize I already feel at home.

Although I am keen to get out into the field to see the local penguins in situ, we won't be able to go until we've spent a week or so at McMurdo, doing mandatory field safety training and readying gear. One of my pre-deployment responsibilities is to develop a basic meal plan for the season and then choose and pack our supplies from among the frozen, canned, and dehydrated foods stocked here in another of the many buildings. And while we'll no doubt be craving fresh fruits and vegetables by the end of our field season, we will be well enough fed that we won't need to eat our study animals, unlike Bill Sladen and some of the earlier human residents of McMurdo Sound and other parts of Antarctica.

In the first part of the twentieth century, penguins were seen as a ready source of food for many a stranded field party. The early explorers favoured penguin colonies for their camps as these headlands and islands were ice-free, and the birds could be killed and their eggs collected by marooned expeditioners in preparation for overwintering—although the edibility and flavour of these provisions were often disputed. American polar explorer Lincoln Ellsworth wrote, "Penguin eggs are delicious when made into omelettes, but ye gods, when they are boiled! Then they are like rubber balls, and fishy besides. My first experience with these eggs was when they were boiled [and] I have never since been able to eat them in any form."[6]

But during their winter stranded in an ice cave at Inexpressible Island in 1912, the members of Scott's Northern Party mixed Adélie meat into breakfast stews to the hearty enjoyment of the starving men. Even a dried-out old penguin flipper—a forgotten pot scraper—eventually made it into a meal. Before that, on board the icebound

Belgica in 1898–99, first mate Roald Amundsen escaped scurvy by mixing raw penguin with his tinned fruit.* But by mid-century field parties were better provisioned and less hungry. In *Hoosh: Roast Penguin, Scurvy Day, and Other Stories of Antarctic Cuisine,* author Jason Anthony recounts the advice of the cook from the Falkland Islands Dependencies Survey (as the British Antarctic agency that employed Bill Sladen was once called): "If, after cutting out the breast meat and washing it, hanging it outside for a few days, washing it again, blanching it, and washing it one final time, it still reeks of penguin . . . sling it out through the nearest window."[7] For many of the early explorers, hunger was the spice that rendered a penguin edible.

One relatively fine day (cold, high overcast clouds, little wind) during our first week, I take a break from field prep and walk with Rachael out to Hut Point to look at Scott's Discovery Hut after signing out the key from the Chalet, as the steep-roofed wooden building that acts as the McMurdo headquarters for the National Science Foundation is known. Rachael is a recent graduate of Cornell University, which as a prestigious Ivy League institution has a reputation for being one of the top spots for bird research worldwide. She is quiet and cheerful, and has long, dark blonde hair that's always escaping from under whatever hat she's wearing at the time. She also has a big smile, and a slow and thoughtful way of commenting on a situation or a research question. It turns out we are both avid readers and on our walk we discuss the books we've brought with us for the season, a mix of Antarctica-focused non-fiction, literary fiction, and trashy novels.

---

* The *Belgica*'s American physician, Frederick Cook, was credited with reasoning—based on his time overwintering with the Inuit of northern Greenland—that in the absence of fresh fruits and vegetables, eating raw meat would stave off scurvy. The *Belgica* was the ship of the Belgian Antarctic Expedition; the expedition was forced to overwinter in Antarctica when their vessel became trapped in sea ice off the Antarctic Peninsula.

The Discovery Hut was built as the storage facility and base ashore for Scott's 1901–04 Discovery Expedition, but for those working at McMurdo Station it's a de facto museum from a time when life in Antarctica was for just a few people, all of them men. Yes, it was the hut of *that* Scott, Captain Robert Falcon Scott, Scott of the Antarctic, the British explorer Scott who died on the Polar Plateau in 1912 after being beaten to the South Pole by the Norwegian Roald Amundsen (who had gained extensive Antarctic experience through his enforced overwinter on the *Belgica*). Before handing over the sacred key its guardian tells us twice about the rules to follow while it's in our possession, and we are warned that anthrax spores have been found (who looked?!) in Scott's other hut at Cape Evans a few kilometres to the north, so we might not want to go to this first hut of Scott's here on the outskirts of McMurdo. The logic of this litigiously minded statement escapes us so we take the key and tell Key Lady we won't sniff the hut's floor.

On its outside the Discovery Hut is a weathered brownish-grey under a peaked roof; the wood is worn but solid, belying the fact that this place has stood here for a hundred years. The first thing that hits me as we open the door is the smell. The odour that escapes is warm and sweet, like a barn occupied by horses. Directly ahead through the doorway lies a pile of decaying straw bales. Perhaps the smell emanates from these, or perhaps somewhere there is still a store of sennegrass—the dried Arctic sedge that was traditionally used by the Sámi people as an insulating and moisture-absorbing boot liner, and was adopted by the early Antarctic explorers. Just inside the main room on the right, a greasy pile of hundred-year-old seal carcasses is slowly disintegrating, and around the corner to the left of the straw is a small storage room with—incredibly—the mummified carcasses of a couple of sheep hanging on the walls. It's a small shock to round the corner and see them there, like the artfully placed display of a talented museum curator, but these sides of mutton are the real thing, left a century ago to feed members of some future expedition. Happily, we aren't that hungry, given the mountains of imported foods that await us back at the Galley.

Apart from the desiccated sheep the hut holds wooden crates with black stencilled lettering proclaiming their British contents as dog biscuits, Fry's cocoa, and Bovril, and on the walls, shelves hold decaying tins of baking soda and processed meat among those of less identifiable foodstuffs, their labels peeling away. This was the hut referred to by Shackleton in his memoir *South* as "a most useful *pied-à-terre* for the start of any Southern journey."[8] Later, in 1968, it was the hut from which Australian author Thomas Keneally filched a hardtack biscuit. Of that voyage, he wrote: "I was able to experience Antarctica in so profound a way that it recurred in my dreams for decades to come. In particular, the huge Transantarctic Mountains . . . returned to me in sleep." The call of those vistas and the crisis of conscience initiated by his theft meant that more than thirty years later he made another trip and returned the biscuit to its box, writing of both journeys in the literary magazine *Granta* (in an issue called, appropriately enough, "This Overheating World").[9]

As we leave the hut, I think of another story about it, immortalized in the book *Big Dead Place,* in which author Nicholas Johnson reports receiving a memorable blow job there. No doubt not the first or last tryst over the years; perhaps that is one reason they so carefully guard the key. Suddenly I'm swamped with loneliness, jealous of the idea of his casual intimacy. In the numb aftermath of my sister's death, I had settled for too many things: a mediocre job as a biologist in government, from which I'm currently on leave; a master's degree in Canada rather than a PhD program in Australia, where I'd been headed to do doctoral research on Antarctic marine birds until my sister was diagnosed with cancer; and a relationship with a man with anger management problems. I've left this future ex-husband behind at home, and I realize that I don't miss him at all. I have taken a tentative step back to my original path by pursuing a prestigious PhD fellowship in Canada, and by returning to Antarctica. But there are few things lonelier than being at the end of the world and awakening to the fact that you are truly alone, with not even a longing for home to sustain you.

2

A COUPLE OF days after our visit to the Discovery Hut, we are scheduled for two days of what the welcome handout calls "your mandatory Field Safety Training." Day one is scheduled for the tenth of November: sea ice school for me and eight other Mactown newbies, Katie and Rachael among them (with Katie having arrived in Christchurch in time to catch our flight to McMurdo). We leave David, Grant, and Viola behind to take their one-day refresher of a previous year's training, mostly, David tells me later, about how to drive a local truck and use the recycling system.

Our group piles into the twin articulated passenger cabins of a red Hägglunds tracked vehicle and we grind off down the hill toward the frozen ocean. First stop is on the sea ice just below McMurdo for our radio checkout with MacOps—communications HQ—and a lesson about field party radio protocols. "MacOps, MacOps, this is . . ." says our driver over the VHF radio, providing our vehicle number to the station's on-duty radio operator; then he states our travel route, number of people on board, trip purpose, and return time. All remote parties away from station for more than a day have a daily scheduled safety check-in call, known locally as our sked. It's mildly sobering to learn that these skeds have an almost non-existent grace period: For travelling field parties, a multi-stage emergency response is set in motion five minutes after a call is late, and for field camps, it's an hour.

The protocol and frequency of skeds were changed to be this precautionary back in the early 1970s, after four students from New Zealand's University of Canterbury went missing in McMurdo Sound after putting to sea in the Cape Bird field station's trimaran in calm weather; they planned to do a few plankton tows. Dirty fuel caused both the main and the backup outboard motors to die almost immediately, and, with their vessel caught in the pack ice and drifting rapidly away from shore, the men abandoned ship to jump from floe to floe in an attempt to return to land. They ended up adrift in the pack for five harrowing days, building shelters from pieces of ice and changing floes as intermittently heavy seas broke apart their refuges. At one point they huddled behind some ice blocks to hide from a hunting killer whale. Miraculously, a McMurdo helicopter plucked all four intact from their last disintegrating floe, close to Cape Royds and just ahead of a gathering storm; and they suffered nothing worse among them than snow blindness and mild frostbite. An inquiry into the near-tragedy recommended mandatory emergency equipment for research vessels, and found that the "two- to three-day interval between check-in radio calls"[10] was insufficient. Now: "Check in *before* your scheduled time," urges the US Antarctic Program's field manual.

After our VHF checkout and a brief leg-stretch on the ice, we get back into the Hägglunds and follow a flagged track out onto frozen McMurdo Sound. The wind is calm, as it has been for the past couple of days, but the sky has clouded over during the night and the air is bitingly cold. The vehicle's interior is as overheated as every other indoor space in Antarctica, so it's easy to warm up once back on board. And then more difficult to strip down once we inevitably grow too hot shortly thereafter. This is the pattern I've already begun to recognize as the norm here at McMurdo; in the realm of overheated buildings we constantly have to guard against overheating, because sweating inside one's clothes makes it that much harder to stay warm once we step outdoors.

We spend the morning out at Ice Hut 19, which feels like it's in the middle of nowhere even though it's just a kilometre or so from shore. The hut is basic and has an outdoor biffy featuring a nice warm toilet seat carved by a McMurdo local from a sheet of blue Styrofoam insulation. Stepping outside the hut to pee, I am alone in a white world, ice sheet against mountains under clouds. The only sounds are the susurration of the wind and the flapping of the flags that mark the sea ice road, with the ever-idling Hägglunds's engine just a murmur against the backdrop of ice and sky.

The day's curriculum consists of sea ice and ice crack theory as it applies to safe travel in a frozen world; how to set up a tent using ice anchors to prevent it from being blown away like a tumbleweed, with a practical outdoors application; and lunch—though in an order designed to bring on maximum stupor: outside activity, back into overheated cabin to eat lots of food, then lectures in soporific tones. Most of us are thus comatose for the next stage of the day's schedule, the clanking hour-long drive north over the sea ice to Cape Evans. There we stop the Hägglunds just below the second of Scott's huts (not the Discovery Expedition mutton freezer we'd visited at Hut Point; this is instead the pestilence-infested dwelling that Rachael and I had heard about from Key Lady). Known as the Terra Nova Hut or Scott's Hut, this is the base from which Scott and his party left for their fatal overland trek to the Pole. Where its wooden sides are visible they are worn to the same weather-beaten grey as those of the Discovery Hut—but the snowdrifts piled against the building give the impression that it is subsiding into the landscape, in the process of becoming one with Antarctica. On the frozen ocean below the shore we learn how to test sea ice thickness in the vicinity of a tidal crack. At these cold temperatures, surface cracks can form and refreeze, form and refreeze, creating a zone of thin ice that's often covered with drifting snow or invisible during a whiteout, a trap door to a watery world for an unwary researcher or even a tracked vehicle. First we clear the snow, and then drill down with a one-metre ice auger—a hand-held tool that looks like a massive drill bit—until the salt water is liberated and gushes up along the moving blades of the screw.

It's so cold and dry here that my fingernails keep breaking at the slightest stress. I catch one on my parka and it snaps off down below the quick, so I find a roll of duct tape in the Hägglunds and wrap some around my finger to avoid snagging the nail again and tearing half of it off. As we sweat over the auger a pair of south polar skuas—fierce, gull-like predators and scavengers—watch us avidly, hoping for a dropped bite of sandwich or a handout from our snack collections. Though penguin sightings are unusual in and around McMurdo, skuas are a regular presence. Out at the penguin colonies, many of them subsist by snapping up penguin chicks or eggs; however, those same predatory skills mean that at McMurdo they are adept at snatching food from unwary humans. I've already seen one instance in town of a frantic resident waving an aggressive skua away from a tray of food as she hastily carried it from 155 to a nearby dorm.

As with many creatures whose behaviours threaten our comfortable existence, a certain mythos has grown around these birds. They are often cursed by McMurdo residents as thieves and penguin-murderers, but a look at local culture tells a story of grudging respect for the skuas and their wily toughness. At McMurdo, "to skua" is a verb, meaning to take and recycle others' discarded items. This ethos of reuse is integral to McMurdo life and in amongst the many recycling bins at each garbage station are those labelled SKUA—places to leave reusable items for others to scavenge, with anything that isn't picked up right away taken to Skua Central, an outbuilding on the edge of town that's open to everyone. Here at our Cape Evans tidal crack we are outside the regular ambit of McMurdo residents and their food trays, but given the hopeful mooching by this particular pair of skuas it seems likely they're getting handouts from somewhere. Feeding them would contravene the environmental measures of the international Antarctic Treaty, but I can see how their beady-eyed persistence might make them hard to resist.

Environmental protection is a complex business in Antarctica, and not feeding the skuas is just the tip of that particular iceberg. The Protocol on Environmental Protection to the Antarctic Treaty, as this measure is fully known, is unique in designating an entire continent "as a natural reserve, devoted to peace and science," and provides a set of rules on how any activities conducted there must protect the Antarctic environment. It was signed by Antarctic Treaty parties in Madrid in 1991, and so is often simply called the Madrid (or Environmental) Protocol, and it entered into force in 1998 via the twenty-six signatory countries' national laws.

The Antarctic Treaty itself, covering all land and ice shelves south of 60°S, was signed in 1959 by the twelve nations* active there in the International Geophysical Year of 1957–58. The Treaty took effect in 1961. Despite being promulgated in the shadow of the Cold War, it initiated the concept of Antarctica as a continent for peaceful use, holding in abeyance the existing territorial claims** (which divide the continent like a pie into seven wedge-shaped pieces) and disallowing

---

* Argentina, Australia, Belgium, Chile, France, Japan, New Zealand, Norway, South Africa, USSR, UK, and USA.

** The seven countries with territorial claims were Argentina, Australia, Chile, France, New Zealand, Norway, and the UK.

new ones. The original signatories, and other nations acceding to the Treaty and "conducting substantial research activity" on the continent, occupy a special place within the Antarctic Treaty system; these are the voting or Consultative Parties, and this ability to vote explains the presence in Antarctica of research stations run by nations with an otherwise limited historical role in the polar regions, such as Bulgaria, Ecuador, and Peru. Non-Consultative Parties are nations with an interest in Antarctica but no physical presence there: These are countries as diverse in nature as Guatemala, Switzerland, and, somewhat surprisingly given its role as one of the eight Arctic nations, Canada.

The Antarctic Treaty is now acceded to by more than fifty nations, representing about two-thirds of the world's human population. Although land claims are in abeyance and mineral exploration is prohibited, the world has been interested in Antarctica's natural resources since the early days of commercial whaling and sealing. In modern times, Antarctica's gold exists in the form of krill and finfish fisheries, and at one point lay in future subsurface mineral rights, until mining was banned under the Environmental Protocol. For its first fifty years the Protocol can only be modified by unanimous agreement of all Consultative Parties, but as of 2048, any one Party can call for a review of its operation (although implementation of any amendments will require agreement by all twenty-six of the Protocol's original signatories).

Just before we leave Cape Evans for the day, Susan, one of the instructors, goes up to the hut to make sure it hasn't sustained any recent weather damage and comes back reporting a female Weddell seal behind the pressure ridge where we've been working. I run over to look from a distance and there she is, sheltering her brand-new pup from the by-now bitter winds. She is fat yet sleek, her silver-and-black coat luminous in the flat light of the late afternoon. The pup is nursing, then nuzzling around its mother to explore this fresh new world—or perhaps just relocating a nipple. Frozen afterbirth still lies on the snow,

now being pecked at by the same pair of skuas that earlier eyed our lunches. Even in the midst of this bleak whiteness, life persists.

Day two of extreme cold weather survival is officially called Snowcraft One Training in our welcome handout, but locally it's known as Snow School or Happy Camper. The main purpose of this training is to make sure researchers working at distant field sites don't fall down a crevasse, that staff working at McMurdo don't get lost in a whiteout on their way home from a late-night liaison at Scott Base, or that anybody doing any travelling has at least a passing chance of surviving an unplanned overnight or two off-station. We're instructed to show up layered in our ECW clothing. "NO COTTON!" read the instructions, and "SORRY—NO ALCOHOL."

We meet up with our instructors from the Field Safety Training Program (FSTP, or F-Stop, as it's known here). Apart from Rachael and Katie, my seventeen fellow students consist of a group of carpenters, a couple of Galley staff, and Zelenda, a blonde-haired, round-cheeked grad student who's off to work as a summer research assistant studying the glaciology of the West Antarctic Ice Sheet. She too is dazzled by her good fortune at being here, and already she wears the dreamy-eyed expression that I later recognize in myself. She is falling in love with Antarctica.

We're all driven in a Delta out to Snowmound City, a site on the Ross Ice Shelf beyond Scott Base where an ATCO trailer and a canvas-sided field shelter called a Rac-Tent form a small encampment against the backdrop of white nothingness. The Delta is yet another large and box-like orange people-mover, this one with tires about two metres high and the sort of vehicle I had previously only associated with a strip mine in the High Arctic. It travels so slowly that some of us get out and walk alongside to our destination.

Fastened to a wooden packing crate on the outskirts of this makeshift camp is a hand-stencilled sign that points to where ice shelf blends seamlessly with lowering sky, and reads "South Pole 1004," the distance in miles to the Pole. The crate is massive, perhaps once having encased a Delta engine, but it is nonetheless affixed to the ice to guard against its loss in the next big storm.

Our instructors are hard-core outdoors experts from places like NOLS, the renowned National Outdoor Leadership School in Wyoming. One of them, Allen, tells us about the time he led an overland trip to the Antarctic Plateau, where it was so windy they literally lost a snowmobile. He is a tall, thin, and energetic fellow with a wicked smile, a semi-groomed beard, and impressive field survival credentials.

This morning there is barely a breeze but the air temperature is around −20°C and a haze of clouds hides the sun; what little wind there is comes from the south, and the cold bites through my thick parka and the layered clothing beneath it if I stand still for too long. Today provides my first objective lesson in the weather patterns here—northerly winds come from over the ocean, and even when the sea is frozen they presage slightly warmer conditions. But winds from the south originate over the frigid Polar Plateau with its brutally low temperatures (days of −20s to −30s Fahrenheit were considered warm by early explorers), and they often bring bad weather in the form of storms and whiteouts. I'm glad of the fleece snood my stepmother gave me just before I left home. The elongated neck gaiter is made of dark green polyester fleece and comes up over my head like a hood. I pull on its drawstrings to fasten it tightly around the high neck of the fleece jacket under my parka, and cinch the face opening across the bridge of my nose so that only my sunglasses are exposed.

Snow School curriculum is full of practical exercises such as how to build a snow shelter, how to follow a flagged route (the flags comprise long bamboo stakes topped with a square of coloured fabric: Green flags equal safety; black flags equal death, in the form of hazards such as rotting sea ice or a hidden crevasse; yellow is known as the pee flag, as in "urinate here"), and how to stay warm at all times.

"I just don't tolerate being cold," says Allen, who frequently demonstrates this by running in frenetic circles or taking on apparently frivolous activities like digging a broad set of steps into a nearby snowdrift. "I'm very task-oriented," he tells us.

We undertake our own warmth-inducing tasks, namely constructing various types of snow shelters, which also keeps frostbite at bay via vigorous exercise. First we add yet another snow mound to the eponymous site, then use it to build a quinzhee—a sort of cheater igloo hollowed out of heaped snow. Snowmound City is already littered with the wrecks of earlier quinzhees built by previous groups this season. To start the construction we pile all our duffel bags in a heap, then bury them with plenty of snow and tunnel through one side to remove the duffel core. Construction takes a long time, and after a couple of hours of shovelling, tunnelling, and general snow-moving we're all personally reminded of the warming power of physical labour on a cold day. It's something we take to heart as the afternoon progresses and the wind picks up, bringing with it a pelting flurry of hard flakes. We are also taught how to wield a snow-saw in aid of snow-block cutting (vital for building a windbreak) and learn how to dig a snow trench for a desperate sort of shelter if your tent blows away. Susan, still with us from yesterday, recommends one of her favourite tricks—that of turning your drinking water container into a hot water bottle before bed simply by filling it with the water left over from making tea, making sure the lid is on tight, and slipping it into the bottom of your sleeping bag.

This is invaluable advice because to emphasize the "field" component of field safety training we are spending the night in the shelters we've built. All of us have brought our sleep kits, issued to us this morning and which I'm soon to learn will travel everywhere with us in Antarctica. These consist of an extra-large duffel bag containing two sleeping pads (a thin foam insulating one and the world's thickest Therm-a-Rest), a fleece sleeping bag liner, and the world's thickest sleeping bag. Eleven of our group decide to prove their hardiness by spending the night in various versions of the snow trench. Some of these are elaborate, roofed with toboggans and sheltered by snow-block walls; others are open to the sky. Everyone else elects to sleep in the quinzhee, except I decide to prepare for life at Cape Royds by spending the night in one of the mountaineering tents we'd pitched during the day's warming exercises, one of a cluster behind another wall of snow blocks. At Royds I'll be sleeping in the same make and model. In the ATCO trailer I make one of Susan's hot water bottles and stick it inside my sleeping bag before cleaning up around camp and making sure my gear isn't lying outside, risking burial by some passing snow squall. By the time I'm ready to crawl into my bag, it is cozy and inviting.

At 3 a.m. I get up to pee. ("Stay hydrated!" say the instructors. "Don't cut back on fluids just to avoid getting up in the night!") The sun has just set, dipping below the horizon for an hour or so, and although it is still broad daylight there is now a muted evening sky with a bright line of light just above the mountains, at the place where the sun will soon re-emerge. In a few days it will no longer set at all, to remain above the horizon for the remainder of our time here. The flag line to the outhouse stands out sharp and clear in a pearly light that is as luminous as a dawn, but brighter. The air is still; although it is sharply cold, the weather has calmed from yesterday's snow and wind. I return to my tent and sleep deeply until shortly before eight, when the sounds of boiling water and breakfast prep right outside my fly wake me from the best sleep I've had since arriving at McMurdo. The worth of the hot water bottle technique is underscored by the fact that everyone else's drinking water containers froze solid beside them while they slept. The snow trench sleepers apparently passed a particularly chilly night, and I am relieved I'd remembered to put my contact lenses inside my sleeping bag so they weren't encased in discs of ice when I woke up.

Later that day we learn how to navigate in a whiteout, how to set up our HF radio for emergency communications from the deep field (as high-frequency radio waves work by bouncing off the ionosphere to travel around the curve of the Earth, we practise by calling Palmer Station, the small US base on the other side of the continent; I briefly chat with a friend who's stationed there for the summer, also working on a penguin study), and how to use the contents of your survival bag to increase your chances of living through a remote snowmobile crash or downed helicopter. I'm intrigued to see that the bags always include a cheap paperback for passing the time (and, as one of the instructors inevitably notes, as a source of extra toilet paper after everyone in the benighted party has read it). These survival bags are present in every McMurdo vehicle that leaves town; back in the early 1970s, American author Charles Neider credited the contents of his with allowing him to survive a helicopter crash near the summit of Mount Erebus. The simulated whiteout exercise is particularly memorable as we are all roped together with white five-gallon food pails over our heads and tasked with rescuing a "lost" co-worker, something that fails spectacularly without a compass.

A key part of all of our training is the "leave no trace" approach to working in Antarctica. This instruction is a legal requirement under the Antarctic Treaty, and we're reminded often—before departing Christchurch, on arrival in Antarctica, and now, as part of our basic training—that we mustn't litter or otherwise dispose of waste products outdoors, disturb or feed wildlife, trample the lichens, alter the environment in any way. In the McMurdo Dry Valleys, even urinating on the ground is forbidden: This is to prevent altering the soil biota and generally affecting these fragile and very stable systems, which are the focus of long-term ecological research in the region. All of this adds to the sense that the entire continent is one giant laboratory, although the effect is spoiled somewhat by the knowledge that for decades McMurdo Station discharged all of its sewage into McMurdo Sound, while all of its garbage was dumped onto the seasonal sea ice to drift away and slowly be scattered over the ocean floor as the winter ice melted. This debris field included an entire aircraft—a US Navy WV-2—that crashed during an attempted landing in near-whiteout conditions in 1960 and was subsequently left to sink through the ice into McMurdo Sound (all crew members survived the crash).

But once you're away from the stations, the complete absence of any sign of human presence is profound—save for an occasional decades-old wooden navigational marker or memorial on a rocky point, or the flags marking the temporary vehicle routes over the sea ice to places like Cape Royds, it is as if humanity does not exist here. We all come away from Snow School with a solemn respect for Antarctica's cold and wind, and a dread of whiteouts. Most summer days the weather here on the coast is no colder than an average winter day somewhere in Canada or the northern USA, but conditions can change in the blink of an eye.

"On our last course, it was snowing hard and a woman went to the outhouse," says one of the instructors over breakfast. "She opened the door to leave and it had turned to whiteout conditions in just a minute or two. What did she do? She stepped back inside and shut the door and stayed in the outhouse until conditions improved enough for her to see the flag line. Good move!" In Antarctica, better a couple of hours huddled in a wind-free shitter than wandering off and dying in an attempt to make it back to the relative comfort of the cookhouse.

An awareness of the consequences of one's actions is a constant companion here. Perhaps it is Scott's fault, dying as publicly as he did, with his death a central part of Antarctica's mystique. Old wooden crosses rise from ice-free promontories, physical reminders of those across the decades who never returned home to their stations. Lost when the sea ice broke up, slipping from a cliff while doing ornithological research, drowning when a boat overturned, falling down a crevasse, succumbing to exposure, gone missing in a whiteout . . . there are many ways to die in Antarctica.

At our hostel in Christchurch I had picked up a stray copy of *The Home of the Blizzard*, Sir Douglas Mawson's account of his 1911–14 Australasian Antarctic Expedition. Despite having formed part of Shackleton's scientific team on the Nimrod Expedition, Mawson is generally not well known in the northern hemisphere, but in Australia his is still a household name. The accounts of death and endurance from Mawson's expedition are perhaps the most harrowing among those told of a continent known for its explorers' epic feats of survival, and tales of loss. His expedition's main base was at Cape Denison, on Commonwealth Bay in George V Land, an exposed portion of Antarctica's coastline far to the north and west of Ross Island. After passing an autumn and a winter enduring constant hurricane-force winds and mapping and collecting geological samples locally, in November of 1912 Mawson led a three-man dog-sledging party eastward to map distant segments of the coast. His companions were Belgrave Ninnis, a lieutenant in the Royal Fusiliers, and Dr. Xavier Mertz, a champion skier and mountaineer from Switzerland. This Far Eastern Party was to use the sled dogs to travel farther afield than the expedition's other field parties, which were travelling and conducting their work without dogs.

On a sunny December day, five hundred kilometres from base, Douglas Mawson had stopped his sledge to calculate their latitude when he heard a distant whine from one of Ninnis's dogs. "When I next looked back," wrote Mawson in his 1915 memoir, "it was in response to the anxious gaze of Mertz who had turned round and halted in his tracks. Behind me, nothing met the eye but my own sledge tracks running back in the distance. Where were Ninnis and his sledge?"[11]

Mawson and Mertz frantically backtracked to find a gaping hole, the broken lid of a crevasse, down which could be glimpsed an injured dog on a ledge one hundred and fifty feet below. It lay next to the body of one of its companions and the remains of some of their supplies. Beyond lay blackness.

"We broke back the edge of the neve lid and took turns leaning over secured by a rope, calling into the darkness in the hope that our companion might be still alive. For three hours we called unceasingly but no answering sound came back. The dog had ceased to moan and lay without a movement. A chill draught was blowing out of the abyss,"[12] wrote Mawson. There was no sign of Ninnis. With him had gone their six best dogs, their tent, and most of their food. They were a month away from base, with a scant one and a half weeks of supplies for themselves, and nothing for the remaining dogs. Of the perilous journey lying ahead of him and Mertz, Mawson later wrote that it "was to be a fight with Death and the great Providence would decide the issue."[13] Mawson, of course, made it back alive to write his memoirs. In the end, like Ninnis, Mertz did not.

But fatal accidents are rare, now, in the heavily structured world of McMurdo and elsewhere in Antarctica, with most accidental deaths in the field in the modern era related to travel decisions gone wrong: an aircraft piloted in deteriorating weather conditions, a delayed return to station meaning being caught out in a storm. At McMurdo, closed-circuit televisions broadcast local weather conditions to base workers, and in Condition 1 storms, when visibility is down to less than a metre, even travelling between buildings on station is forbidden. Despite improvements in technology and training, the reality of Antarctica's harshness remains, and our field training instills in us the realization that things can fall apart in an instant if we're unprepared. In the vast, white, open spaces, whether out on the sea ice or traversing the flanks of Mount Erebus, it is hard to get away from the feeling that Death is standing behind you, ready to tap you on the shoulder if you make the wrong move.

3

IT'S MID-NOVEMBER. Yesterday the weather reminded us it is still only late spring here, with lows of −19°C and the wind chill approaching −35. I've been here a little more than a week and already I feel the hold of The Real World slipping away. It is normal to see everyone around me, men and women alike, sporting bunny boots and insulated coveralls, shaggy hair and sunburned faces. Life is busy but languid, run at a fast pace under an endless empty sky. Time moves at a different velocity here and it feels as if we exist in a different place, some sort of distant realm. "The Real World" or "The Other World" is how we refer to the normal life left behind at home, but it's about more than just what is "normal"—these terms capture our feeling of being outside of time, suspended in a corresponding reality into which the outside world cannot intrude.

With field training behind us, our waking hours are now consumed with organizing supplies in advance of our scheduled field deployment to Ross Island's three Adélie penguin colonies. David and I are to be heading to Cape Royds as a team of two as originally planned. Katie is going to the two-person camp at Cape Bird on the northwest coast of

Ross Island, to a research station co-run by the Kiwi collaborators in our study; they'll be our programmatic link with New Zealand's Scott Base. The Cape Bird colony is an order of magnitude larger than the one at Royds, about thirty thousand pairs to the three thousand or so that David and I will be studying. Rachael will go with Grant and Viola to Cape Crozier, the remotest site of all, far to the east and abutting the northwestern edge of the Ross Ice Shelf.

Crozier is the place immortalized in English explorer Apsley Cherry-Garrard's book *The Worst Journey in the World*, a title that makes me wonder whether any human should be going there, even in the modern age. Cherry-Garrard was stationed at Cape Evans as part of Scott's 1911–12 expedition to attain the South Pole, and the book chronicles his eponymous midwinter journey with Birdie Bowers and Edward "Bill" Wilson. On that trip the three explorers man-hauled sledges from Cape Evans to Cape Crozier, in the constant winter dark, to collect the egg of the emperor penguin—a species then barely known to science. According to Cherry-Garrard, their trip was "the weirdest bird's-nesting expedition that has ever been or ever will be."[14] Today, Crozier is clearly a top spot for Adélie penguins as well as emperors; at about three hundred thousand pairs, it is one of the largest Adélie colonies on the planet.

And also: "It's one of the power spots of the world," says David one day.

I consider asking him why, since he doesn't strike me as someone disposed to what seems to me to be a flight of fancy, but as we've approached deployment day he has grown increasingly taciturn so I don't broach the question. He's been irritable because he and Grant have been struggling, so far unsuccessfully, to get one of the automated penguin weigh-stations to work. Faulty equipment is the bane of any field researcher's existence so I can understand his frustration, especially after he has endured the inconvenience of travelling with it from halfway around the world.

But his silences have begun to have the flavour of something that may weigh on me later, and I ponder what I'll do about being stuck in the deep field with someone so non-verbal. A book of yoga poses; a draft of a paper from my MSc research I intend to finish writing and submit for publication; headphones and the music on my computer—I suddenly realize that the mental occupations I have planned for any downtime may also be a bulwark against a season of silence. But it's just silence and solitude, I tell myself, not the true physical hardship for which the continent has been known for well over a century.

In an example from the modern era of Antarctic travel, in 1993 British physician Mike Stroud and explorer and writer Sir Ranulph Fiennes completed the first unsupported crossing of the continent on foot. Theirs was a hazardous ninety-three-day journey during which they traversed more than two thousand kilometres, each dragging nearly a quarter of a tonne of supplies behind them on their sleds through crevassed and icy terrain while temperatures dropped to −60°C and below. As they ate their way through their supplies and the loads on their sleds decreased, their bodies disintegrated from frostbite, gangrene, and starvation, and their loads seemed no lighter. And as their bodies disintegrated so too did their relationship, the tiny daily torments of personality differences as corrosive as the cold.

Yet they finished the traverse and went on to collaborate on other expeditions in subsequent decades. If they could pull through such extremes together, surely I can endure a couple of months in what are bound to be fairly comfortable conditions, with or without deep daily conversations with my campmate. In point of fact I am not a talkative person either, and a chatty companion would be more likely to grate on me, to the point of insanity, than a quiet one.

—

For this year's deployment, Viola is taking care of the Crozier gear while I deal with the Cape Royds equipment. I rely on lists others have saved on the project's computers from previous seasons to ensure I don't forget any of a multitude of essential field camp items: propane heater, cooking kit, dishes, buckets, rope, crampons, various electronics, tools, the power supply set-up, food for the season, a hundred other things. Before I can do this I need to obtain a McMurdo driver's licence, granted after a briefing about the station trucks—some of them normal four-by-fours and others equipped with Mattracks, triangular treads installed in place of wheels—and a test-drive around the icy streets of town.

Much of our gear I simply check out from the Berg Field Center, or BFC, a barn-like warehouse named after American geologist Thomas Berg, who was killed in a helicopter crash while doing fieldwork back in the 1960s. In the BFC's food stores I go through my list and peruse the shelves, lingering over chocolate treats, high-fat foods, and the canned, frozen, and dehydrated ingredients for easy-to-prepare camp meals. There's a selection of supplies sent over from Scott Base, Kiwi field favourites like Raro drink powder, Bumper Bars—a superior and calorie-rich muesli bar made with real butter, chocolate chunks, and dried fruits—and yoghurt-making kits with full-fat powdered milk.

After I complete our food order I undertake the task of finding which of McMurdo's many barracks-like buildings house esoteric items like picric acid (an indelible liquid dye for marking study birds, explosive when crystallized, so packaged for shipping to our camp over at Dangerous Goods), cross-country skis (at the Recreation Department in 155), and obscure bits of hardware (the Heavy Shop can machine them if need be).

At dinner David asks if I'd like to share a bottle of whisky and gives me some US dollars to pick one up at the station store. "We don't need much," he says. "Just enough for a nip after the occasional celebratory dinner."

Viola and I stockpile mountains of supplies in preparation for our big weigh-in over at Helo Ops: Before we can be deployed via helicopter, everything down to the last pair of down booties must be put on the scales. Cargo weight determines how much fuel can be put into the aircraft, with the helo pilots measuring fuel in pounds instead of gallons. For Cape Royds, we weigh one ton of gear.

Viola tells me she's heard that the Cape Royds hut is new this year, and that this is good news. Apparently the canvas-sided ones last only a few years, the constant exposure to UV radiation degrading their fabric quickly.

"You know Josh and Hannah?" she says, referring to two of our colleagues in the world of seabird research. "A couple of years ago they were at Cape Royds during a hurricane and their hut—it was a Polar Haven that year—just blew apart."

I look at her askance, imagining a small tear or two turning into gaping rips, disbelief turning to fear, then the entire hut exploding into the sky as shreds of canvas. Apsley Cherry-Garrard wrote of his own version of this experience in his book although in his case it was midwinter a century earlier, and he and his two companions were alone at the Crozier colony in a makeshift rock-and-tarpaulin shelter, nearly out of supplies: "[The] green Willesden canvas flapped into hundreds of little fragments in fewer seconds than it takes to read this. The uproar of it all was indescribable. Even above the savage thunder of that great wind on the mountain came the lash of the canvas as it was whipped to little tiny strips."[15]

"Seriously?" I say to Viola.

"Yeah, it just disintegrated. Apparently they both sheltered inside the hut's packing box until the winds let up enough for them to get over the ridge to the Kiwi refuge hut."

"Well, that would be exciting," I say. "I'm glad ours is new."

In the rush to prepare for our departure from McMurdo, the luxury of unscheduled time shrinks to scraps snatched here and there. In my dorm room I develop the habit of stockpiling any trash I generate during the days—used dental floss, pieces of notepaper, candy wrappers, a worn-out earplug—to be disposed of in the evenings, when I can visit the hallway waste depot en route to the building's shared bathrooms. Each night before bed I multitask, brushing my teeth or drinking a glass of red wine in front of the waste station's many bins, reading their instructional labels like a fingee—a newcomer to this complex system of sorting the disposable remnants of my days. After midnight I check emails at one of the shared computers in the hushed science library upstairs at Crary Lab; at this time of night the silence presses on my ears, unexpected in the pearly spring twilight that makes it feel as if the station should still be bustling. The library has a wall of windows that are full of the sky and the Transantarctic Mountains, more than sixty kilometres away but towering above frozen McMurdo Sound in the gloaming.

On our last morning in town I get up at 6:30 a.m. to finish packing my personal gear—strewn about my dorm room—into the two standard-issue orange duffle bags I received back in Christchurch, do a final email check in Crary, drop off a form at the Post Office that gives Helo Ops permission to collect and deliver my mail, and use one of the McMurdo trucks to drive David and our bags down to the helipad in time for our scheduled 9:15 departure. Most of our ton of gear has already been loaded into the Bell 212 by a helo-tech and now forms a wall of boxes, parcels, and sundry objects that looms over our backward-facing seats in the rear of the machine. A few bulkier items wouldn't fit and so remain in the Helo Ops hangar, ready to be dropped off next time there's an underloaded helicopter flying north to the Dry Valleys. David and I do a final weigh-in, us plus our personal gear and helicopter helmets, then shoehorn ourselves into the aircraft. Even our own weight is factored into determining how much fuel the helicopter will use.

We lift off at 9:15 a.m. precisely, heading into the white blankness. I feel something heavy fall away as McMurdo recedes and with it all the hustle and bustle, the institutional impersonality and bureaucratic nonsense. This is it, I think: nearly three months of pure isolation ahead. Although as it turns out, I couldn't have been more wrong about the isolation.

4

WHEN THE HELICOPTER touches down on our first day, Cape Royds is bleak and stark under a grey sky. The pilot and his helo-tech rush to help us unload our mountain of gear while keeping an eye on some incoming weather, and then they lift off, leaving David and me alone.

My first impression of the place is that of a moonscape with penguins. The terrain is composed of black kenyte lava formed into flows and boulders and pillows. Kenyte is known only from the slopes of Mounts Kilimanjaro and Kenya in eastern Africa—and from here, on the slopes of Mount Erebus, whose volcanic presence dominates the inland sky above our camp like a glacial god from some formidable polar pantheon. The pillow lava cascades voluptuously down the Royds headlands and bluffs, like the rolls of fat on a sumo wrestler's arm.

Our field camp is just uphill from the Adélie penguin colony, at 77°34′S, 166°11′E. I walk to the ridge that shelters our hut and hides the view of the colony, which is situated at the end of the cape. There the frozen ground between the black lava mounds is mud-brown, a colour derived from centuries of well-trampled penguin shit. The effect is one of a sepia-toned world under the lowering sky. A token amount of ice remains in sheltered cracks where it is not ablated by the winds, but the terrain is largely blasted free of snow, making it a veritable paradise for nesting Adélies.

Ice-free areas such as this one comprise less than 1 percent of Antarctica's land mass, meaning that few places on the continent are suitable for penguin colonies, or, for that matter, for human encampments. Sure enough, at the inland edge of the Cape Royds Adélie colony sits the historic hut of Sir Ernest Shackleton, tucked into a contour of the landscape like it belongs there. Built a century ago by the men of the Nimrod Expedition, the wooden building has weathered to a silvery sheen but looks younger than its hundred years. It too has been preserved by the cold and dry, like the seal carcasses at Hut Point. It gives me a small thrill to think that Cape Royds was the first place that penguins were ever studied, by members of that same expedition.

That the Nimrod Expedition's hut was built here at all was a function of the competition that existed between Scott and Shackleton in the race to get to the Pole. In the months before his departure Shackleton had promised Scott—who in 1902 had already built the dwelling at Hut Point about twenty nautical miles farther south—that he would not base his own expedition's effort out of McMurdo Sound. However, ice and weather forestalled Shackleton's efforts to land at the Bay of Whales on the Ross Ice Shelf, or in King Edward VII Land to the northeast, forcing him to turn south to Ross Island or cancel his expedition entirely. When the *Nimrod* arrived at McMurdo Sound in January of 1908 the pack ice was heavy and Cape Royds was the southernmost point of ice-free land they could reach. With summer drawing to a close, Shackleton decided the ship should offload its supplies and the crew establish a base there in preparation for their attempt on the Pole the following spring. Though they did not reach that destination, by turning back only ninety-seven nautical miles from it, and thus returning with all in his party alive, Shackleton achieved a knighthood and, some have argued, greater success than

Scott, who reached the Pole only to perish with his men on the return journey.

I have a physical sense of the history of this place as I take in Shackleton's hut. The windows are shuttered and the crates of supplies piled outdoors on its lee side are disordered, but if I squint sideways I can almost see the man himself leaning against the door, his pipe clamped in his teeth as he gestures to one of his crew. I already feel a strong sense of kinship with them despite having only just arrived. As Australian explorer John Béchervaise wrote in the 1970s, "In one sense all Antarctic explorers are contemporary, for the continent does not change in man's scale of time."[16] And his sentiment applies equally to scientists working on the frozen continent.

Sixty-five years after Shackleton's men built the hut at Cape Royds, the American writer Charles Neider spent time there while documenting the work of Operation Deep Freeze, the US Navy program that initiated the US presence at McMurdo and ran Antarctic science there from 1955 to 1999, when most support was formally handed to a civilian defence contractor. Neider was one of the few to have stayed there in the mid-twentieth century; Cape Royds was essentially free of human presence from the end of the Heroic Age of Exploration until the 1950s, when the establishment of Scott Base and McMurdo Station as part of the International Geophysical Year (or the IGY as it's usually known) provided a scientific toehold on Ross Island.

"Few people have resided for a substantial time at Cape Royds since Shackleton's day," wrote Neider. "All in modern times have been scientists . . . To modern residents home is McMurdo Station or Scott Base [but in] Shackleton's time the Cape meant home." And little has changed since then.

Our own abode is hidden in a gravelly little hollow upslope from Shackleton's hut and surrounded by low ridges of the ubiquitous volcanic rock, out of sight of the colony yet within earshot of it. The harsh staccato braying of the penguins is attenuated by distance and the muted cadences that reach the hut sound almost musical. *Uh-uh-uh-uh-uh-uhhrrr, uh-uh-uh-uh-uh-uhrrr, uh-uh-uh-uhrrrrrrr,* they sing. David and I spend our first day setting up camp against the background murmur of Adélie calls, slowly stowing away our mound of field gear before the weather changes.

A few days before we arrived a crew of carpenters had come out from McMurdo to erect the hut itself, a one-room sixteen-by-twenty-four-foot Rac-Tent like the one out at Snowmound City. It's a daffodil-yellow half cylinder that looks like a canvas Quonset hut, with a windowed door in each end and clear plastic panels in the roof. When the sun is out from behind the clouds the filtered light inside is buttery, soft, and cheerful. Beside the hut the carpenters have set up two solar panels, now tilted upward and mounted on a rotating metal pole set in a heavy base. Our electricity needs are minimal; given the constant daylight we don't need lighting. But enough power to run our electronics—laptops, various penguin-monitoring devices, a small weather station, the VHF radio for our nightly safety calls to MacOps—is vital. A couple of times a day we turn the panels to face the sun as it wheels about the sky, never setting. In this desolate landscape of black rock and blinding snow, the movement of the solar panels reminds me of sunflowers, mutely echoing the yellow of our Rac-Tent by always seeking the light in the sky.

Lashed to the base of this solar array sit two fifty-gallon steel drums. These are empty for now, but one is destined to fill up with our grey water and the other with our urine, both due to be retroed out by helicopter in a couple of months and then shipped off the continent by supply vessel at the end of the summer.

And behind the hut the carpenters have set up a bank of one-hundred-pound propane tanks connected via a hose under the canvas hut wall to a free-standing heating stove, our sole source of warmth for the season.

The heater will also be the indirect source of our water. Immediately outside the back door towers a snowdrift that is twice the height of the hut, and layered with Erebus's ubiquitous black volcanic grit; one of my first tasks on arrival is to grab our blue Coleman water jug and fill it with snow, then bring it indoors to melt. We've brought ten gallons of potable water from the McMurdo desalinator, enough to last us a couple of days, but for the rest of the season we must drink and wash with the clear, cold, gritty meltwater provided by the local snow. The jug's home is the kitchen shelf just over our heating stove, the warmest place in the hut, where its contents will melt quickly enough to provide a constant trickle from its spigot. Every couple of days from now on one of us will have to take the shovel and fill the jug from our snowdrift. This will provide enough water for cooking and drinking, but as a fuel-saving measure we'll clean dirty dishes all season by wiping them with paper towels—I've brought stacks of them from the BFC—and for personal washing a daily scrub with a damp facecloth will have to suffice. In the extremes of dry Antarctic cold, and the roughness of a field camp, these measures are enough.

On the north side of the hut, in its sheltered lee, we store the camp supplies that are impervious to the cold—rebar; the shovel, pickaxe, and sledgehammer; our cross-country skis; some two-by-fours. Weighted down next to these is the stack of white buckets that we'll use for our open-air toilet, separate ones for liquid and solid waste. The two we've already readied for service are tucked into the lee of the hut and have large volcanic rocks on their lids to prevent them from blowing away. Like the U-barrel and grey water, our filled solid waste buckets will be shipped off the continent at the end of the season. Several metres away from camp, out in the open, we stash the HF radio and a survival bag—close enough that we can hope to find them in a whiteout, far enough away to escape unscathed should our hut burn down.

On the windward side of the hut, to the south, I erect the yellow mountaineering tent that will be my sleeping quarters for the next two and a half months. This is a snug and inviting place that, like the main hut, is filled with a golden light when the sun is out. I had moved to erect it on the hut's lee side prior to realizing this was where the toilet buckets would be situated.

"Don't put it there!" says David. "The snowdrifts pile up in the lee. You'll have to dig out every time there's a storm."

The proximity to the toilet zone doesn't seem to figure into this advice, and I have a sense of the lack of privacy we will have from each other, here in the middle of nowhere. I take a break to make us tea, and sit alone out on our little front deck, a rough wooden pallet set on rocks and lashed down against the elements. From the front door of the hut we have a clear view of McMurdo Sound and the Royal Society Range, the portion of the Transantarctic Mountains that forms the west side of the sound. When I look out over the frozen sea I realize that I can hear emperor penguins out on the ice, their distant calls blending with the plaintive honks of the Adélies. They sound tantalizingly close yet are too far away to be seen.

The wind picks up over the course of the first day, and by the time we've eaten dinner the anemometer shows the wind speed at the hut at over twenty-five knots, despite our sheltered hollow. David suggests I sleep with earplugs to mute the flapping of the tent's fly. I get into my bag and its liner wearing the fleece snood over my head, and two layers of long underwear. I drift off feeling as if I'm wrapped up inside in a cozy nest and sleep deeply, without dreams.

The next morning I awake with the sun now high. It is still far too windy to go down to the penguin colony, so I get up, go into the hut to eat breakfast and do some yoga to work the kinks out of my back, then return to the tent and sleeping bag until it's time for lunch. I try to talk with David about the upcoming work but he is engrossed in a book and monosyllabic in his replies, so I turn instead to the camp's binder of fieldwork protocols, trying to sort out my tasks for the next week or so. By mid-afternoon the wind has dropped and we walk down the slope to the Adélie colony for our first visit of the season.

At the tip of the cape the colony extends along the raised edges of a gully leading up from the sea, over the headland called Flagstaff Point, and onto adjacent rocky bluffs overlooking the ocean. Here the terrain is well drained and with plenty of pebbles for nest-building, just the way the penguins like it. The colony is made up of a mosaic of smaller subcolonies that occupy the patches of elevated and snow-free habitat unaffected by meltwater runoff. In each subcolony the penguin territories are contiguous, spaced so that each bird sitting on its nest is just within beak-locking distance of its adjacent neighbour or neighbours. In between the subcolonies are unoccupied areas of mud and rock, with these sometimes used by nesting skuas, or more often by penguins travelling through the colony on their journeys to and from the sea. From the edge of the colony David points out the boundary of the Antarctic Specially Protected Area, or ASPA. ASPAs are designated under the Antarctic Treaty system, this one to protect the world's southernmost Adélie penguin colony. Our research permits allow us to enter it, but any visitors to camp will have to remain outside its boundaries.

All around us the birds go about their business, oblivious to our presence. The males are the first to arrive each spring, and the colony is still largely occupied by unpaired birds on their territories, each awaiting the arrival of a female. Adélies build their nests entirely with stones, and throughout the colony male penguins bustle about, busily trundling to and fro carrying small rocks prised from the frozen debris of last year's nests, or stolen from the piles gathered by their neighbours. The birds carry a single rock at a time in their beak, so the back-and-forth activity is constant.

When these males are not nest-building they stand guard at their half-formed piles of stones, or engage in what is known as an ecstatic display, their primary courtship behaviour. This begins with a penguin throwing back his head and spreading flippers wide, then swelling his chest with air and stretching his neck to its full length while slowly fanning his wings back and forth, looking just like a conductor standing on his toes to call forth some gentle notes from the back of his orchestra. Then the sounds begin to issue forth from the bird's throat, at first a quiet sputtering *put-put-put-put* like a small outboard motor starting up in the distance, then, with little warning, the small motor metamorphoses into a loudly braying donkey, the increasing volume accompanied by more vigorous wing movements and a general pumping up of the entire penguin, as if he is trying to reach some sort of crescendo where he might burst. As suddenly as the ruckus starts it is over again, the bird slowly deflating while he lowers his head and wings to look around shyly as if expecting applause, or accolades in the form of an approaching female.

The female penguins will soon be returning to the colony en masse to find last year's mate, or to try to meet a new male if last year's has died or been delayed, with time being of the essence here in this land of the briefest of summers. Each pair will then copulate, with the female initially remaining at the nest until she lays her two large and yolky eggs, about eight days after her arrival. The male takes the first incubation shift, which commences as soon as the eggs are laid. With each egg weighing about 120 grams, or one-quarter of a pound, egg production is a physiologically demanding task and after laying the female must return to sea as soon as possible to replenish her fat reserves, in preparation for the rigours of the rest of the breeding season.

We spend the rest of the day deploying the penguin weighbridge. This is the device that was making David so grumpy back at McMurdo, and along with its data-logging computer, solar panels, and plastic snow fencing, it comprises one of the season's main pieces of research equipment. The weighbridge itself is essentially an electronic scale enclosed inside a low ramp-like structure with a gentle incline designed for stubby penguin legs. Once it is levelled in place with the help of a lot of broken volcanic rock, we peg out the orange fencing to corral the adjacent subcolony of Adélies so that the bridge is the only way for them to come and go to and from the sea. This way we can log the length of each bird's foraging trips and, later in the season, the mass of each chick meal—all part of studying the demography of the Cape Royds colony. Cables snake from underneath the weighbridge to its computer, which we have sheltered inside a mountaineering tent that looks much like my sleeping quarters up at camp. Each individual bird traversing the bridge will be identified via a passive integrated transponder, or PIT tag. These subcutaneous devices are essentially the same ones used by vets and livestock breeders—tiny encased microchips with individualized IDs that allow for identification of lost or stolen animals. In the case of the penguins, their PIT tags will allow the weighbridge computer to assign each pulse of data to its own individual for later analysis.

By the time we are done it's nearly dinner time and my back is sore from lifting large rocks to secure the weighbridge tent's guy lines. Dinner is a largely silent affair, with David staring into the mid-distance, immersed in his thoughts, again responding monosyllabically to my questions about how the research work will unfold. I retreat into my own thoughts and memories. It has been over fifteen years since my father died, but there are still days when I miss our friendship profoundly. I briefly imagine what it would have been like to call him on our camp's satellite phone and share stories about being isolated with others—in his case, on ships servicing navigational aids in the Arctic; in mine, here in a polar field camp on the edge of the world. But even in this otherworldly place he is as far away as he ever was, and I instead retreat early to my tent with a book.

5

IT IS STARTLING to see how quickly the sea ice has cleared. On our arrival at Cape Royds two and a half days ago, McMurdo Sound was solidly iced in as far as the eye could see. By this morning, we were clearly situated near the interface where frozen sea meets liquid ocean: Open leads were visible in front of the colony and the ice had a rotten look to it, with a sickly greyish pallor and many smaller cracks in evidence. Now this afternoon the wind has pushed the broken ice to the north and the ice edge has arrived at Cape Royds, open water lapping against the frozen sea ice that stretches southward from the colony.

The rapidity of this change makes me nervous, given that the sea ice track from McMurdo is still flagged as operable all the way to Backdoor Bay on the south shore of Cape Royds, just around the corner from the colony. Since I've arrived, I've found myself haunted by the voice of an old shipmate mournfully recounting the loss of three colleagues who disappeared during a dogsledding trip back in 1982, before dogs were banned from the continent under the Antarctic Treaty. He too had been a dogsled driver, exploring and mapping the Antarctic Peninsula for the British Antarctic Survey.

"They went through the sea ice, mate," he'd tell me over drinks, clearly tormented by the old memory each time we saw the commemorative cross on a rocky rise near Lemaire Channel on the Antarctic Peninsula. The men were away from base on an overnight trip to a nearby island when a sudden midwinter storm blew out the ice. They stayed at the island's refuge hut for a few days, running low on supplies yet waiting for the sea to refreeze before attempting to travel back. But the deep midwinter cold was no match for the channel's strong currents, and the newly formed sea ice was weak. The next storm came quickly, the sea ice was blown out once more, and the three were never seen again. This event took place on the other side of the continent a long time ago, but the men were caught by the sort of rapidly changing ice conditions that are in front of us today. This evening the water in front of Cape Royds is white with vicious wind-whipped whitecaps, not ice, and only the occasional bergy bit or flotilla of brash ice serves as a reminder that we saw a group of McMurdo snowmobiles travel across the frozen sea past the cape just yesterday.

Whether the ice is safe for travel is a moot point at present. The same wind that is blowing out the ice is keeping us inside again, enduring the tedium of yet another weather day stuck in the hut, and the local conditions are visible only in brief glimpses when we step outside to visit the bucket. Here in camp it's blowing thirty knots, with the temperature below −10°C. Down at the colony the wind will be gusting much harder and the risk of frostbite to binocular-holding fingers is high enough that we'd only be able to work for short periods of time.

But the hut is a snug enough place to be marooned now that we've finished unpacking all our gear. Food, books, and electronics line the shelves fitted along each wall, and on two makeshift desks—each comprising an extra-wide shelf set at hip height—sit our laptops, charging off a bank of batteries that are in turn being charged by the solar panels, at least when the sun is not hidden by cloud. The hut won't win any home efficiency awards as items sitting toward the backs of the shelves tend to freeze, but the propane heater keeps it cozy and there are remarkably few drafts despite the fact that the walls are made of just a single layer of canvas.

Before cooking us a late dinner I pull on my thickly insulated moon boots and several more layers of clothes and venture outside for a break. It is all I can do to walk up the height of land that shelters our hut. As I crest the ridge I emerge into the full force of the storm, which shoves me backward like a push from a strong pair of hands. I consider crawling down the other side, but make it on foot by leaning bodily into the wind with such force that if it stops I'll crash flat on my face.

When I return from my wind-blasted stroll I dig out the box we've buried in the snowdrift outside our back door, retrieve some frozen halibut, and cook it with packaged pasta alfredo and Surprise brand dehydrated peas, another field camp staple from the Kiwi section at the BFC food room. Already I'm finding our diet a struggle, heavy as it is in packaged and canned foods. The majority of these provisions are of US origin and full of sugar or high-fructose corn syrup, making them unbearably sweet to my Canadian palate, so I'm grateful for the New Zealand component of our food supplies. Raro, the Kiwi drink mix powder, is less sweet and more fruity than its North American counterparts. Its flavour makes me crave our over-mineralized and flat-tasting meltwater, and makes bearable the ever-present volcanic grit that eddies in the bottom of my water bottle. This is a good thing given the need to be constantly sipping water to combat the dehydration brought on by our high daily levels of exertion and the desiccating air of the world's driest continent. Its icy countenance notwithstanding, much of Antarctica is a desert, with only about fifty millimetres of precipitation per year falling across the Polar Plateau on average.

The challenges of staying warm also contribute to our dehydration. Each night is cold enough that I wear multiple layers of clothing to bed and do vigorous sit-ups inside the sleeping bag to warm my feet before going to sleep with the bag's hood and my fleece snood closed tight around my face. Each morning the temperature has inevitably warmed just enough that I awake twisted in my garments and coated in sweat, mouth dry and papery despite the sub-zero temperatures outside my bag. My morning routine has quickly become established around warmth and hydration: I pull on extra clothes over those I've slept in, stagger out of the tent to the pee bucket, then go into the hut to gulp down half a litre or so of frigid meltwater while waiting for the kettle to boil and coffee to drip through the filter.

Along with their effects on my water intake, the constant physical work and the cold are already shaping my eating habits as well. I'm ingesting much more butter and sugar and chocolate than normal in the name of getting enough calories, and I think of my friend Henry, a veteran traveller of Mongolia, with his stories of drinking hot tea laced with rancid yak butter. Suddenly it doesn't sound as disgusting as when he described it to me, and I begin adding butter to my own mid-afternoon tea. The extra fat is delicious and I wonder how many calories per day I am burning. Certainly nothing like the 11,500 that physician Mike Stroud calculated as their maximum daily caloric intake when he and Sir Ranulph Fiennes traversed the continent on foot. However, I'm eating far more than at home and still losing weight. The strange food, the ongoing struggle to stay hydrated, the unfamiliar surroundings, and an erratic schedule are all making me feel off kilter and vaguely nauseated, and though I'm constantly hungry I struggle to have an appetite at mealtime. In contrast, David, Antarctic veteran, ploughs stolidly through each meal and each night appears to sleep solidly on his bedroll in the corner of the hut.

—

It has taken a couple more days but the wind has finally subsided enough for our penguin work to begin in earnest. For me this work includes beginning to map and monitor B-REF, the abbreviated name of the reference subcolony of banded birds. There are 101 Adélies in this subcolony today, including a banded individual from last year, and there will be more there tomorrow: New birds are arriving from the sea each day as the breeding season gets underway. The mapping and monitoring are tasks I'll undertake almost daily through the season, and they require close attention as the B-REF birds are those whose reproductive data we will use to estimate annual reproductive success for the entire colony. For the penguins everywhere else at Cape Royds, we will only be banding a subset of the close-to-fledging chicks late in the season, but at B-REF, each breeding adult will be individually identified with a numbered metal band so we can record the details of his or her reproductive success.

Penguin bands are unusual. With their stubby lower limbs, penguins can't wear the numbered leg ring that has long been favoured in ornithological studies worldwide, so, thanks to the pioneering work of Bill Sladen, researchers mark birds with flat, hydrodynamic metal bands on their flippers instead—although it is increasingly common to substitute PIT tags because even the flat profile of the flipper band adds some extra drag to the birds in the water. These bands fit loosely but securely around the narrowest part of the flipper, mid-humerus, above the bone's widening at its joint with the radius and ulna.

Flipper bands mean that for penguins, unlike for most other birds, band-searching consists of looking at wings. Each day from now on I will be using my binoculars to scan the left flipper of hundreds of penguins to look for the banded ones, recording each band's numbers and the breeding status and exact location of the bird that is wearing it. The daily band-searches are central to the study and they will also be carried out by our colleagues based at Capes Crozier and Bird—all of us searching for Adélies that were banded as chicks at these colonies in previous seasons. As the vast majority of penguins are not banded in a given year, this is definitely akin to seeking a needle in a haystack, although maybe it's more like seeking a needle in a sea of needles.

Even more difficult to find than the bands are the fifteen tiny light-sensing data-loggers that had been fitted to birds' legs—using a sort of cable tie attachment, which is different from the permanent metal leg bands fitted to other species—at the end of the previous season. These daylight loggers, also known as global location sensors or GLS tags, record ambient daylight when the bird is on the surface of the water or resting on the ice; subsequent calculations with the downloaded data will estimate a bird's location over time, based on day length and the time of sunrise and sunset. The small size of these tags—they each weigh about a gram—is both an advantage and a disadvantage. On the pro side of the equation they are so lightweight that they have no impact on the birds, but the minimal size is achieved at the cost of eliminating any satellite component for uploading data remotely; this means that the study birds must be recaptured months later for tag retrieval, with tag size making them very hard to relocate. These relatively simple data-loggers revolutionized migration ecology when they first were used in the 1990s, when they were pioneered on seabirds such as penguins and albatrosses.

We are undertaking the band-searching portion of the study to help estimate important demographic parameters like survival rate and breeding propensity—values that are crucial for estimating population changes over time—and to track the Adélies' movements among colonies from year to year. Penguins exhibit what appears to be a high degree of natal philopatry, meaning that they tend to return to their place of hatching when it is time to breed. But when conditions are particularly harsh, all bets are off.

In the early 2000s, iceberg B-15A broke off from its parent berg B-15, which in turn had broken from the Ross Ice Shelf a couple of years before. At about 11,000 square kilometres in size, at its calving B-15 was the largest iceberg ever recorded, at least during the era of satellite imagery. Even as a mere child of B-15, B-15A nonetheless started out its icy life at 6,500 square kilometres, meaning that when formed it was larger than Prince Edward Island, an entire Canadian province. It is unclear whether the original berg's calving was due to the effects of climate change or natural variability, but one thing that is obvious is that over their multi-year tenure, B-15 and its offspring have been dramatically—and sometimes catastrophically—affecting the penguin colonies at Ross Island.

B-15A has been wedged up against the north coast of Ross Island for a couple of years now, changing the oceanography of the Ross Sea and creating a giant natural experiment on penguin breeding biology and foraging ecology. Last year the grounded berg's alteration of regional ocean currents rendered the summer sea ice so extreme that penguins had to walk as many as seventy kilometres each time they returned to Cape Royds to feed a chick—whereas in a normal season the ice edge would be right at the cape, as it is today. This year there are already signs of a colony-level response to the berg. Royds is the smallest of the Ross Island colonies, and by David's estimation there are only about 2,500 pairs of Adélies here this year—one thousand fewer than at the start of the previous breeding season a year ago—so it's likely many have given up in anticipation of another unfavourable ice year and shown up en masse at the more accessible Cape Bird and Cape Crozier colonies instead.

"Way fewer birds here than last season," David stated over dinner last night. "Penguins don't like walking."

Still, as he has mentioned to me, this may just be part of the ebb and flow of penguin life at Ross Island: The West Antarctic Ice Sheet (with its regional remnant form being the Ross Ice Shelf that surrounds most of Ross Island) has been spawning such bergs since it began to retreat at the end of the Last Glacial Maximum, twelve thousand years ago. As a species, these penguins have lived with this icy flux for millennia, and we now have the opportunity to observe how they will have responded on numerous past occasions, and over geologic time scales.

All our plans for daily band-searching are weather permitting, of course: There is nothing like a long period of holding up metal binoculars in wind-blasted sub-zero temperatures to bring on frostnipped or frostbitten fingers, gloves notwithstanding. In my daypack I carry hand-warmers, and today I stuff one into each glove to combat the bitter cold, pulling the drawstring tight on my snood so it covers all of my face but my eyes, protected behind glacier glasses. I start band-searching from an outcrop above the colony, and find four banded penguins attending separate nests up at its northerly edge. From my vantage point I can hear more emperor penguins out on the sea ice at the tidal cracks, calling to each other in voices that are somewhere between a flute and a kazoo. The most distant group is nearly a kilometre away, their calls carrying clearly to where I stand. Perhaps natural selection has honed these vocalizations for their capacity to carry over the vast open spaces. Hearing their voices lifts my spirits, an otherworldly counterpoint to the harsher calls and the aggressive hustle and bustle of the Adélie penguin colony, with the onset of breeding season in vigorous full swing.

On my way back to our hut at the end of the work day I see a skua copulation, the first I've seen this season; it's the pair at the edge of the colony near Shackleton's hut. If one can describe such things as tender, it seemed to be so—perhaps it was the contrast to the speedy balancing act performed by mating Adélies.

—

Tonight it's David's turn to make dinner. With the weather letting up we will be working long days and shifting to a later supper schedule accordingly. He's a methodical cook, chopping ingredients carefully, engrossed in the task, but not wasting time either. He never takes long to make us a simple but decent camp meal. While he cooks I make a large funnel entirely out of duct tape to replace the plastic one that blew away in yesterday's gale. This may be another first for duct tape. A funnel is a vital piece of equipment out here—without it, we can't pour our grey water into the fifty-gallon storage drum, or our urine into the fifty-gallon U-barrel, without running the risk of a spume of the stuff blowing fifty metres downwind, or, worse, into our faces on an unpredictable gust. Yesterday conditions were too windy for us to decant liquids even using the funnel, and today it is gone. Now our urine is sitting in a frozen lump at the bottom of the piss pot outside the back door of the hut. We're either going to have to bring it inside to melt or return it to town as a frozen cylinder in the helicopter. Sure to induce loathing in the pilots, especially once it starts melting on board.

Right after the meal, we have our nightly radio sked with McMurdo and a radio check-in with the Crozier crew. They tell us that this morning there was a team out there from Mactown to do a cleanup of the old hut, where David lived while doing his PhD research decades ago. The crew had picked up 110 pounds of rusty nails—using a magnet—from the place where the old dwelling had stood until it was deliberately burned down in the 1970s to get rid of it, rather than taking it in pieces back to McMurdo. They sure did things differently in those days.

I go back down to the colony for the last task of the day, the hour-long shoreline watch, where every other evening it is my turn to huddle up on one of the bluffs to watch for hunting leopard seals and record their interactions with penguins, fatal or otherwise. Apart from a few barely open leads in the ice and a shoreline crack, the ocean in front of Cape Royds is again frozen after a couple of days of calm winds and exceptionally frigid temperatures—the surface in the leads just thick enough for the Adélie penguins to scamper across, thin enough to be almost invisible. Three of the emperors have come close to shore and are swimming in one of the leads. They submerge and surface, submerge and surface, hunting under the sea ice, where small fish are plentiful and not yet depleted by the seasonal depredations of seals and other penguins. Through their activity these three birds alone are keeping open the still-freezing leads, stopping the nascent ice from forming every time they emerge, and incidentally keeping it open for the Adélies to use. I can see the thin and elastic skin of sea ice stretch, break, and re-form with each emperor's surface and dive. The Adélies follow their bigger cousins to their breathing holes so that they too can forage close to the colony—they would be doing a lot of walking back and forth across the ice to more open water if it weren't for the emperors being here.

Tucked into a niche in the rocks on the bluff during the shoreline watch, I am out of the way of the slight three-knot breeze that is moving the frigid air here tonight. Grant, Viola, and Rachael told us during the radio check-in that at Cape Crozier they are currently hut-bound and being blasted by a punishing easterly, but here, today, we are sheltered beneath the towering slopes of Mount Erebus and I am warm and even comfortable in my nook. Across McMurdo Sound the mountains and glaciers leading to the Dry Valleys gleam in the clear golden light of evening, and the sunlight sets the ruffled sea on fire. Leisurely groups of Adélie penguins enter and leave the water via the open tidal crack at the edge of the glistening expanse of ice holding fast to the shore. With the air still cold enough to continue to freeze the sea, circles of pancake ice collectively wheel there in a slow ballet, their edges ever thickening where they touch and push together. Even the skuas are languid in their flights, perhaps caught up in the serenity of this limpid Antarctic evening and the clarity and brightness of light and mountains, sea and ice, glaciers and sky.

Late the next afternoon David and I are down at the colony when about a dozen emperor penguins casually waddle ashore from the sea ice and then travel single file up the slope in an apparent visit to Pony Lake. Pony Lake is a frozen meltwater pond that lies in the middle of the Adélie colony and was named after the Shackleton expedition's ponies, which were tethered near it all those years ago. On the lake's ice the emperors congregate in small groups or bow to each other in pairs or rest alone on their bellies, ponderous yet graceful, all calling to each other in their delightful voices. They go about their business seemingly unconcerned by our presence but occasionally regard us briefly through their black-button eyes as we go by them on our way to mark an Adélie nest or carry past some rocks to weigh down equipment.

None of these individuals will breed here—the closest emperor penguin colony is at Beaufort Island, about twenty kilometres northwest of Cape Bird, while the Cape Crozer colony is situated on the far side of Ross Island over one hundred kilometres away by sea—but emperor visits to Cape Royds have been documented since the days of Shackleton's Nimrod Expedition, when Scottish biologist James Murray described the behaviour of these visiting birds. Today they largely ignore the resident Adélies, who, when they cross paths with these larger birds, nervously peck at the emperors just below the level of where their midriff would be, if they had one. Once in a while an emperor's flipper lazily waves in the direction of the Adélies' flailing beaks but most of them stare above the smaller penguins' heads at the horizon, regally oblivious to the havoc being wreaked around their feet.

A timeless dance, it seems, with these same interactions described here over a century ago by Murray, who wrote of Cape Royds, "While the Adélies were nesting [the emperors] began to come in numbers to inspect the camp. Passing among the Adélies, the two kinds usually paid no attention to one another, but sometimes an Adélie would think an Emperor came too close to her nest, and a curious unequal quarrel would ensue, the little impudence pecking and scolding . . . the Adélie knew the value of discretion whenever the Emperor raised his flipper."[17]

Though the light is mediocre I decide to fetch my camera from the hut after dinner, enticed by the emperors' synchronous bowing displays against a snowy backdrop. In the time it takes me to go from colony to hut and back again most of the emperors have left for the sea ice, and the three that remain stand motionless in the middle of frozen Pony Lake, apparently contemplating life. As I draw near they drop their meditative and disengaged air and stretch up their heads to follow my approach and then advance, almost as if to say, "Hey, it's you! You're back!" They then proceed to shuffle along behind me as I skirt the pond's perimeter, stopping when I stop, starting when I start again, occasionally moving a few paces closer to bob their heads and call at me melodically. When I sit on the ice nearby to take a couple of photos I begin with my telephoto lens, but in short order have to switch to a 35mm and then to the wide-angle zoom as the curious birds come closer and closer. Soon one is pecking at my camera case beside me, and then peering right into my face while bowing to me and calling, and I realize I am being courted by an emperor. I feel inordinately flattered, as if this courtship event says something profound about my value as a human being. As perhaps it does, at least from the penguins' perspective. "They seem to regard men as penguins like themselves," Murray wrote.[18] And perhaps women as penguins like themselves too, given their behaviour. Our *ménage à quatre* only ends when I grow too cold to stay still any longer, and hike back up to our hut, and to bed.

—

A couple of days later I'm entering data after dinner and am startled by a knock at the door of our hut. It's the director of New Zealand's Antarctic program.

"Hello!" he says from the doorway, sticking out a hand after removing his glove. "Lou Sanson."

"I know you from somewhere," I say, shaking hands while mentally coming to terms with the shock of seeing another human being who is not David Ainley.

It turns out his group arrived yesterday on the back of another departing weather system and is out for a couple of days' escape from Scott Base. With typical Kiwi hardiness they are camped out just over the ridge at the wanigan, a cube-shaped emergency refuge made of moulded fibreglass and resembling a walk-in freezer unit, painted a shade of hospital green for greater visibility. The wanigan is there for any New Zealand field party that gets stuck out at Cape Royds in bad weather—or for field parties that just want to get away from the crowds at Scott Base—but its tiny single room is so cramped it seems that most visitors just pitch their tents outside and use the wanigan as a windbreak, cook shack, and gear depot.

Lou is a large, hearty fellow who likes to chat. After a lengthy conversation I realize that we crossed paths when working as cruise ship lecturers on the Antarctic Peninsula; shared participation in illicit tobogganing on steep icy slopes with the hardier of our ship's passengers comes to mind, and memories of someone's cracked rib following a sled crash. He is rather pleased to have come across David here. This is because the Kiwis apparently have a trip planned in a few days for high-level VIPs, including the prime minister's number one aide, the head of the fisheries ministry, and a gaggle of conservation types.

Portions of the New Zealand government are keen to support the proposal to designate the Ross Sea as a global marine protected area. This marine protection plan is all tied up with interest in the toothfish fishery, minke whale hunting by the Japanese, the potential for a scallop harvest, and a recent controversial paper written by David in which he set aside scientific detachment and called for the Ross Sea to be protected as the last unexploited ocean in the world, before it's too late. He published an earlier paper in the same vein in the scientific journal *Marine Ornithology*, entitled, in his trenchant style, "The Ross Sea, Antarctica, where all ecosystem processes still remain for study, but maybe not for long."[19] Over the ridge at the Kiwi camp-out is a reporter from one of the major New Zealand newspapers and Lou is keen to have David talk to him. After more chit-chat he leaves on the promise to return tomorrow, and the hut's silence closes in again.

The next morning, I've only just got up and am heating water on the propane cookstove for a wash and a cup of coffee when the door opens and a balding, bespectacled man in New Zealand blue field garb stands hesitating on the threshold, peering forward through fogged lenses and turning his hat in his hands. It's the journalist in the flesh.

"Come in, come in," David and I both hurriedly say a couple of times before he stops hovering and enters, mercifully shutting the door on the wind.

I make him a cup of tea and continue with my ablutions, pouring half the hot water into a coffee filter and half into a plastic bowl, washing my face with water as hot as I can stand it: the best moment of each day. Shortly thereafter, Lou's cheerful face appears at the door and he steps inside to join the confab, or perhaps to stage-manage it. His drink of choice is hot chocolate so I make him some along with my breakfast—today, cream of wheat—while we chat about our respective backgrounds.

"This place is like the crossroads of the world," I say to David after the two Kiwis have departed for the comfort of their tents.

I'm being slightly facetious, but the fact is that whenever there are bigwigs in Antarctica visiting McMurdo Station or Scott Base, they hop on a helicopter or climb into some weird tracked vehicle to fly or drive over the sea ice for a visit to Cape Royds and the closest penguins to town. In a few days we're due to experience a plague of US congressional staffers, flying in via McMurdo for a whistle stop on their budget appropriations tour—presumably related to the National Science Foundation and the Office of Polar Programs, the federal body that funds US research here. These sudden transitions between utter isolation and intimate bouts of socializing threaten to give me whiplash, but the company is nonetheless welcome. Royds is also a favourite place for the few tourist vessels that make it this far south, given the presence of Shackleton's hut and the added bonus of the world's southernmost Adélies. The tourists are scheduled to show up here later in the season, after the US Coast Guard icebreakers have bashed the annual supply route through the fast ice to the stations at the southern end of McMurdo Sound.

The following day I slowly awake from a nightmare on the moan of the rising wind, my eyes full of tears. In the dream, I am with my sister, weeping. She has just told me that she has been diagnosed with stage four cancer and wants me to take care of her two young sons after she dies. The older one will need braces; the younger one still likes to have stories read to him before he goes to sleep. I can't bear the thought that she will soon die, and I cry unconsolably. Then everything shifts and I am flooded with relief when I realize that this is just a dream, that my sister is safe and sound at home; I tell myself that I will call her and tell her about it. When I really do wake up the relief seeps away, to be replaced by an echo of the grief from the dream's beginning. It's only in these nightmares that the numbness is erased and I truly feel the devastation that my sister's death has wrought.

I go into the hut feeling off kilter emotionally but also physically, extra hungry and calorie-deprived, and decide to make a bowl of instant lentil soup with a fried egg in it for breakfast. David, usually the early bird, is still curled up in his sleeping bag on the floor in the corner of the hut, neck gaiter pulled up over his face so that just his shock of greying hair is visible. He stays there, apparently sleeping, as I drink my second cup of coffee and begin perusing the week's data on my computer, trying to ignore the wind.

It is 2:30 p.m. before David eventually emerges from his bag, and who can blame him? It's another crappy day and it seems to be getting worse. Here in our sheltered hollow we are protected from the worst of the wind yet I just saw the anemometer on our little digital weather station register a gust of thirty-five knots, and stronger gusts periodically hammer the hut's walls. The Kiwis left yesterday—just in time, it seems. Out on the water the sea state shows that the winds are approaching storm force, one of our worst days yet. It is noisy in the hut, with its canvas sides flapping in and out, metal and wood ribs squeaking, and the occasional can of food being bounced off the shelves to fall clattering onto the wooden floor. I finally have to stuff a wedge of cardboard between the booze bottles on our liquor shelf as they are clinking together mercilessly in an unbearably maddening concerto, and each time I try to separate the bottles they jiggle back together like a winter huddle of emperor penguins and start clinking again. Funny that with all the other racket in here this is the one sound in particular that is irritating me; in comparison to the vibrating bottles, the roar of the wind and the squeaking and rumbling of the hut has faded to mere background noise. Well, almost. It would be nice to be able to hear the "the call of the vast empty spaces [and the] silence," as Robert Falcon Scott's sister Grace called it when dissecting her brother's motives following his death.[20]

Yet any hardship imposed by an Antarctic storm is indubitably part of what draws men and women to this punishing place. As Grace Scott also wrote of her brother—and perhaps of adventurers more widely—Antarctica also represented a striving for "the beauty of untrodden snow; liberty of thought and action; the . . . seeming infinitude of its uninhabited regions whose secrets man had not then pierced, and the hoped-for conquest of raging elements."[21] David and I are not here to conquer anything, but I admit to a certain fundamental satisfaction in pitting ourselves against such abysmal conditions, and thriving.

6

WE'RE JUST GETTING back into our routine. Three days ago, and ten days into our stay at Cape Royds, the flagging storm still rattled the hut and we were halfway through a silent dinner (more pasta) when David made some throat-clearing noises, then "Hmm, err, umm." Since we've been out here I've noticed a tendency for him to start and punctuate his sentences with such dysfluencies, and I think fancifully that he sounds not unlike a penguin himself as he makes them.

"Urr, we're going into McMurdo in the morning," he said. "The helo's coming at eleven thirty. Be ready."

I looked at him blankly.

"I thought we were out here for the duration," I told him.

"I need some help with the weighbridge," he replied, and went back to eating his fettuccine.

During post-dinner cleanup I had fantasized about the shower I would have—with our limited water I had only washed my hair once since our arrival, in the dish tub, and it was again feeling lank and disgusting. In camp I mostly keep it tied up on the top of my head so I don't feel its greasiness against my face and neck as a reminder of how much I dislike this side of remote fieldwork.

David cleared his throat again.

"Bring that case of wine," he said. "It'll freeze if we leave it here."

My day in town was hectic, with laundry and shower to catch up on, supplies to round up (more hot chocolate), and above all, messages to download and send on the slow Mactown system. It was simultaneously weird and normal to be back to the hustle and bustle of McMurdo, wearing fresh inner layers of clothing while I laundered the long underwear and other items I'd worn twenty-four hours a day since arriving at Cape Royds a couple of weeks ago. Best was communication with friends at home, and the glass of wine at the Coffee House was a treat, but I had a stiflingly long sleep in an overheated, windowless dorm room decorated with abandon in all known shades of the colour brown, and I missed my bright and cozy tent and its warm sleeping bag.

I woke the next morning to gusty winds and called Helo Ops on the Mactown phone system, who told me to check back for an updated departure time. Pilots here don't like flying when blowing snow obscures the horizon: They can't tell where land ends and the sky begins, which can have bad results if you are flying a helicopter. But by late morning the winds had calmed and I met David at the hangar on schedule. His mop of grey hair looked clean and fluffy. It had been strange not to see him for twenty-four hours. Well, I had glimpsed him in the corner of the Coffee House the night before, drinking wine with an attractive dark-haired woman, but I hadn't approached their table. I think it was one of the NSF program managers but I was not in the mood for talking shop, and anyway seem to have lost any previously held social skills.

"Did you have a good time in town?" I asked.

"Erm, yeess," he said, repressively.

Our helicopter left at noon under a sullen overcast sky and we followed the sea-ice road along the coast to Cape Royds. Even without blowing snow, distance is difficult to judge in this monochromatic land—white sea ice, white mountains, white sky—and I was surprised to realize that the tiny dot below us was a Pisten Bully, another tracked vehicle, crawling along its flagged route over the frozen ocean toward Cape Evans. It hadn't felt as if we'd climbed that high.

This is Antarctic transportation in the modern age. One hundred years before, the icy route below us was traversed by Scott and by Shackleton, man-hauling their sleds and practising runs with their hardy Manchurian ponies. (These animals, which were fed a meat-based ration to decrease the volume of their fodder, were favoured by the earlier British explorers over dogs—and were probably the source of the anthrax spores at Cape Evans because the modern anthrax vaccine for livestock wasn't used widely until the 1930s). It was only in the mid-twentieth century that travelling via aircraft and tracked vehicles became the norm in Antarctica. But even motorized vehicles are not immune to Antarctica's hazards; this season we've already heard of one helo crash—or "hard landing," as it was euphemistically called.

Now we're back in camp again, catching up on research and chores, and toward the end of the day a group of Kiwis arrive by tracked vehicle, drifting in off the sea ice like emperor penguins to set up camp down by the wanigan. They're from the school of veterinary science at Massey University and are here because the emperors are still periodically hanging about at the Adélie colony. They are hoping to catch the birds to collect blood for a study on corticosterone levels that John Cockrem, the PI, has been doing to determine whether different capture techniques can ameliorate any stress response—something that's relevant for penguin researchers in general to understand. Their team had been at Cape Crozier trying to work with the emperors from the colony there and had heard from Grant about the birds hanging out here at Cape Royds.

"It's too bloody cold and windy for us to work at Cape Crozier," John grumbles over a cup of tea at our hut that evening. Apparently getting a few drops of blood from the flippers of the emperor penguins has been nearly impossible out at the Crozier colony because of peripheral vasoconstriction, meaning that the extreme cold was restricting circulation to the birds' extremities. Even when they would manage to get a bit of blood going it would freeze before they could get it into the centrifuge tubes. Based on studies on Adélies they estimated that they had three minutes before elevated corticosterone, the stress response, would show up in a bird's blood and affect their results, so they needed to be quick and the cold wasn't helping.

"You'll be all right here, though," says their guide, a tall and rugged individual with a shaved head and what sounds to my ears like a rather British-sounding accent for a Kiwi. All the New Zealand parties arrive out here with a safety guide from Antarctic Field Training, or AFT—Scott Base's equivalent of FSTP—to make sure nobody falls through the sea ice or goes missing behind a hill. "This place is the banana belt of Ross Island."

I'd heard Grant say the same thing back at McMurdo before we all parted ways and thought he was joking; now I see David nodding his shaggy head in agreement from his corner of the hut. It dawns on me that it's not that the weather is particularly good here; it's just that it's never quite as bad as it gets elsewhere on Ross Island or in McMurdo Sound.

"Hi, I'm Paul," the guide says to me in an aside, and starts to ask me about my photography gear and whether I've got any good shots of the emperors yet; it turns out we use the same camera.

"I've got a great telephoto lens with me you can borrow if you want," he tells me. "I'll be back out again in a week or two. I'll get it back then."

—

Back at the colony, it's clear that spring is progressing. We've been at Royds for nearly two weeks and many more of the lone male Adélies have paired up with a mate. There has been a great influx of females over the past few days, and single penguins are now in the minority. Pairs of birds waiting for eggs to be laid or lone males taking the first incubation shift are now the norm. The place is as noisy and crowded as a bustling town. The breeding season is well and truly underway.

I've been noticing other new things too, my eye refreshed after the hubbub of McMurdo. Snow petrels, as white as their namesake and with a sooty black eye, are periodically flying along the edge of the sea ice and past the cliffs of the colony. They have flown here against the heavy southerly winds we've been having again, a detour along the route from their foraging grounds at sea to the nunataks where they breed, far inland.

"D'you think they're prospecting for nest sites here?" I ask David.

"Errm, nope," he says. "Attracted by the smell. They come here on the southerlies."

These days the colony certainly has a fishy guano reek to it that the petrels must find reminiscent of their food; unlike many birds, those in the petrel family have excellent olfaction and use it to forage at sea.

We're up early today as we need to count every pair of Adélies currently on nests at the colony, along with our other daily work. HNO, one of the two Kiwi helicopters at Scott Base and with Kiwi researchers on board, will be doing the annual flyover to photograph the entire colony this afternoon. They'll do the same at Cape Bird and Cape Crozier, and we will validate their oblique-angle aerial photos with our ground counts, either of the entire colony (as at Royds, with an average count of only about 2,800 pairs since the 1980s), or of a set of subcolonies at the two larger colonies of Bird and Crozier. These colony counts contribute to an impressive historical dataset that goes back more than fifty years. Tomorrow at Cape Crozier, Grant, Viola, and Rachael will be counting all the nests in Area M, a portion of the Crozier colony that is home to about fourteen thousand pairs. All in all, it'll be a lot of counting.

David and I take roughly 50 percent of the colony each and use tally counters, field notebooks, and pencils to complete our census by lunchtime, just before the helo arrives. Counting every nest is a feat of intense concentration, albeit one that is aided by the fact that the subcolonies divide the large areas of penguins into countable units. Each subcolony was numbered in the early 1980s by the Kiwi biologists who implemented the aerial surveys, and their numbering is still used in the study today. These photo-monitoring flights are done under permit, of course; in the normal run of things helicopters are not allowed to fly over the colony. Nonetheless the Kiwis fly high enough that their passes don't disturb the birds, and the colony is small enough that they are done quickly. Before they leave, the helo flies over our hut, coming in low so the pilot can give us a thumbs-up from the cockpit before heading back to Scott Base.

While band-searching at the colony later the same afternoon I watch a skua steal an egg from an incubating Adélie. As the penguin stands up to shift his incubation position, the skua swoops in out of nowhere to fly circles around him. The penguin gamely swings his beak around to confront the circling threat, but makes the mistake of standing up off his two eggs to do so. The skua continues its circling until the penguin loses his bearings, and then the skua darts in to take an egg on the wing while the dizzied penguin is still facing in the opposite direction. All of this in just a couple of blinks of an eye.

The skuas don't really fly in out of nowhere, of course, but the ones with the Adélie subcolonies within their territories spend a great deal of time sitting on the ground near the nesting penguins, staying out of the wind and watching for an opportunity to grab an egg. Much of the time they are not successful. Often enough, they are. They're frequently all but invisible on the ground as they blend in with its mud-brown colour and hide from the wind behind small rocky protuberances, looking like miniature nunataks rising from a sea of hardened guano. I worry about stepping backward onto one of these birds as I circle the busy subcolonies looking for banded penguins. They are completely unafraid of us and often don't move until we're half a pace away; then they shuffle sideways with an indignant cluck and settle back down in the lee of another insignificant piece of rock.

Walking up on the top of the bluffs overlooking the sea I hear one making a high-pitched keening sound that I haven't heard before. I look around and there sits a skua on its nest, calling to warn me away. The breeding season has begun for them too.

View of McMurdo Station from Hut Point, with Robert Falcon Scott's Discovery Hut in the foreground.

Storage shed at Snowmound City on the Ross Ice Shelf, about five kilometres outside McMurdo Station, with Snow School participants building snow shelters in the distance.

Unloading a Bell 212 with field camp supplies at Cape Royds.

Adélie penguin, Cape Royds. Penguins' flippers are rigid and paddle-like, designed for a life of swimming.

Adélie penguin coming ashore at Cape Royds, feathers still sleek and wet from the sea. Note its short-billed appearance resulting from head feathers extending far down the beak, an adaptation to a life in extreme cold.

Courting Adélie penguins overlooking frozen McMurdo Sound. Their streamlined body form helps to reduce resistance in the water and increase swimming speed.

A group of emperor penguins resting on frozen Pony Lake, Cape Royds. Virtually all the nesting colonies of this species are on fast ice rather than on land.

Two curious emperor penguins on Pony Lake.

South polar skua. These fierce birds will aggressively defend their nesting territories from intruders.

A south polar skua pair at their territory on the edge of the Cape Royds Adélie colony, from where they will prey on penguin eggs and chicks. As generalist foragers, like many species in the gull family, skuas will also hunt for fish and krill, and scavenge seal placentas and carrion.

Cape Royds field camp following a storm—the author's sleeping tent is on the left, and the larger Rac-Tent provides the main accommodation and living area.

Shackleton's hut at Cape Royds. The hut was originally constructed and erected in England, then brought in sections by ship. Volcanic Mount Erebus is visible in the background.

Adélie penguins making their way to Cape Royds through the open pack ice.

The incubation period, Cape Crozier. Each incubating bird is situated at the edge of the pecking range of the surrounding pairs. The white lines are squirts of guano; Adélie penguins do not like to soil their nests.

View from the south over the Cape Royds Adélie penguin colony and into McMurdo Sound. Here the colony is transitioning from incubation to the "guard stage," with some birds still on eggs and others guarding young chicks. The melt stream from Pony Lake runs toward the ocean in the lower right of the photo.

Tobogganing is the fastest way for penguins to move over ice or snow-covered land. These Adélies are travelling over the sea ice near Cape Royds; the edge of the open water of McMurdo Sound is visible in the mid-distance.

An Adélie penguin parent with a single young chick.

Adélie penguins raise one to two chicks in a successful breeding season. A newly hatched chick's plumage ranges in colour from dark grey to pale silver.

Visitors to Cape Royds looking out at the Transantarctic Mountains. The fast ice has broken out, but temperatures are still cold enough for the surface of the ocean to begin refreezing.

Adélie penguin portrait, midsummer. Note the species' distinctive white eye-ring and feathers extending down the bill.

New Zealand's Scott Base, Ross Island. Some of the specks on the ice surface beyond the pressure ridge at the shoreline are Weddell seals, gathered around an area where they can access the ocean through cracks in the ice.

South polar skua pair, away from their nesting territory following the earlier failure of their nest.

Beginning the day's work at the Adélie penguin colony on remote Beaufort Island in the Ross Sea.

The Cape Royds field camp on a fine midsummer evening, with Mount Erebus peeping through the clouds.

David skiing around the bow of the Russian vessel *Kapitan Khlebnikov,* a Soviet-era icebreaker repurposed for polar tourism.

The Kiwi wanigan and a visiting group's temporary encampment of Scott and mountaineering tents, following a midnight blizzard.

An Adélie chick approaching the crèche stage and showing the typical pear shape of a well-fed young penguin. Their thick grey downy feathers keep the chicks warm even when soiled with guano, something that tends to happen as the season progresses.

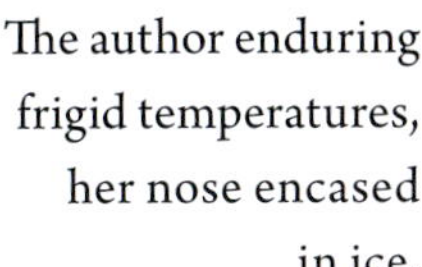

The author enduring frigid temperatures, her nose encased in ice.

Man-hauling a supply sledge from the Adélie penguin colony up the hill to the research hut, Cape Crozier. Debris from the mega-iceberg B-15A towers along the shoreline.

The author and colleague Rachael Orben visiting the Kenn Borek Air office at the Willy Field airstrip.

7

I AM SURE that if I'm asked about the worst part of being here once I'm home, I will reply that it had to be our toilet system, set up to facilitate shipping waste out of the field to McMurdo and then, bizarrely, back to the US at the end of the season. We discussed this arrangement more than once over dinner at McMurdo—the amount of natural resources required to ship all those frozen buckets of human excrement halfway around the world. It's one of the more arcane aspects of the national polar programs, but there are many of these and we have come to accept their multifarious weirdnesses.

My growing dislike of this system is instead aimed at the realities of separating liquid and solid wastes in the field. The latter are deposited in a bag-lined plastic bucket in the lee of the hut, which we invariably require when the wind is blasting down from the South Pole. It's deathly cold outside; your hands are numb in no time (or wear gloves and risk soiling them in the land of no laundry, no thanks); loosened clothing flaps around your ankles; and the liner bag flaps noisily against exposed skin, threatening to disrupt the whole process. We each seem to have fine-tuned instincts about when the other might be out at the bucket and so nobody ever walks around the corner unannounced, but the whole experience nonetheless feels more like being left outside like a sacrificial goat than answering the call of nature, despite the unparalleled views. And once in a while the wind boldly snatches the toilet roll from the pocket of your parka to send it bouncing merrily up the slope, unfurling a festive streamer of paper as it goes and leaving you scraping the corners of your pockets for a replacement wad of tissue.

The other day we had to bring our piss pot into the hut to thaw its contents because another storm had kept us inside and away from proper toilet facility management, which includes emptying urine into our fifty-gallon U-barrel—the one lashed to the solar panel array next to the grey-water container—before it has frozen. This was the day after I made the duct tape funnel to replace the real funnel that had blown away in the previous storm. We sat the pot on a chair in front of the propane heater like some welcome guest so that we could begin to decant our urine into the fifty-gallon drum where it belonged.

Before going to bed I decided to take the bucket outside and pour off what had melted, just to get the process going. The duct tape funnel worked well until the middle of my test pour, when the frozen lump in the bucket's bottom lost its icy grip and slithered free. The funnel was dislodged and the frozen disc of urine lay broken on the ground like some shattered piece of crystal. It was a dilemma—I briefly considered leaving it there to melt into the ground, in likely contravention of the Antarctic Treaty, but then realized that conceivably might not happen until next summer. Finally I went indoors and found a plastic bag to wrap my hand, then picked up and deposited the chunks back into their bucket to continue warming before the fire. The smaller pieces I left for the wind to desiccate, concluding another day of Cape Royds urine duty.

Today is American Thanksgiving, apparently. Ted, the MacOps radio operator, just wished David a happy one when he called in first thing to check for messages. "Thanks, same to you," David said, in a voice that has grown increasingly hoarse in the last few days. I wonder if it's possible for vocal cords to thicken from lack of use; I have not heard that many words from him all morning. But it's not as if I'm particularly chatty out here either, and I think my voice may be coarsening too.

By some unspoken agreement our communications have lapsed into a near-telepathic state, monosyllables over dinner about fieldwork logistics, and the minimal words necessary throughout the day to discuss camp chores. From initially wanting more interaction I've rapidly progressed to finding this monk-like state to be rather restful, interspersed as it is with our frequent visitors providing intense bouts of stimulus. Despite this we occasionally exchange snippets of personal information.

After the radio call I wish David a happy Thanksgiving also, and then ask whether he misses anything from home.

"Umm. Err, my little dog," he says.

"What kind is it?" I ask.

"An Australian terrier," he replies. "Digby."

This is not the sort of pet I would have associated with David if I'd thought about it, and it seems incongruous to imagine him walking with a small dog along some northern California beach. On the other hand, down here it feels alien to imagine anything that isn't to do with penguins, ice, and snow.

It's yet another stormy day, getting up to the usual forty to fifty knots, whitecaps with the foam being shredded off them out on the water. It's because of the wind and its effects on the sea ice, David tells me, that this colony is here at all—so there is some consolation in experiencing the storm. In fact all Adélie colonies are associated with a wind-driven polynya, which is a Russian word meaning "open area in the sea ice."

I briefly go outside to shovel snow for our meltwater container before breakfast, although a shovel is the wrong tool. First I use it in an attempt to remove the layer of black volcanic grit that has accumulated overnight, a scattering of chocolate sprinkles on a white cake. David never bothers to do this and while I'm swiping futilely at the hard snow, shovel blade bouncing off ice, I have to admit that it is probably a waste of time: Little pockets of grit are studded throughout the snowbank so it finds its way into our water regardless of how diligently I try to scrape it away. Next I use the shovel to chip icy chunks from the solid surface of the snowbank, jarring my shoulders, and then watch most of these blow away each time I attempt to transfer them from bank to bucket. Even our basic camp chores take longer in bad weather.

After breakfast I sweep the morning's accumulation of gravel from the floor of the hut, then settle down to write about the weather in my field notebook, procrastinating so I can delay going outside in the gathering storm. The constant moan of the wind—a droning, menacing sound like an approaching train—is setting my nerves on edge, and I jump as a gust bashes the tent and knocks a couple of cans of tomatoes onto the floor. There's a bang at the door and John, the emperor penguin researcher, and his colleagues traipse in, trailing a fresh layer of grit from the soles of their insulated boots. They've packed up camp down at the wanigan and are waiting for a group of New Zealand national media to arrive to document Cape Royds, Shackleton's hut, and some penguins. Today's medium is television. We've already had print and radio out here, or at least the Kiwis have. The filming will need to be quick if the researchers and TV crew want to get back to Scott Base ahead of the storm.

We feed everyone tea and hot chocolate in exchange for gossip and conversation, and John tell us that they've just finished rounding up six emperors out on the sea ice for blood-collection purposes—more of a test run for next year, in the end. The team claims to have perfected their restraining method, which involves two people, a leg hold, and a sack over the head (of the penguin, not the researchers). Reportedly the emperors were unfazed by the experience, focusing their energy on retaliation rather than escape. A story from my old dogsledding friend comes to mind of how more than once he'd seen an emperor penguin drive off a hungry dog. "It is well to keep clear of that flipper when he strikes, for it is very powerful, and might break an arm," wrote James Murray, Shackleton's biologist.[22]

One of the Kiwis, whose first name happens to be Murray, bears some battle scars from the morning's activity, attesting to the aim and determination of the penguin. A long and bloody beak mark runs from the corner of his eye and across the bridge of his nose, down to its tip. The gash is an angry red colour and his nose is still covered in blotches of blood, as if he'd mopped up the rest of his face but had been afraid to touch the tender area around the wound. He is also covered in penguin shit, demonstrating the primary drawback of the leg-holding method, at least from the point of view of the team member at the aft end of the whole process. Everyone else in his group is looking relatively unscathed, albeit sun-beaten, dishevelled, and cold. Apparently their original piece of restraining equipment—a specially designed bag—did not work well. It was built back at their lab around a stuffed penguin, and the Kiwis deride its size and the skills of the taxidermist who had originally prepared and shaped the bird model, adding that the emperors they had handled today weren't even the largest birds, which can reach forty kilograms—these ones weighed in at a mere twenty-five kilos or so.

Murray pulls a Bumper Bar from a pocket in his parka and munches on it along with his tea.

"I love those things!" I tell him. "I've only just discovered them."

"Oh yeah?" he says. "We've got loads left. Everything's packed but if I can still get at them in our mountain of gear I'll leave you some. If I head off now I'll have time to look."

The Kiwis' helo arrives in the nick of time, discharging the television crew for a brief tour, then reloading and clattering away through the sky shortly before I make it down to the colony in the middle of the afternoon. Their pilots must be more intrepid than the Americans—I can't see Helo Ops flying in these conditions. It is already too windy to band-search (reading bands clearly through vibrating binoculars is impossible), but new birds are arriving from the sea every day as the breeding season progresses and I need to update my mapping and notes for B-REF, which has been commensurately growing in number.

Before finally venturing out I don an unbelievable amount of clothing in the hope of staying warm: two pairs of long johns; thick fleece pants; merino undershirt; two long-sleeved merino thermal shirts, one thin and one extra thick; my thickest fleece jacket—all under insulated windproof overalls and down parka, plus two pairs of gloves (thin liners under thick outer windproof mitts), fleece hat, neck gaiter, and the ever-present fleece snood cinched about my neck and face so that only my eyes are exposed.

Down at the colony the wind buffets me in icy blasts and at the end of the first hour I am chilled to the bone, the wind's fingers finding their way through all of my clothes. I'm reminded of the description by the Australian explorer Sir Douglas Mawson of how their multiple layers of clothing felt "distinctly porous" in stormy weather. I take a break and consume a bar of chocolate to help me warm up, the segments waxy in my cold mouth, like chocolate chips in ice cream.

On my way back home from the colony I stop by the Kiwi wanigan and find a large bag of rich, buttery, chocolatey Bumper Bars on one of the bunks, Murray making good on his promise. Today is the first day I've thought of our camp as home, welcomed here by this act of kindness from the Kiwis. I haven't yet decided if my favourite flavour is apricot chocolate, raspberry white chocolate, or chocolate banana, but all of them are what an energy bar needs to be in this kind of climate. They are so superior to their North American counterparts that they seem to be from a different family of foods altogether, like comparing Christmas baking to sawdust. In the shelter of the wanigan I bolt down one of the apricot chocolate variety, sip some water, and again feel the cold begin to recede. I love the Kiwis.

I do have to crawl over the ridgetop into our camp this time. A concerted blast sweeping up from the ice and down from the continent threatens to blow me off my feet.

"At least it's nearly summer," I say to David when I get back, securing the hut door while the wind tries to rip it out of my hands. "It can't get much worse than this."

"Just wait," he replies from behind a mug of something hot.

And by evening the conditions are indeed worse. At our sheltered hut the anemometer has maxed out at a gust of thirty-eight knots, at least when I've been watching it, but during a brief moment outside on our makeshift deck after dinner I can see that over McMurdo Sound the wind is gusting to a solid Beaufort force 11, storm- to borderline hurricane-force winds, snatching giant handfuls of spray from the tops of the waves and flinging them viciously downwind in a welter of white. ("Force 11. Violent storm. Everywhere the edges of the wave crests are blown into froth" says one seaman's guide to the Beaufort wind force scale. "Very rarely experienced on land," reads a landlubber's guide. "Serious devastation.") Now, back in the hut, the wind sounds like a giant's fist repeatedly pounding on the walls.

Most people are surprised to learn that Antarctica is the driest continent on earth, but nobody bats an eye to hear that it is the coldest and windiest. In *The Home of the Blizzard*, Douglas Mawson described the site of his expedition's base, Commonwealth Bay, as "the windiest spot in the world," a place where they learned "the art of 'hurricane-walking.'" A famous photograph in that book—taken by expedition photographer Frank Hurley and called, simply, "A blizzard"—vividly depicts this sport: Two men struggle forward through a foreground filled with a fury of wind-whipped snow, the first bent double, about to drive an ice axe into the frozen ground ahead of him, while behind him, on all fours, crawls his companion.

Mawson devotes much of his book to accounts of the extreme wind, cold, and frostbite that were their constant companions for two years, describing regular periods of winds over ninety miles per hour, and, in one cyclonic storm, gusts they estimated to approach two hundred miles per hour. Anemometer tracks published in his book for May and June show that the average daily wind speed often approached seventy or eighty miles per hour; the average wind velocity for their entire first year was fifty. Mawson—familiar with Cape Royds from his time on Shackleton's Nimrod Expedition—perhaps also saw Royds as a banana belt of sorts. At least, he took pains to point out that on only three days over those two midwinter months did the maximum wind speeds there ever reach the lowest daily speeds recorded at their Cape Denison hut.

The following morning I wake to what is definitely the worst weather day since we've been here. It turns into another indoor day, though on this one I don't go outside at all except to pee, check on my tent, and take a quick photo of our hut all but obscured by driving snow. David, unfazed after years of Antarctic work, goes down to the colony late in the afternoon to download the weighbridge computer. He comes back reporting that its sheltering tent—the same design as the one I sleep in—was ripped to shreds by last night's blasting winds. He's temporarily shored it up, but hopefully I'll be able to go and see for myself tomorrow how bad it is. David estimates that it is blowing seventy to eighty knots out on the water this afternoon. Steady Beaufort 12, hurricane-force winds. "Force 12," reads the deadpan Beaufort Scale guide, "effects on land, violence and destruction."

Whatever the speed of the gusts, at bedtime I am glad to have earplugs. Being in my tent is like sleeping in a high-speed wind tunnel with a wet sheet flapping on a clothesline. "I hope this weather trend doesn't continue," I write in my journal the next morning. "Today is worse than yesterday, which was worse than the day before." The moaning wind sounds like a mad thing outside our canvas walls. The anemometer currently says it's blowing a steady twenty-five knots, gusting to fifty. Not that I trust it anymore, especially given the sheltered location of our hut. I frequently look out the window and see snow blasting past at a speed that could literally scour rust off metal, and the weather station display will be reading a modest seventeen to twenty knots.

After breakfast we relocate many of our cans of food plus the meltwater container to the floor for a safer passage through the hurricane—which it now clearly is. I estimate that even in our sheltered hollow it's currently more like a steady forty knots, gusting to over sixty, and the visibility remains as poor as it's been all day—a whiteout. The snow worsened this morning, miserable hard little pellets of graupel, and conditions have been down to about five metres of visibility. If we could see the ocean I know it would appear torn to shreds by the wind.

If I didn't go outdoors yesterday it was partly from choice—David did make it down to the weighbridge tent after all, so I could also have chosen to crawl over the ridge and brave the elements. Today, staying inside was a necessity. Between the cold, blasting winds and the poor visibility, travelling more than a few steps from the hut would have been foolish in the extreme; when I go out there to check my tent or use the bucket, I've literally been hanging on to the hut's steel guy wires so as not to be flung about by the gusts. Five metres of visibility means that if something is farther away than the length of our hut, it disappears from view, and there is no predicting when visibility may further decrease in the swirling maelstrom of wind and snow blasting at us from over the continent. Our whiteout survival exercise with buckets over our heads in Happy Camper survival school now seems charmingly naive, occurring as it did on a sunny, windless, and warmish day. In a snowstorm over the monochromatic and undulating volcanic landscape of Cape Royds, it would be trivially easy to miss the faint path we have trodden between the penguin colony and the Rac-Tent, get turned around, and be lost.

Inside, sheltering from the violence of the storm, even David is growing increasingly agitated, sitting at his desk in the corner and staring unseeingly at his computer screen while incessantly jiggling his knee. Stuck as I am in my own twisting anxiety brought on by forced inactivity and the mad groaning and creaking of the hut, this begins to annoy me almost as much as the shrieking wind. In a bid to occupy myself I reorganize the food shelves and tidy our indoor equipment corner, where I notice that our battery bank is holding up well despite the absent sun. Chores exhausted, I turn to my laptop, and, as I'm almost caught up on data entry, manage to bore myself rigid with endless games of solitaire. I've heard a mountaineering friend say that being stuck on the side of a mountain in a tent in a storm is like spending days in the trunk of your car. It's not quite that bad here—the hut is not that small—but the claustrophobic feeling of not being able to leave these four walls is bearing down on me.

During dinner we talk to Cape Crozier over the VHF—they have been even more pummelled by the weather than we have these past couple of days. The iceberg B-15A has been grounded there for weeks, and despite its size being equivalent to that of a minor island nation it is now moving in the hurricane, ponderously bashing the shoreline.

Such is its mass that the wooden Crozier hut, a kilometre or more up the mountainside, shakes each time the berg rams into the cape, as if in an earthquake. We all take turns talking and Rachael tells us she is currently reading Cherry-Garrard's account of the trek to Cape Crozier in *The Worst Journey in the World*. It was so cold on that winter journey that Cherry-Garrard's teeth split.

"Whenever conditions get bad here, I think of them and remind myself it could always be worse," says Grant when it's his turn on the radio.

Today the Crozier crew resorted to tying the hut's outer door shut, peeing in a bucket in the pantry, and duct-taping the window seams to stop the spindrift from leaching through. Here at Cape Royds we have a small spindrift pile accumulating in one corner of the hut but it isn't so bad. My mountaineering tent was still standing on last check, but from the mad flapping noise outside our canvas walls it sounds as if the fly has unzipped again, despite the carabiner I've clipped into its drawstrings. Each time I go out to check on it I return covered in a thick dusting of powdered drift, like icing sugar on a cake or concrete dust coating the survivors of a bombing attack.

The snowstorm is underscoring the wisdom of David's advice to pitch my sleeping tent on the windward side of the Rac-Tent—despite being buffeted by the blasts it is weathering the storm, while in our hut's lee snow is piling high in drifts and beginning to bury the gear we have stored there. I have to dig out the toilet bucket each time I want to use it. Tonight I've brought my sleep kit inside and will be spending the night on the floor of the Rac-Tent, which I'm optimistic isn't going to disintegrate like the old Polar Haven that Viola told me about back in Mactown. As I fall asleep loose gravel starts blowing against the side of our hut. Sleeping in the Rac-Tent is like trying to drift off inside a sandblasting facility.

—

The next day is the first of December, and after lunch the snow suddenly stops, the clouds lift, and the winds die down in a matter of minutes; it's as if the storm never happened and the weather has changed its mind about how to behave now that a new month is here. We can see the ocean again through the clear plastic pane of our front window; pieces of blown-out fast ice are drifting past as they would have done all night, unseen behind a wall of white. Exposed areas of ground have already been swept clear of snow by the scouring winds, and the icy coating that had formed on the inside of the hut's transparent roof panels is melting, dripping onto the floor in neat rows.

David is talking to MacOps on the radio, the sun is breaking through the clouds, and it's as if the world is coming back to us again. My tent survived the night but I'm glad I slept in here. Its vestibule is literally full of snow, driven in through tiny gaps in the fly by the relentless wind. At four thirty in the morning I had woken and listened to forty-five knots banging against the side of the hut, the wind still loud but dropping off, the light changing as the cloud thinned.

We go down to the penguin colony to check on the weighbridge. This part of the colony must have seen the full force of the hurricane. The computer's tent is destroyed, converted into a pile of snow and rubble with tent poles sticking out at odd angles. Several rocks hold the whole mess down, placed there by David when he paid his visit during the lull of a couple of days ago. It looks like a burial mound, although surprisingly, the weighbridge computer is still alive and working.

Shortly after we arrive I see a thick wall of snow rolling in across the sea ice from the south, obliterating surface visibility to the height of several metres.

"David, there's a ground blizzard on the way," I say nervously.

David mumbles something I don't catch, and continues tying up the torn plastic weighbridge fencing. His casual grumpiness is comforting but I feel a little less blasé and decide on a craven retreat to the hut, watching the leading wall of the blizzard advance and retreat as I walk back up the hill. On my way a snow petrel wheels around me, so close that I can see the faint dark markings along the leading edge of its wings, its black eye staring curiously at me as we pass each other.

Back at camp I dig out the mound of snow from underneath my tent fly and fix the hut's door latch, which the winds have nearly rattled loose from its moorings. David returns from the colony just as the ground blizzard rolls over us and the winds pick up once more. The storm does appear to be clearing up, but it's dragging a series of squally little systems in its wake. By dinnertime we're confined to the hut yet again and David recommences his knee-jiggling, sitting at the table and staring blindly into the distance as I clean up. I've been listening to Thievery Corporation on my headphones but instead decide to connect to my travel speakers and play Yo-Yo Ma's unaccompanied Bach cello suites, their swooping cadences a civilized echo of the screaming wind. Somehow their wild abandon renders the wildness of the storm less threatening, as if we're moving in time with it instead of hiding inside.

"Nice music," says David after a while. I notice his knee-jiggling has stopped, and I too feel less agitated; I can sit and focus on data entry and writing, instead of pacing.

At least the sun has periodically appeared today, but at bedtime the weather is still bad enough that I leave my bedroll in the hut and sleep there again.

Thank god, the storm has abated. After four days of it the silence is an unbelievable relief—just the quiet jazz of Thelonious Monk emanating from the speakers on my laptop in the late afternoon, and the susurration of the snows drifting past our walls on a slight breeze.

Time to do things, now that the wind and the snow have both stopped. I've already moved my sleep kit back into the tent, happy to contemplate sleeping in its cozy confines again after two nights on the floor of the hut with David gently snoring in his corner. Bedding down there is too much like sleeping at the office. And it will be possible to empty the piss pot, which we have filled well past the halfway mark these past three days, despite our chronic state of borderline dehydration. (I can never drink quite enough fluids to combat the exertion and the desiccating air, despite sipping from my water bottle constantly.) During the hurricane the urine bucket sheltered outside the back door behind a pile of gear; emptying it into the unsheltered U-barrel was not something that bore thinking about, given the wind.

I am also itching to spend more time outdoors after ninety-six virtually uninterrupted hours of confinement in our one-room hut. I imagine David feels much the same. We did both emerge for that couple of hours yesterday to survey the wreckage of the weighbridge shelter, but other than that it's been Rac-Tent Central except for as few visits as possible to Ye Olde Human Waste Buckett, as someone back at the Berg Field Center had written on the side of the one we currently have in use. David goes down to the colony after dinner at around 9 p.m., and I follow shortly thereafter. I want to do a nest count post-storm and see what its effects might have been.

When I get to B-REF I see that all the unpaired birds have gone, as have the paired birds who have yet to lay their eggs. There were 120 Adélies in this subcolony prior to the hurricane; immediately following it there are 69, all of them incubating. Their mates and the other birds have all departed for their true element, the sea. But that count is increasing again very rapidly—there are 82 birds by the time I walk back through that part of the colony an hour later.

Throughout the colony, penguins are still incubating despite being half buried in snow. Other individuals in more exposed sites are unburied but remain facing into the direction of the prevailing wind, eyes tightly shut; this is how they weathered the hurricane and their front half looks like it has been sugar-coated by the spindrift. I see an incubating skua encased in snow, just head and a tail feather and a smidgen of back sticking out. I am only a pace away when I notice the bird, so neatly does it blend in with the surrounding skua-sized rocks. It eyes me casually, seemingly unfazed by its white cocoon.

The Adélies are tobogganing across the fresh snow on their bellies, and their foot and stomach tracks are everywhere, recording the flurry of penguin activity that has been underway since the skies have cleared. There is also a burst of activity on the part of the skuas—they are all suddenly mating and building nests and incubating at a compressed pace. It seems that the hurricane has blown out the remnants of winter.

Another ground blizzard louring in the mid-distance eventually drives me fearfully back to the hut again, but it is a false alarm and now the breeze is but a whisper, the late evening sun shining from behind the thinnest layer of cloud and gleaming brassily on the wrinkled, lead-coloured ocean. At midnight I sit on the deck sipping a whisky before turning in. The world is ethereal, breathtaking, pure, and crystalline, sun glinting on fresh snow, the silence simultaneously piercing and remote. It's not a silence that would swallow up a human shout, if one could bring oneself to the point of being irreverent enough to cry out in the face of such indomitable beauty. It's a silence that would render a human shout completely, utterly, and irredeemably inconsequential. Despite this, I can hear the things that do matter: a nearby skua calling to its mate with the squeaky mewing cry they give from their nest; the slithering of melting snow; and the distant guttural squawks of the Adélies as they toboggan through the colony to and from the sea.

8

IN THE WAKE of the storm, the weather has turned to what passes for warm, with temperatures hovering just above zero during the day and dipping slightly below freezing as the sun makes its evening descent toward the horizon. The wind has blown itself out in a last gasp and summer is suddenly here. I performed triage on our frozen food earlier today—it is starting to thaw—and stuffed everything that was still solid into the big heavy-duty cooler, packed tight with snow and ice, and then stuffed it into a hole in the same big snowbank we use for our water. We've been using the thawed items as quickly as we can, but as it's still much colder outside than the interior of the average refrigerator there's no huge rush.

I finish work at the colony early and decide to take advantage of the weather to go for a late-afternoon ski on the still-thick sea ice to the south of us. The sky is the same clear blue it has been for several days, and from where I put on my cross-country skis at the top of the slope leading down to Backdoor Bay, I can see the flags that mark the tracked-vehicle route to McMurdo growing smaller and smaller as they march southward to the horizon. With the tricks that distance and light play in Antarctica's crystalline air it is hard to tell whether some of the smaller dots are far-away flags, or penguins in the mid-distance neatly arrayed on the ice.

The push-off down the gentle slope and onto the frozen sea is like cutting a line to shore. Although there is little distinction here between snow-covered land and icy ocean, the knowledge that the hut is on land, but I am not, suddenly leaves me feeling alone with Antarctica in all its immensity. The edge of the sea ice and the beginning of the floating pack stretch along to my right like a blank space. The smoking, glacier-clad slopes of volcanic Mount Erebus tower into the sky and dominate the views on my left. I ski out toward where the infinite horizon eats up the flagged track. Every so often I stop and hold my breath to listen to the complete silence. Occasionally a distant penguin's call breaks into the stillness, and once, unnervingly, I hear the trickle of running water as I pass near a refrozen tidal crack. But I'm on the route to McMurdo and the field safety crews have been testing it regularly. Cloudless summer sky above, somewhere not too far away the darker blue of the ocean emerging from its winter case of ice, but everywhere else the boundless negative space of glaciated peaks, snow, and frozen sea—so vast it is as if the world has swallowed itself up and left nothing but emptiness behind. In this place I know myself to be an insignificant speck, yet it is at my smallest that I feel most at one with the world—and with those I have lost from it.

We head back to McMurdo for two nights. The roads there are knee-deep in slush and meltwater. It seems that we'll be going into town on a semi-regular basis, something I hadn't anticipated at the start of the season.

At dinner in the Galley the first evening a man with a beard sits down next to me.

"Aren't you one of the scientists working out at Cape Royds?" he asks.

When I answer in the affirmative he introduces himself.

"Brien Barnett. I write for *The Antarctic Sun*?"

"Oh right," I say. "I've seen your byline."

The *Sun* is the continent's only newspaper, funded by the National Science Foundation and produced out of a small room at McMurdo. It comes out weekly in hard copy and online, and is another one of those cultural peculiarities found in Antarctica, quickly normalized by its residents but improbable to outsiders, like the bank machines. Dropping in at McMurdo can feel like parachuting in to stay with some remote and seldom-contacted tribe. Brien tells me it would be great if we could do an interview for a penguin story and I suspect that he is hoping to wrangle a day trip to Royds, but that is fine with me.

"Do you want an ice cream?" he asks as we clean our plates. "I'm heading for the Frosty Boy machine."

"It's broken again," I tell him.

I head to the library after dinner and enter the building as a woman wearing sandals is leaving. "It's spring!" she says, stepping over a small meltwater stream as she crosses the threshold. Funny how our relative concept of warm can change.

This time our trip back to Royds is over the sea ice by Hägglunds, accompanied by a group of galley staff from McMurdo who won the trip in a Field Safety Training Program bingo game. The ride out is marred by the apparent beaker-hatred of the FSTP driver, the rudest person I've met down here so far. "Beaker" is Mactown slang for scientist, a term that is sometimes affectionate and sometimes not. The official term is "grantee," as in a recipient of an NSF grant, but the only people who use it are the bureaucrats in the Chalet. Back in November, when I was first at McMurdo and working on field prep in the Crary Lab, there was a cautionary photo making the rounds, some research program's truck that had rolled down into the gap between the raised roadbed and the lab building because the driver hadn't chocked the wheels.

"Typical beaker move," said Viola at the time, rolling her expressive eyes. "Or at least that's what the locals will say."

While we are all loading up the vehicle in preparation for our trip out, our Hägg driver gets shirty when I tell him which boxes can't freeze.

"I'm not a valet," he snaps. This sentiment is patently bullshit, as everybody who works outdoors here pitches in to help load and unload vehicles. Knowing which boxes can freeze and which cannot is a fundamental part of the task in this world of sub-zero temperatures, expensive science gear, and non-freezable comestibles, and "DNF" is a ubiquitous acronym, seen written on the outside of most of the containers that warrant a "Do Not Freeze" label. This is my first (and, as it eventually turns out, my only) exposure to an anti-beaker attitude . . . or perhaps he is just having a bad season or a bad day.

We arrive back at Cape Royds in early afternoon. As I disembark from the Hägg at Backdoor Bay I notice some glycol dripping from the back of the vehicle and mention it to the driver. He snarkily replies that if he'd been in the back he would have tightened the lid on the glycol container, apparently thinking that scientists and the galley crew are too stupid to figure out that lids are closed clockwise even in the southern hemisphere.

"I've only just noticed it," I tell him coolly, and leave him to stew over the pool of antifreeze in the Hägglunds cargo area as the excited bingo winners help us carry our gear up to the hut. When we walk inside there are more Bumper Bars sitting on my chair, a sure sign that the Kiwis have been here again.

I stop by the wanigan on my way down to the Adélies—David is giving our visitors a colony tour, I will be catching up on band sightings—and a couple of Kiwis are there: Paul Rogers, the AFT guide from Scott Base who had loaned me his camera lens, and the painter Grahame Sydney,* down here with Antarctica New Zealand's own Artists and Writers Programme, and who's just arrived to work on a book. As an introvert, I should be reserved upon meeting someone of such renown—Grahame's paintings have been in the collections of such personalities as Nelson Mandela and Elton John—but my beloved father was a talented visual artist as well as an engineer, so I have a soft spot for hearing painters talk about their work. Over a cup of tea we end up making evening plans for wine and Scrabble, and then I head off to the colony.

After dinner Paul and Grahame stop by the hut to collect me. It turns out that my ears hadn't deceived me in thinking ten days ago that Paul's accent was British—he tells us that despite having lived in New Zealand for years, he's originally from East London and in fact is related to the Kray brothers, East London's notorious gangster twins of the 1950s and '60s. We wander back to the wanigan along the slopes of Mount Erebus, watching the fine powdered snow whipped across the harsh landscape by the scouring winds. Something about the three of us really clicks, and we spend the evening wrapped in conversation by turns witty, serious, rude, hilarious. We laugh uproariously for much of the night; after the monastic silence of much of the past month, this repartee is the sweetest thing imaginable.

I'm confident of a Scrabble win—my skills were originally honed by many boring days at anchor waiting for the west coast salmon fishery to open, alone with a skipper who was some sort of Scrabble savant—and Grahame claims to be a good player also. Despite this Paul handily thrashes both of us. After his triumphant finish Paul says he's going down to look around Shackleton's hut and asks magnanimously if

---

* Now Sir Grahame Sidney: In 2021, he received a knighthood for his service to the arts.

Grahame or I want to go with him. The Kiwis always seem to bring Shackleton's key with them to Cape Royds, something that mystifies me as the Americans' copy is guarded jealously at the NSF Chalet in town and we are never allowed to have it.

Grahame has retreated outside following our humiliating defeat and is trying to sort out how to paint with freezing paintbrushes, so declines. Paul and I set off over the thin layer of snow that's blowing across the black lava moonscape. Tonight I'm wearing my "indoor" boots, a pair of ankle-height insulated Sorels that are less bulky than the blue issued FDX boots I wear most days and which are currently back at our hut in front of the propane heater, drying their damp insides. Although I mainly use the Sorels indoors, their rubber soles are already shredded from occasional treks across the abrasive volcanic ridges immediately around our camp.

This is my first time inside Shackleton's hut, despite the fact that David and I trudge past its shuttered and weather-beaten exterior multiple times a day. In the dim light from the doorway, everything in its interior is a washed-out sepia—floor, walls, stacked packing cases with stencilled names of contents, rusty cans of food balanced on wooden shelves with their faded labels barely legible. I peer curiously at a few of these and can make out words like parsnips, Irish stew, mutton, and tongue, alongside classics like Lyle's golden syrup and digestive biscuits. The most striking thing to me about this dwelling is its familiarity, with food items from my British childhood, and cans arrayed on the shelves as they are at our own hut up the hill.

It is a relief to be out of the wind. Paul has left his gloves off after unlocking the door, and he reaches out and lays the back of one frigid finger against my cheek. "Cold?" he asks. It's a physical and emotional shock to be touched by another human being, one that's almost electric in its intensity. I stare at him for a moment, stunned by the sudden realization of how much I miss human contact.

"Thanks," I say to his apparent invitation. "But no thanks." Paul shrugs, unflappable, and I move away to investigate another corner of the hut: decrepit century-old footwear, more rusting cans (here, Irish brawn and kippered herrings), and intact packets of Lifebuoy soap all sitting in corners or lining the walls on the open shelves. Shackleton himself described this place in *The Heart of the Antarctic*: "It was not a very spacious dwelling for the accommodation of fifteen persons, but our narrow quarters were warmer than if the hut had been larger."[23] I imagine dinner being cooked on the stove, and how crowded this place must have felt with all the men working inside through the stormy days and into the long winter nights.

We head back to the wanigan for the evening's last glass of wine and somehow the subject of flannel pyjamas comes up. Perhaps whether they are suitable bedtime wear for a sleeping bag. Grahame blames them for the demise of his marriage. I protest and say that flannel can be sexy, especially when it is being taken off.

"Anything can be sexy if it's being taken off," retorts Grahame. "But you've got to be with someone who wants to be undressed."

The next morning I stop by to say so long, and Grahame gives me a hard hug and a kiss on the cheek. Even the farewell turns into an hour of chatting and drinking tea.

"I'm about to sit on my lawn," says Grahame in his posh accent, driving the legs of his rusty metal chair into the snowdrift outside the door of the wanigan and seating himself facing Mount Erebus where it fills the sky. "Won't you join me?"

So I drink tea and filch bites of Paul's hash brown patties, and the three of us laugh and talk some more while Paul wanders in and out of the hut serving breakfast and Grahame makes notes with his eyes full of Erebus. Our brief time together has been one of those perfect travel moments when everyone has an almost spiritual connection and laughter is plentiful and everything falls into place. I'm suddenly reminded of the bittersweet autumn following the summer when my dad died, when I dropped out of my undergrad program and headed south for six months to buffer the shock of it all, wandering through the US, Mexico, and Central America. In California I met up with two friends, Glenn and Mark, and we drove to the Mexican border via Yosemite at the end of October. I carved a pumpkin, and each night the jack-o'-lantern's candle flickered on the dashboard of the van as the darkness rushed by outside. It was one of those times when the love of life expands inside you like a drug and you feel big enough to encompass everything, despite understanding that your role in this world is infinitely small. Last night at the wanigan felt the same.

I wave Paul and Grahame goodbye as their helicopter lifts off for Scott Base, then make my way back to our hut. David hasn't yet left for the colony and he just mouths a hello in response to my greeting as I come in—but the ensuing silence feels peaceful instead of oppressive, and I contentedly brew a cup of coffee before beginning the work of the day.

9

IT IS NOT always easy being a skua with a territory adjacent to an Adélie colony. Some researchers have suggested that these birds will likely do better than the pairs nesting away from the colonies—the hypothesis being that access to penguin eggs provides important early-season food on which the skuas can grow fat prior to laying their own eggs, and dead or alive penguin chicks to eat through the rest of the season. However, there's a classic book by the New Zealand biologist Euan Young, entitled *Skua and Penguin: Predator and Prey,*[24] in which Young reports his extensive Ross Island research and his finding that the skuas whose territories include penguin nests do not necessarily thrive. An earlier study of David's also documented numerous Ross Sea skua colonies existing independently of penguin colonies—suggesting there's no strong benefit to being near one—and today during my band-search rota I observe one of the disadvantages in the form of an irate penguin.

As I approach the colony from the north I look for the skua nest there, as I always do to make sure I don't get too close as I pass. Skuas are vigilant and assertive defenders of their territories against all incomers, penguin or human, and the more aggressive individuals (which is most of them) attack by screaming and flying straight for one's face. Anyone imprudent enough to stand their ground finds out that the attacking bird veers up only at the last second while raking the intruder's head with beak and claws.

Instead of being on or by their nest, both adults are flapping up into the air and down again, agitated. A particularly irascible penguin has crossed the empty space between subcolony 14B and the skuas' territory and is making repeated little charges at each parent as it tries to land back at the nest. The penguin gives up with an angry squawk as I draw closer, but I've come close enough to see the skuas' new eggs before one parent takes another skyward leap and then drifts back down to resume incubation. The eggs are a lovely fat globular shape, a warm greenish colour with dark blotches that look like they've been splattered at random with a paintbrush, a couple of Jackson Pollock ovoids. I find myself silently cheering on their survival.

The Adélie colony is slowly leaving behind its post-hurricane lull. Now that I'm familiar enough with the landscape and our work to have time to look around me while recording data, I can enjoy the individual reactions of the penguins as I wander through the subcolonies looking for bands and the last couple of unlocated GLS tags. I've still not located any of those since we've been here, despite trying hard. David will periodically show up at the hut and place one on his desk in quiet triumph, one less to find, but I have yet to master the search image, the picture I need to hold in my mind as I seek them. Grant has recently received and plotted last year's coordinates (with the photoperiod or light-level data translated to geographic positions by the British Antarctic Survey, the loggers' vendor), and the tracks show that the birds wintered out on the edge of the sea ice, far to the north in the twilight, where ice and daylight levels are optimal for a winter-foraging penguin.

The penguins' responses to us range from aggression through to curiosity, shyness, or sleepy-eyed indifference. Some of the young birds are the most bashful: two- to four-year-old non-breeders here to check out the colony for a subsequent year, on their first visit since they departed Cape Royds as fledglings. They are arriving en masse now, big groups of them bounding through the waves and ejecting themselves from the sea to the ice like corks shooting out of a champagne bottle. The undersides of their wings are flushed a delicate blushing pink from their exertion (due to dilation of the blood vessels closest to the skin) as they enter the colony in twos and threes—some timidly, unused to all the hustle and bustle and noise now around them in this penguin town—and some less so, but all of them wide-eyed and still bursting with the energy they tapped into to get here. It is these neophytes that most often give a dowager-like croak in horror at my approach, and run off to a safe distance to stand and watch me passing. Their flippers gently wave in agitation as they do so, like Victorian ladies fanning themselves to ward off swooning.

Then there are the bold and curious birds, my favourite personality type. These are the ones I sometimes see when I stop and turn to look around me as I'm band-searching or walking along the edge of the colony. A pace or two behind, a penguin will be following me, stopping when I stop, moving along again when I pick up the pace. These may simply be short journeys where we are both coincidentally travelling in the same direction rather than me being followed per se, but the birds show no fear at my presence and are certainly intrigued—or annoyed—by my being there. Occasionally one of them will rush up to me and stop abruptly just shy of the toes of my boots, slowly turning its head to stare earnestly up into my face, wide-eyed, aggressive, and curious.

This range of reactions is exemplified by a couple of incoming groups I pass on my way home this evening. Instead of coming in via the west beach, the colony's main point of access, the first group of penguins has come over the cape from Backdoor Bay and are making their way downhill toward the raucous voices of their compatriots along the shore. The birds are delicately picking their way across the gravel below the Kiwi refuge hut when they see me approaching and freeze in horror. I give them a wide berth as I pass, and they all stand silently, their heads moving to follow me like spectators of some slow-motion race. As soon as I am safely distant they turn as one and trot down toward the colony with wings splayed wide, emanating shocked outrage as they go. I feel like a slovenly teenager who's just walked past a coterie of the village's social elite, who are even now engaging in horrified gossip about me as I trudge out of earshot.

And then around the bend comes a smaller group, the birds tobogganing on their bellies across a small field of snow. Both they and I stop simultaneously, until one of them tentatively takes five, ten paces closer, halving the short distance between us as we gaze at each other. A meeting of eyes across the fresh snow, bridging who knows how big a gulf in our ways of seeing the world. We look for a while, the penguin and I. It waves its wings ever so slightly, a butterfly fanning the gentle evening breeze, and I stand still to take in birds, sea, ice, and sky, an infinite panorama around me, as our worlds briefly merge. Then the bird turns to waddle slowly back toward its companions, and breaks the spell. When it rejoins them they toboggan slowly down the last half of the snowbank toward the colony, and I prosaically make my way uphill toward the hut and dinner.

10

MAIL DAY. I go into the Kiwi wanigan to take a short break from the wind on my way back up the slope in the afternoon, and discover that five parcels with our names on them have mysteriously been deposited there. Mine are from my stepmother and contain a few requested comforts from home—books, more ground coffee, gummy bears, stronger sunscreen, some art supplies.

"What did you get?" I ask David later, back at the hut after I've left our boxes there and gone out again. "Early Christmas presents?"

"Oh, I got some chocolates and magazines." A pause. "A box of mouldy brownies."

"Mmm, my favourite," I say.

"Well, they're there if you want them." He indicates the food waste container, where they are already subsiding beneath leftovers, hairbrush cleanings, and orange peel.

"Oh well," I say. "It's the thought that counts."

We are approaching mid-December and it has remained warm for the past week. Each day has brought clear skies and temperatures hovering right around freezing. Gentle northerly breezes persist in the vacuum that is left when southerlies aren't screaming down from the continent and over the ice shelf, so there's no wind chill to speak of either. Like our frozen food, the frozen ground around the colony is starting to defrost. Slopes that were rock-hard a week ago now subside slightly under our boots, squishy top layers of formerly solid soil turning into icy muck. In front of Shackleton's hut, Pony Lake is still solidly frozen but each day when the sun is at its highest some murky meltwater appears around the edges where the lake ice touches the dark volcanic earth.

Perhaps linked to the earlier weather and its effect on the pack ice, which has been blown beyond the northern horizon by the storms, there has been a big influx of new penguins over the past couple of days. The B-REF colony has suddenly increased in number by about 25 percent, and the rest of the colony appears to have done the same. These newcomers are a mix of delayed breeders—older birds held up by sea ice conditions, or by the big iceberg, or both—and the two- to four-year-old non-breeders, young birds coming in prior to the reoccupation period, when penguins who lost their eggs return to the colony for a while.

Whichever the cohort or the reason, the colony has briefly reverted to the bustling chaos of the early occupation period, underway when we first arrived a month ago. Newly arrived young birds run in their panicky way through occupied areas of the colony, dodging pecks and flipper-slaps from angry nest occupants and trailing a wake of aggravated squawks behind them. Throughout the colony, the older late-arriving males stand erect at their new nests—some of these neat bowls of symmetrical stones, others a slapdash collection of a few small pebbles—and ecstatic displays are again being performed everywhere, in the hope of attracting a mate before the season progresses any further. It's once more the in thing to do at Cape Royds.

Until this new influx, the birds remaining after the hurricane had been getting down to the serious business of incubating eggs. Most of the pairing up, at least by the birds who are actually going to manage to produce chicks before the summer ends, occurred a while ago. Eggs have been laid, females have gone to sea to forage and then returned to relieve their mates, who have in turn gone to sea to feed themselves. Now, the female of each pair sits on her nest and pants in the sun, patiently taking her turn with the eggs and awaiting their imminent hatching.

The next morning I awake to the wind rattling my tent—the weather has changed yet again and it's another blustery day. The temperature dropped overnight from 0° to −6°C, and the snow from a storm to the south is blowing along at waist height under a clear blue sky: another ground blizzard. This cold weather is welcome after the airless "warmth" of the past few days. It is unfortunately too windy to wander about reading penguin bands, but by noon I am so restless I can't stay in the Rac-Tent any longer, so I layer on my clothes and go out to face the day.

As I'm leaving, Katie Dugger arrives from Cape Bird via a Kiwi helicopter. Her field season is a short one this year because she's heading home to Oregon and her husband in time for the holidays, and to begin teaching at the start of the new year. As planned, she has just handed off her time at Cape Bird to a Kiwi project collaborator, Kerry Barton. Katie wears her habitual big grin as she disembarks with a mound of gear, and I greet her with a hug, happy to have additional company in camp for a couple of days.

The combination of sun and blowing snow makes for a spectacular afternoon. Each pebble and piece of gravel stands out in sharp relief against the miniature snowdrift that has formed behind it. All the footprints—penguin and human—marring yesterday's landscape have been filled by the snow and smoothed by the winds, the ground now covered with thousands of these sculpted undulations all catching the sun on one of their many angles, glistening like a rippled lake on a cloudless day.

Down at the colony, the recent noisy chaos is already beginning to subside and the prospecting penguins are returning to the sea by the hundreds each day, their visit a practice run for a subsequent year. The active breeders are now the only ones arriving. Two days ago I saw a severely injured bird—apparently the survivor of a leopard seal attack—slowly dragging itself up the main beach and into the colony. It couldn't walk or even stand; a huge gash was open in its side and blood pooled on the ground wherever it paused. The penguin's right leg dragged uselessly and its right flipper twitched as it inched forward on its belly across snow and gravel, a pathetic imitation of the healthy birds around it whizzing over the snow, tobogganing quickly and smoothly on chests and abdomens to and from their nests.

It was wearing a band and I was dismayed to discover that this was one of the birds from B-REF—number 1091, a female. Her mate, 1096, has been faithfully incubating their two pale eggs since she laid them around the twenty-seventh of November, fasting for nearly three weeks as he waited for her return from foraging at sea. There she had been growing fat again, eating fish and krill and recovering from the effort of courtship and egg production. Now it appears that all this will be for naught as the male will soon leave, forced by incipient starvation to choose his own survival over that of the offspring rapidly developing inside their eggshells as the Antarctic spring races by. I imagine her suffering to be immense and long to ease it somehow—penguin palliative care. My mind turns to my sister and her pain-filled decline, her moments of lucidity amongst muddled morphine dreams. What does a penguin know of the future? Likely nothing, yet still she strives to return to her nest and her mate.

Then yesterday morning I saw her on my band-search rounds, and it appeared that she was not simply going to give up and die now that she had reached the colony and was within striking distance of her nest. She appeared near B-REF on the route up from the main entrance beach, having dragged herself into a nearby subcolony to rest for a while. Perhaps that would be as far as she would make it, I thought. But perhaps not—despite her fearsome wound, she looked more alert than the previous day and her right leg showed a little movement, though she was still unable to do anything more than drag herself clumsily along on her belly, listing to the left like a disabled ship. But later in the day she appeared at the top of the hummock that forms B-REF, where she lay a couple of nests away from her patient mate, blood crusted all over her once-white breast. Perhaps there she would die, I thought. Almost home.

Today I tell David and Katie about the injured bird over lunch, veggie burger patties with melted cheese, eaten on bread toasted over the Coleman stove and slathered with butter and mustard. This is currently a favourite afternoon meal, as dictated by the contents of the slowly defrosting cooler; David and I have eaten the same thing three days in a row so far. He chews and swallows a mouthful of burger before responding to my tale.

"Prepare to be amazed," he says.

"I hope so," I reply. "But she's lost a lot of blood."

I'm intrigued by his optimism. He hasn't seen this particular penguin yet, but on the other hand he has witnessed far more of these odysseys than have I.

Sure enough, this afternoon I see her on the nest, and her mate, 1096, has returned to sea. She isn't doing a particularly efficient job of incubating as her body still lists to one side and her leg still protrudes at a funny angle; part of one of the eggs is exposed to the elements rather than being cozily tucked up against the unfeathered and supervascularized skin of her brood patch, where it's supposed to be. But she is on her nest even though it took her nearly two days to get there from the sea edge, in a journey that would normally have taken her ten or fifteen minutes. I am indeed amazed. Perhaps the pair will successfully hatch and rear a chick or two and I will continue to be astounded. Really, I'll be surprised if she does no more than survive the season. But life is tenacious here, and the fact that the penguins persist at all is a testament to their toughness.

As 1091 perseveres, the season continues unabated in the rest of the colony. After watching her for a while, I head over to subcolony 10AB for some band-searching and there I register a new sound, a sibilant far-off whistle: It is the first penguin chicks, calling from their eggs. Chicks first start to vocalize as the egg is pipping, when they are still ensconced in their shell and just beginning to chip their way into the world. Sure enough, an egg with a hole near one end the size of a quarter is being carefully turned by a parent at a nearby nest. The chick's bill is poking out, breathing and calling in the chill air of its new world. The sound comes from several directions, multiple hatching eggs. I imagine the colony full of them, penguin chicks safe within the confines of their shell for another day or two, calling to their attendant parent and the world, readying themselves to emerge.

With Katie in camp, David becomes more talkative. He wants to hear how things have been going at Cape Bird, and on the second day, as we're all doing post-breakfast chores—tidying Katie's bedroll into the corner of the hut, cleaning dishes, data entry, sweeping volcanic grit off the floor yet again—he mentions some post-Christmas plans for us and the Crozier crew: a trip to remote Beaufort Island, in the Ross Sea twenty kilometres north of Ross Island, to retrieve last year's GLS tags and search for banded birds at the Adélie colony there. This is new information to me. Apparently we'll be getting a ride on one of the US Coast Guard icebreakers that are somewhere nearby, on their way south to bust a channel into McMurdo Sound ahead of the arrival of the annual supply vessel.

Katie and I sit on the porch after dinner, sipping our evening glass of whisky and chatting about her plans for the holidays, her excitement at seeing her husband soon, what she'll be doing next semester at the university, people we know in common in the world of avian science. It's another breathless evening, the sun still high in the sky.

"How's it going with David?" she asks. "He's not exactly talkative, is he."

"Ha," I reply. "I've probably heard more words spoken today than I've heard out here all season."

"Well," Katie says, "if it makes you feel any better, he's like this with everybody in the field. He's just being chatty today because I'm a fresh face."

"I know, everyone knows what David's like—his inscrutability is part of his mystique. But I guess I didn't envision him being quite this lacking in conversation," I say glumly.

"Well," she says, "don't take it personally. He and I would have stopped talking by now if I'd been based here." Given Katie's chattiness and David's introversion I can see that being the case; perhaps he and I are a good match after all.

And it's not as if various levels of friction among remote crew are a new phenomenon. Though it was seldom discussed because it went against the popular perception of the day, examples of interpersonal conflict and even outright antagonism regularly featured in the journeys of the early Antarctic explorers of the Heroic Age. On the Nimrod Expedition's attempt for the Pole, surgeon Eric Marshall wrote of Shackleton and his leadership that he was like "an old woman, always panicking,"[25] while expedition member Frank Wild wished in his turn that Marshall "would fall down a crevasse about a thousand feet deep."[26]

In modern times the emotional difficulties faced by people on isolated polar expeditions have been more formally studied, in part to improve preparations required for space missions: Antarctica as analogue for Mars. It has also been important to understand these responses from the perspective of better preparing personnel for the often grinding demands of life in Antarctica. In 1984, the commander at Argentina's Almirante Brown Scientific Station reportedly set fire to the base as the season's final supply ship was departing, in a desperate bid to avoid another overwinter. Researchers studying the negative mental health aspects of working in remote Antarctic sites have described the small and large irritations that contribute to field camp stress.

"Say there's somebody you go to lunch with and you don't notice the way that they eat. But if you ate with that same person day in and day out for six months, suddenly the way they chew their food is enough to drive you crazy," one of these researchers, University of Southern California's Larry Palinkas, has said.[27]

In a paper in the medical journal *The Lancet,* he and Canadian co-author Peter Suedfeld noted that "interpersonal conflict and tension is the greatest source of stress in polar expeditions"[28] and write about the fate of the Greely scientific expedition to the Arctic in the 1880s, in which the crew reportedly resorted to mutiny, suicide, and cannibalism . . . helped along by personality clashes and poor leadership. Palinkas also describes examples of this "polar madness" at modern research stations, one of which included a staff member clubbing a co-worker with a pipe. "There was a saying at the station for the remainder of the winter that 'If you've got a gripe, use a pipe,'" Palinkas said.[29]

Knowing McMurdo's denizens, I'm convinced that this would have been more than a saying if it had happened there—someone would have mocked it up to look like an official safety bulletin and posted it on a bulletin board outside the HR office.

So in the grand scheme of things David's silences are pretty mild, driven as they presumably are by his extreme introversion, and by being generally lost in thought about the many logistical and intellectual aspects of the research project. And who knows what personality quirks of my own may be irritating him. Everyone I get to know well eventually comments on my stubbornness, so maybe that's it—and nor am I always good with social cues. David is probably dropping hints all over the place about meals he'd like to have, ways I should enter data differently, a better place to keep the toilet paper, and I'm blithely ignoring all of them, doing everything my own way as usual. At least we are both tidy and respectful of each other's personal space. At a field camp on an island seabird colony in Canada I had an assistant who suffered from frequent nosebleeds. He regularly left blood-soaked tissues lying on the table in the hut's eating area, alongside the decaying plant and insect specimens he would leave sitting half processed for days. Eventually, after he slept in my bed when I was off-island and helped himself to my laundromat money, we fired him.

Nor is David remotely sexist in any aspect of his dealings with me, something that is deeply refreshing here on a continent where women were generally not even permitted to conduct work at British or Australian research stations until the 1970s or 1980s (the first women entered the US Antarctic Program somewhat earlier, in the late 1960s), and discriminatory attitudes persist. "Women are not seen as researchers but as women" was one written response to a recent survey on gender barriers in Antarctic research, published in 2019.[30] And in 2022, a report by the National Science Foundation found that 72 percent of women—nearly three-quarters of those surveyed—reported that sexual harassment was a problem in Antarctica. There are also independently verified reports of egregiously misogynist behaviour at remote Antarctic field sites—like women being repeatedly sworn at, pushed, and publicly denigrated by male superiors.

That thankfully hasn't been my experience this season. To David, always deep in his thoughts, I'm simply another pair of hands to help with the work in and around camp. In team development theory it is posited that effective teams need both a common goal—here, the collection of high-quality research data—and team members' ability to respect each other's strengths and work styles, something that is particularly important when individuals are strongly independent, as is the case with David and me. When I contemplate all this I realize that I feel fortunate in my assignment of campmate.

"I'm reading about Mertz," I tell Katie, sipping my whisky.

"As in the Mertz Glacier?" she asks.

"As in Xavier Mertz, the Swiss guy it was named for," I say. "He died on Mawson's Australasian Antarctic expedition." I take another drink of Scotch. "It's an unforgettable story. "

"Unforgettable how?" asks Katie.

"For its extremes of human suffering. This is three weeks after their companion Belgrave Ninnis has been lost down a crevasse. It's just Mertz and Mawson, struggling back to base, still a month away. It's very cold—the temperatures are zero Fahrenheit and below—and very windy. They're almost out of food, eating their remaining sled dogs to survive, and because they've lost their ground sheet they are sleeping directly on the snow. Their sleeping bags won't dry, and they are both so wet and malnourished that their skin starts sloughing off in sheets."

"Ugh," says Katie. "Ugh! What do you mean?"

"Here, I'll read you that bit so you can hear it in Mawson's own words." I walk back into the hut and retrieve *The Home of the Blizzard* from my desk. The book is already open to the page. "'The skin was peeling off our bodies and a very poor substitute remained which burst readily and rubbed raw in many places. One day, I remember, Mertz ejaculated, "Just a moment," and, reaching over, lifted from my ear a perfect skin-cast. I was able to do the same for him. As we never took off our clothes, the peelings of hair and skin from our bodies worked down into our under-trousers and socks, and regular clearances were made.'"[31]

"Ewww!" exclaims Katie.

"Mertz is growing weaker," I tell her. "He declines to the point of incontinent delirium, then dies in his sleeping bag. Shortly before he dies he bites off half his little finger in some mad demonstration of courage."

Katie stares at me wordlessly, her glass halfway to her mouth.

"Later on," I continue, "when Mawson is heading back to base alone, the soles of his feet fall off and he has to smear the raw skin with lanolin, bandage the soles back on, and hold them in place with his socks. I can't stop thinking about it."

"I think you should stop reading that book," says Katie, an incredulous half smile frozen on her face.

"I realized the other day that my fingernail clippers are made by a company called Mertz," I reply.

11

TWO DAYS AFTER I hear the first chicks peeping from their eggs, I see the first hatched individuals of the season. At the same time I watch one of them being nabbed by a skua. The bird lands in the midst of several penguin nests and pounces before the parents can put up a fight, seizing the chick by the head and flying off. From being grabbed from the nest, where the parent has just sat half upright to shade its two offspring from today's sun, to being devoured by the marauding bird and its mate, takes all of a minute. How can something go so quickly from being alive and vital to filling another creature's stomach? The skuas' eyesight must be eagle-sharp to spot a tiny day-old chick the instant its parent stands up—it was a split second between the time that the penguin adjusted its position and when the skua landed next to its nest. It is a hard thing to witness—with their wobbly little heads, quivering flippers, and soft downy feathers, the penguin chicks epitomize cuteness and vulnerability—but the skuas will die and sustain other things one day, and they too have chicks to feed.

There's nowhere quite like a seabird colony—penguin or any other—for instilling a sense of the harshness of the natural world. All of life is on display here. Mates desert each other, eggs and chicks are taken by skuas or whatever the local predators might be, offspring are deserted by parents and starve. Even adult penguins, which, like most other seabirds, are long-lived once they attain breeding age, are not immune to untimely death or misfortune—as I've seen here with the injured bird 1091, and with the other individuals who occasionally stagger into the colony with sprained limbs or grievous bodily wounds. The other day I saw a one-footed penguin in the colony, its wound long since healed, stumping among the nests like a peg-legged pirate. These are tough birds. Death and injury are just one aspect of the tide of life, however, and a seabird colony is also full of pairing and mating, hatching and growth, life force in full swing.

And today, 1091 is prevailing. She is still incubating a single egg, the other one having been grabbed by another of the skuas. She is now able to stand clumsily if she uses her bill to push herself upwards, and is currently balanced sturdily on her bum and legs, like a tripod.

Early this evening it snows heavily for about an hour, a big dump of fluffy flakes drifting down on a calmer wind than this morning. It's the heaviest snow that we've had since we've been here, but the most noteworthy thing about the squall is its departure. The thick flakes stop falling in a matter of minutes, and as the clouds recede northward it's as if a hand is drawing back a thick grey curtain to expose the Royal Society Range on the distant coast of Victoria Land. On the left of my field of view and dead ahead, glaciers glisten, while on the right stands the dark wall of the receding blizzard, nothing visible behind it.

We are heading back into McMurdo tonight, with pickup scheduled for 19:00 hours. All three of us—David, me, Katie—are antsy waiting for the helicopter, already half an hour late. Here, a late helo is a distinct source of anxiety for would-be passengers: Are we stranded because it has been grounded somewhere by local weather? Has the dispatcher forgotten about our flight? Has it crashed en route? All of these scenarios are not outside the realm of the possible, especially the weather delay or a crash. Katie is pacing back and forth ahead of the last hurdle before catching her flight out of town on the eighteenth of December, the day after tomorrow. This should get her home just in time for Christmas, barring any travel delays. She's scheduled to go on a ski-equipped LC-130, the slowest thing still flying to and from McMurdo, so she is facing at least an eight-hour flight back to Christchurch, assuming it doesn't boomerang. I am simply ready for a break from camp, and David wants to get to a meeting he's arranged at Crary Lab.

The helo eventually arrives, apparently delayed by local weather conditions during a drop-off out in the Dry Valleys—the tail end of this evening's blizzard. I still have the key to my previous room in Building 155 so upon arrival in Mactown I go straight there, only to discover it occupied by three male roommates. But they are fine (enthusiastic even) with the idea of someone of the opposite sex taking up the last bunk for the night, and they ply me with questions about penguins and Cape Royds while I unpack. It's a balm to talk to these strangers with their laid-back friendliness, a brief respite before I'm swept up in the whirlwind that is a twenty-four-hour stopover in town.

I take a long and delicious shower in the communal bathroom down the hall. After I've dressed in clean clothes, dried my hair, and thrown my dirty field gear in a machine in the laundry room, I grab a snack in the galley and head to the Coffee House for a glass of wine. I savour each one of these mundane activities, which have a spa-like quality after the austerity of field camp. I walk over to the library to check email in the midnight stillness, then to our lab space in Crary to pick up a couple of pieces of gear we need in camp, a head start on tomorrow's chores.

Molly Miller's research team, some of whom we flew with from New Zealand back in early November, nearly six weeks ago now, have just returned to McMurdo from the end of their season out at the Beardmore Glacier, and there are wild-looking people wandering in and out of the building with excited eyes, dirty clothes, skiers' tans, and hair sticking out in all directions. All of them have stories to tell. They seem to be physically manifesting the madness of extended time in the deep field. Come to think of it, I probably look like they do every time I get into McMurdo from Royds. It's a wonder tonight's roommates were so welcoming.

Eventually, back at my room, I turn in, but thanks to an overstuffed pillow, a sore neck, a too-late cup of coffee in the library, the stimulation of being in town, and the protruding bedsprings of the top bunk—all overlaid with copious snoring—I am unable to fall asleep until nearly 3 a.m.

I am groggily grabbing some early lunch in the Galley lineup the next morning when a cheerful woman with short reddish hair approaches me in line.

"Hi," she says. "I'm Jennifer."

I stare at her mutely, my mouth already full of a biscuit I've grabbed en route. Bad manners on my part, I think, but note that at least I haven't degenerated to the point of serving my meals directly onto a dining room tray like the more iconoclastic of the Mactown locals. On the other hand, at Cape Royds we just wipe down our dirty dishes with paper towels to save on water and propane so I probably shouldn't be throwing stones about people living outside the bounds of civilized society.

She sees my blank look. "I'm joining you at Cape Royds this week," she says.

I swallow some biscuit. "Oh, really," I reply. "Why?"

"I'm with the NSF Artists and Writers Program," she says, "researching a book on ice."

"Oh, great," I say. "I hadn't heard. Well, our flight leaves at seven o'clock tonight, so I'll see you before then for weigh-in at Helo Ops. I've got to go and deal with supplies right after lunch. Any food in particular you like?"

Jennifer is waiting with her pile of gear at Helo Ops when David and I arrive. I almost never see him on these trips into town—we part ways at the helicopter pad and meet back there again at our prearranged departure time. As the assistant I deal with most camp logistics, driving a station truck to transport our supplies to the helicopter pad—which I'm happy to do since it's easier than trying to coordinate division of in-town tasks between the two of us, and it gives me a chance to explore new corners of McMurdo. This trip I've augmented my liquor supply with a couple of new bottles of wine and, somewhat reluctantly, a one-litre bottle of Jägermeister. I've been wanting something less demanding than the tot of whisky I sip after dinner, and given the store's dwindling supply it was either that or syrupy retro flavours like crème de menthe, limoncello, or crème de banane.

The flight back out is breathtaking. The prevailing southerly winds have stilled, and as a result McMurdo Sound is once again clogged with the pack ice that has drifted in from the north, filling the ocean (and the eye) from sea ice edge to distant glacier-laden mountains to northern horizon. Even the sky is pale tonight, thinly veiled by skeins of cirrus cloud. I stare through the window of the helo, devouring the view.

Despite the visual stimulation of the flight, by the time we land my bad night's sleep and the post-town adrenaline slump have caught up with me and I am exhausted. My stomach is acting up too—from the camp water perhaps, or from our rudimentary outdoor refrigeration not functioning well at this time of year—which contributes to my general malaise.

But as I started to realize last night as I tossed and turned, my sudden wretchedness is as mental as it is physical. As spring has turned to summer I've found my resistance to Antarctica's enchantment waning and I spend more and more time just staring at all of the wildness, drinking it in. Now each night after work I sit on the cold volcanic rock outside the hut in a meditative trance, and feel as if I could gaze forever into the nullity of ice-filled McMurdo Sound and the distant Transantarctic Mountains, any sense of self slowly draining away. I sometimes wonder what would happen if we didn't go back into McMurdo every so often to break the spell of this place. Would I become like an empty shell, consumed by all the purity and emptiness? Succumbing to this landscape feels like giving oneself over to some sort of exquisite delirium that is far more welcome than the narrow confines of sanity. Is this what polar madness is actually like, how it starts?

After more than a month of being high on this endless daylight, I realize I am abruptly crashing. Since arriving here my daily schedule has been advancing; each night I have been getting to bed a little later than the night before, and getting up a little later each morning. There's a name for this physiological slippage under continuous daylight (or continuous darkness). It's called "free-run," where melatonin levels desynchronize from the regular circadian rhythm and lead to cycles slightly longer than the usual twenty-four hours. Left unchecked, this means that you're eventually going to bed at breakfast time and awaking for a late lunch. There's less slow-wave sleep—what we commonly think of as deep sleep—and more light dozing. No wonder I feel increasingly out of control, like someone skiing down an icy slope with the brakes off. The constant daylight is beginning to seem unrelenting and there is nothing I can do about it. At McMurdo the associated sleeplessness is colloquially known as "big eye" and can be associated with the thousand-yard or Antarctic stare, a glassy-eyed look with a slack jaw that is reportedly common in overwinterers.

I'm starting to feel scraped raw by this place, but have a real sense that I don't ever want to go home. There lies busyness, distraction, complexity, the boredom of meaningless short-term work. I wish I could use some of my allocated satellite phone minutes to call my sister and tell her all about it, like I used to do occasionally from South American phone kiosks when I worked in that part of the world. These are the moments that make her absence tangible, leaving me grasping for a reality that is no longer present.

So where better to be in the world than here, now? Melatonin deprivation aside, I manically cling to wakefulness each night because I'm afraid I'll miss something of the perfection of this place, as if I might sleep through enlightenment.

It turns out that Jennifer is a writer of children's books, and unlikely though it seems to me from someone in such a genre—I'd somehow expected earnestness—she brings a spark to camp. Her trip to Cape Royds is a pilgrimage of sorts. She once wrote a YA book about Shackleton and decided on a whim that she wants to visit his hut while waiting for a flight to the Pole.

The morning after her arrival I take her down to see the hut and the penguin colony and show her the boundaries of the ASPA so she can stay outside them; she has a permit for her work here, but it doesn't allow her to enter any of the protected areas. Jennifer comments on how different the terrain in the colony proper appears from the unoccupied land around it, and I point out where the ground is cemented together by ornithogenic soil, mainly formed by hundreds of years of penguin guano. Out at Beaufort Island, where we are going after Christmas, this soil is reportedly a metre or two thick. "Ornithogenic" literally means "produced by birds," but it is not just composed of guano. The top strata will also be full of the decaying carcasses of dead chicks from previous seasons, like raisins studded through a disgusting pudding. This place looks like a mausoleum even at this time of year, when natural mortality is low but the desiccated bodies of last year's dead remain scattered about the landscape, adding to the half-buried corpses of the past decade or two. Ornithogenic soil is laid down slowly. I mention that later some of the present year's chicks will die as well, their corpses adding to the process, continuing to build the soil and feed the skuas.

"It all sounds like some sort of zombie movie," says Jennifer.

As we walk around the colony I notice that the pace of chick hatching has picked up even over the day we've been away, in a highly synchronized process thought to confer overall advantage to seabird hatchlings by "swamping" predators with potential prey. I can hear the shrill voices of the chicks all over the colony now. The sound reminds me irresistibly of the noise one's nose makes when it whistles—high and breathy and so faint that you're never sure if it's within you or something louder but very far off. And at B-REF, 1091 is still at her nest. While I'm watching she stiffly pushes herself upright with her beak and reveals that both her eggs are now gone. She is still too slow and sore to have defended them from the agile depredations of the skuas. I suspect that she will remain on the nest, growing strong again while awaiting her mate's return.

From Shackleton's hut we stand and look out on the pack ice, mellow in the morning sun. With no southerly wind again today to push it out to sea it keeps drifting in on the currents and the northerly breeze, growing denser and denser, until it looks as thick as fast ice, as if we could walk on it without slipping beneath the surface. In the vista beyond the two hillocks framing the main entry to the colony, a black shape suddenly slices through the whiteness—a killer whale hunting among the floes. We walk to the cliff and watch the pod move north, an adult male and female, a young male, and a new calf, the latter surfacing behind the adults in a sprightly and debonair manner with the joie de vivre of young killer whales everywhere. The dorsal patches of these whales are so dark grey as to be almost black, and their narrow white eye patches tilt upward like a bold slash of eyeshadow, characteristics typical of Type C killer whales, the race most commonly found in the Ross Sea. These animals are denizens of the deep pack ice and, at least in the southern Ross Sea, are thought to eat mainly Antarctic toothfish.

This reminds me of the superlative "most untouched," which is often applied to Antarctica along with "highest," "driest," "windiest," and "most remote." It is true to a point, particularly for the southern portion of the Ross Sea, which is the most inaccessible part of the world's oceans, but the story of the Antarctic toothfish (marketed in the world's wealthy countries as Chilean sea bass) is one example of how even Antarctica is being changed by the far-reaching hand of humanity.

In the evenings and on bad-weather days David has been reading a book entitled *In a Perfect Ocean*,[32] the cover of which caught my eye because one of the co-authors is Daniel Pauly, the renowned Franco-Canadian fisheries scientist based at the University of British Columbia, in a department I've been considering for my PhD program. It was Pauly who coined the term "shifting baseline"[33] to refer to the phenomenon of the intergenerational amnesia that affects each subsequent cohort of biologists, such that every generation sees the environmental condition that existed at the start of their career to be the norm, or the baseline. He also coined the phrase "fishing down marine food webs"[34] to describe the process of fishing and depleting the larger, longer-lived, and more marketable species, then consecutively switching to ever smaller and shorter-lived ones, a process that leads to upper-trophic-level animals disappearing from many areas of present-day oceans.

It is in these ways that vast but incremental ecological losses (a "creeping disappearance of . . . species," as Pauly called it[35]) are observed and accrued. It is the fate of all field biologists to be able to cite personal examples of these losses; one of mine lies in the sea ducks I would see flocking in the thousands near my childhood home in coastal British Columbia. Today I see them in much smaller flocks and lament their decline in my lifetime, but Pauly would say that the baseline we should be considering instead is one from an earlier time. Of such earlier days, Indigenous knowledge—in this instance told by coastal Saanich (W̱SÁNEĆ) Elder Dave Elliott—says that in the waters off British Columbia in the spring, "so many [ducks] would come that they would darken the sky. They would blot out the sun like a big, dark cloud."[36] Some would dismiss such information as no more than a story, but in fact Pauly suggests that recognizing anecdote is the solution to such historical data gaps.

In a Perfect Ocean thus draws on historical accounts to describe the North Atlantic Ocean before industrial fishing and whaling took hold, and the book's description of the Atlantic's early riches reminds me of the teeming life I have observed in Antarctic seas. However, great swathes of the waters around Antarctica—particularly around the Antarctic Peninsula but also the Ross Sea in the past—have seen their own share of industrial fishing and whaling. Even now the commercial toothfish fishery is extracting its catch from the northern portion of the Ross Sea, with the impacts of this trickling south to affect the population dynamics of Antarctic toothfish in McMurdo Sound, in the southernmost part of the species' range.

These and other Antarctic fisheries for species like krill are managed by the Commission for the Conservation of Antarctic Marine Living Resources (its acronym is pronounced camel-R), a regulatory body set up under the Antarctic Treaty. CCAMLR's provisions appear precautionary—and indeed the body sees itself in this way, with its website using terms such as "ecosystem-based," "best available scientific information," and "ensure the long-term sustainability of the fishery."[37] Yet CCAMLR arguably has approved commercial fisheries for Antarctic toothfish without sufficient biological data to determine whether the fishery meets its own definition of sustainable. Historically, commercial extraction of fish from waters on the other side of the continent, around the Antarctic Peninsula, drove some marine fish species to such low levels that fishing of them is no longer economically feasible, and populations have not recovered decades later. In fact, in a subsequent year David and I will write about this, in a paper published in the scientific journal *Fish and Fisheries*.[38] From the 1960s to the 1980s, key finfish populations on the Peninsula were reduced to less than 20 percent of their original size, and numbers are still low.

I've been mildly surprised that as an Antarctic scientist David would be spending his time reading about the history of the Atlantic, but it turns out to be about a study in contrasts, or a cautionary tale: Antarctica offers the possibility for humanity to learn from its past mistakes. Here, despite humans having left their mark, the sea still boils with krill, penguins come ashore to breed in the hundreds of thousands, and whales, seals, and certain bird species such as king penguins—once harvested as a source of blubber and feathers—are recovering.

When I first asked David about the book, he carefully placed his coffee cup on the corner of his desk and turned toward me, his normally reserved manner falling away; he has known and loved this place for decades now. "The Ross Sea is the last intact marine ecosystem on Earth," he said passionately. "So it's the last place to study how marine systems really work."

In the next year or so David will emerge as a leading voice for the protection of the Ross Sea from fishing and other industrial exploitation, and as a major force behind the science and global campaign that will lead to the 2016 decision by Antarctic Treaty states to adopt much of the region as the world's largest marine protected area. As part of its quest to bring Antarctica to the world, this campaign will produce the award-winning documentary *The Last Ocean*. "You can't be a doctor of the ocean without knowing what a healthy patient looks like," states David in the film.

In the here and now he feels the same. "Marine scientists elsewhere in the world always make generalizations about how marine ecosystems work but they're mostly wrong, because they are all working in systems that are broken. All of the other oceans are broken."

I can hear the subtext: To David, here on the shore at Cape Royds we are lucky enough to be conducting research on an (almost) perfect ocean.

The next day there's another Scott Base group out here, this time a group of twenty or so grad students from the University of Canterbury, escorted by Paul Rogers (who is enthusiastically helping the female component) and another AFT guy called Rob, who is busy trying to reach Scott Base via hand-held radio. I ask him what the ice track conditions are like going back into town, particularly the refrozen tideline cracks in the sea ice near Cape Barne. This is one of the jobs of the AFT and FSTP guides: to check the condition of the ice road on a regular basis, feeding information back to base when breakup begins or where cracks are forming or changing. Rob tells me there's been no change from when he drilled the cracks earlier in the spring, at which point they were still solidly frozen from last winter. "There's one spot where it drops off to a metre but everywhere else is really thick," he says.

This information is imparted as we walk back to the hut, where I've invited Rob for a quick tour and a hot chocolate. I pass the news on to David as I'm bringing the water to a boil, already planning my next ski.

"What? I told you yesterday that the ice was fine—you believe this guy because he's got radios hanging off him?" he says, gesticulating at

Rob and glaring at me from under thick grey eyebrows. I think he is joking, but sometimes it's hard to be sure with David.

"You didn't exactly tell me it was fine; you hummed and hawed about it," I reply.

I am sure that in David's mind he'd provided a definitive answer, but even though we've been living together for a while, his manner of communication is sometimes still opaque to me. I reflect on my own unemotional communication style—like David, I'm highly literal and at my best when focused on the details of work or data—and wonder if he finds me similarly hard to read at times, despite the proximity of our lives.

Jennifer and I walk down to the colony, and I leave her behind at the edge of the ASPA. At the skua nest nearest B-REF, I see a vigilante squad of three young penguins harassing the adult until it has to get up off its eggs and retreat. Before she left for home Katie told me that at Cape Bird she has seen penguins run at skua nests and trample the eggs. The skua nest that is up on top of Cape Royds, up by subcolony 11/12, has failed, but all the other skua pairs are doing fine, despite penguin attacks and whatever weather extremes the season may be bringing them. They currently seem to be keeping a preferential eye on the penguin nests where the chicks have already hatched—small chicks are easier prey than an egg that's being closely brooded.

Not all of the skua territories at Cape Royds border the colony, and the species feeds on marine prey other than penguins—krill or the silverfish *Pleuragramma antarcticum*—though I've yet to see one fishing despite watching them regularly when they are flying out over McMurdo Sound. In the 1980s the skua population in McMurdo Sound was widespread, and estimated by David and colleagues at fifteen thousand birds overall. This high number was thought to be due to the open dump at McMurdo Station, in place since the early days of Operation Deep Freeze in the 1950s. Skuas scavenged there constantly, as evidenced by the many discarded chicken, beef, and pork bones that in those days could be seen scattered around their nesting areas. Since the dump closed in the 1990s, McMurdo skua numbers have declined and the birds have returned to eating natural food, except when they manage to dive-bomb a McMurdo resident and frighten them into dropping a food tray, or otherwise convince a human to feed them.

One of the skuas' more repellent (and fascinating) dietary habits these days involves pulling the semi-frozen carcasses of last year's dead penguin chicks from the thawing ice around the edges of Pony Lake, in front of Shackleton's hut. This is usually accomplished with much tugging and accompanied by much excited vocalizing to a mate once the treat is free. Although the dead chicks seem like a revolting meal, in reality they often look freshly dead, presumably flash-frozen by the cold weather already rolling in last February at the start of the chicks' fledging period and the time of their mortality.

Pony Lake itself is really starting to look disgusting. With the advent of near-zero temperatures, the ice around its edges has slowly been retreating and now, during the daytime hours when the sun is high, its western edge is rimmed by a metre or more of open water. This is currently the colour of very strong, slightly murky tea. Fluorescent green algae patches are visible on the bottom and among them eddy sundry parts of long-dead penguin chicks. Evil-looking mats of bacteria and blue-green algae have already risen to float on the surface of the open water, looking like giant pieces of skin shed from a scrofulous elephant. So far the lake's smell is not distinguishable from that of the rest of the colony, but I have no doubt that it will become so as the season progresses and the ambient temperature rises.

And yet even that vile lake is a thing of beauty to some. Witness the odes to cyanobacteria sprinkled generously throughout the weathered old guestbook in the Kiwi wanigan. I've been perusing it lately whenever I stop by there to eat my snack or take a rest out of the wind. The organisms of Pony Lake, and of nearby Green Lake, just over the hill, probably have more logbook space devoted to them than any other subject covered by the multitude of visitors over the years—peppered with charming hand-drawn illustrations. One early entry from an unspecified year in the 1980s reads:

> *26 Nov–19 Dec.* Good to be back at Royds continuing to look at the algae (slime!) in the ponds . . . These are all "blue-green algae" (though they don't all look blue-green—most here look orange-red)—scientific name Cyanobacteria, in the family Oscillatoriaceae (how about that then!). These were first studied in 1912 on material sent back by Shackleton's expedition. We've come back to re-examine the same ponds in considerably more detail and will be growing these bugs in cultures back in NZ. Pony Lake, Green Lake, Coast Lake and Blue Lake are all places from which species of the above were first described. These microscopic plants are the most abundant form of life on the whole continent (a good reason for a trip to Antarctica . . .) . . . P.S. Not very impressed with whoever left their shit bag under a rock in the middle of Backdoor Bay.

I ponder the accuracy of this stranger's comments on the abundance of "plants" here. There has been a sea change in scientific classification since those words were written, and cyanobacteria are now considered to be bacteria, not algae, the writer's colloquialism "bugs" perhaps being closer to the mark. Taxonomy has also long since changed for lichens, another plantlike life form at Cape Royds. The author of this logbook entry would have described these as plants too, instead of the strange composite life form we now understand them to be: fungi living symbiotically with photosynthesizing cyanobacteria or algae.

Lichens are among the hardiest life forms on the planet and several species are widespread here, fertilized by wind-borne particles of penguin guano; many of them are obscure enough to lack common names, going only by their Latin binomials. The most noticeable of these at Cape Royds are *Xanthoria elegans,* tinted rich and satisfying shades of burnt sienna or cadmium orange, and species of *Candelaria* and *Candelariella,* splashed across the black rocks like flaking blotches of yellow safety paint—all of them providing bursts of colour to relieve the eye in this monochromatic landscape. They seem to prefer the northern or lee side of boulders where they can catch the sun, absorb greater moisture from drifting snow, and escape the worst of the abrasive winds.

The lichens are the most widespread of the plant-like lifeforms at Cape Royds, but it amazes me that true plants also grow here, in the form of mosses, small dark green cushions of *Bryum* scattered through the colony and nearby. In some areas these are plentiful, and Shackleton's party referred to one area of prolific moss and algae growth between their weather station and Backdoor Bay as "the green parade." When fall arrives the penguins will swim north to the edge of the pack ice and the skuas will fly farther north still, with some migrating as far as the North Pacific. But the mosses and lichens must remain, with their presence a colourful reminder of life's ability to flourish just about anywhere on Earth, even here on the coast of Ross Island, where darkness prevails for half the year and winter temperatures descend to −50°C.

A helicopter arrives to take Jennifer away and in exchange leaves a Pulitzer Prize–winning science writer. Cal is a large, enthusiastic man with abundant floppy dark hair that seems to get in his eyes a lot. He too is down here on the NSF Writers and Artists Program and will be visiting us for three days. I offload all our trash and the latest full shit bucket on Jennifer, who is a good sport about taking responsibility for its fate at McMurdo.

I realize I'll miss her—her presence these past few days has been uplifting, open as she has been to thoughtful conversation on a wide range of topics, from children's literature to the intricacies of the Antarctic Treaty System. But not too much conversation. Cal is already demonstrating that he is very chatty, and I hope he discovers that silence too can be golden, especially here in the Wide Open Spaces. Three days can be a long time when you just want someone to stop talking.

The weather this afternoon has turned closed-in, moody. Clouds the colour of dirty sheets sit low on the mountains, nearly touching the far edge of the sea ice across McMurdo Sound. Because of the overcast it is not as warm as it has been the past couple of days. The air temperature is hovering a couple of degrees below zero as I walk around looking for banded birds. Cold is relative, though, as attested to by the shimmer hovering over the colony's dark rocks as they release the sun's heat into the still afternoon air. Nor is it cold enough to stop me sweating when I go for my post-work ski over the sea ice. Perhaps I'll make it to Cape Barne this time, that dark hump of land protruding from the sea ice to the south. Each time I go for a ski I travel farther and feel that this time I must reach it, but so far it has eluded me, inching away as I draw near so that at my turnaround point it still seems nearly as far away as on the previous day, like some fantastical landmark in *Alice in Wonderland.*

Cal wastes no time settling in and volunteers to make us dinner. He cooks an odd assortment of things that need to be used up from our makeshift freezer: partially defrosted salmon, asparagus, hash browns, and a few cheese tortellini. Last night David cooked up some defrosting green beans and shrimp, and served flaccid strawberries in syrup for dessert. Once the meal is on our rickety folding table David and Cal move forks from plates to mouths with a workmanlike efficiency until their food has gone, but I pick at the meal and realize I'm losing my appetite again. While our frozen food is lasting a long time in its semi-solid state it certainly isn't being kept as cold as it should be, and the textures are breaking down into an unappetizing uniformity.

On the other hand, at least we, unlike the skuas (and many explorers of the Heroic Age), are not subsisting on defrosted penguin flesh—nor surviving on starvation rations. In but one of Antarctica's many historic tales of privation, Shackleton wrote in *South*—his account of the Imperial Trans-Antarctic Expedition of 1914–1917—of a man who "searched for over an hour in the snow where he had dropped a piece of cheese some days before, in the hopes of finding a few crumbs. He was rewarded by coming across a piece as big as his thumb-nail, and considered it well worth the trouble."[39] Marooned on the ice after their ship *Endurance* sank, Shackleton's crew subsisted primarily on seal meat, the occasional emperor or Adélie penguin, and a small supply of dog-pemmican, as the cakes of sled-dog food were called. Of the same trip, storekeeper Thomas Orde-Lees wrote in his diary that "one wish[es] now that one could have many a meal that one has given to the dog at home . . . when the cook upset some pemmican on to an old sooty cloth and threw it outside his galley, one man subsequently made a point of acquiring it and scraping off the palatable but dirty compound."[40] And it was commonplace for marooned explorers to kill penguins by the hundred to see expeditions through an approaching winter. On the 1901–03 Swedish Antarctic Expedition, led by Otto Nordenskjöld, one benighted party of three men killed seven hundred penguins to get them through to the next year, while a larger group of their companions—marooned nearby when their ship sank off the very large Adélie colony at Paulet Island on the edge of the Weddell Sea—killed 1,100 birds, and slept on beds of decaying penguin skins.

In contrast to such hardship, our defrosting food is of course merely unappetizing, and on our last trip to McMurdo I picked up one of the yoghurt makers from the New Zealand goods section of the BFC and added it to our food order. Now every few days I mix some full-fat powdered New Zealand milk with hot water and yoghurt starter, wrap the container in a sweater to stop the heat from leaching out too quickly, and set it on a shelf above the propane heater overnight. Opening the lid on each successful batch is a small satisfaction based on having made it myself in our rudimentary living quarters, and consuming it is a tiny luxury.

As we clean up after dinner, Cal and I begin a lively discussion about Canadian politics. I find him an intriguing mix of politically savvy (he used to be a science policy advisor to government), worldly (he has recently worked in several foreign nations, and written a couple of deeply erudite volumes on science and society), and naive (he tells me he had never been outside North America until he'd finished his PhD). Our conversation meanders along some fascinating byways but the flow of words starts to feel relentless, and I edge out the door to my sleeping bag early.

I check the weather station on my way out and see that this evening's temperature has dropped to −3.5°C, which makes me think a weather change may be in the offing. The winds I feel on my face from the south are mere zephyrs, but I suspect a stronger system isn't far behind. The clouds on the horizon tonight are tinged with a hint of rich purple. They look like some exotic flower, or so I tell myself, starved as I am for the sight of vegetation that is not lichen plastered to a rock. I can hear the sound of Cal chatting away to David as I read in my tent, the low grumble of David's voice occasionally coming in reply. I put in my earplugs and for once fall asleep before 3 a.m.

12

IT IS THE longest day of the year, or would be if we weren't here in the land of twenty-four-hour daylight. When I sit at my makeshift desk with my breakfast—a large mug of strong coffee, instant oatmeal with lots of butter and brown sugar stirred into it—I look at the calendar pinned to one of the wooden wall supports and there it is: solstice, the twenty-first of December. Back at home in the northern hemisphere, the days will now slowly begin lengthening toward spring.

Here, with summer progressing and penguin traffic increasing as parents more frequently visit the sea to obtain food for their growing chicks, leopard seals have begun showing up at Cape Royds. David noted one yesterday on his shoreline watch, the first either of us has seen this season. Leopard seals have a well-deserved reputation as ferocious penguin-killers and are fearsome-looking creatures, over half a tonne in weight and with a mouth that opens to a reptilian gape approaching ninety degrees. The same individual, a large female, is back again this morning, swimming along with her snakelike head out of the water as she patrols the shoreline for penguins and her next meal.

And while these seals subsist on a range of smaller prey, including penguins, young seals, squid, fish, and even krill, they have also attacked humans on occasion. In his memoir *South*, Ernest Shackleton reports that one leapt onto an ice floe and attacked a member of his expedition (the seal was shot, with the starving men subsequently eating both the seal and several undigested fish found in its stomach). Decades later, Canadian Gareth Wood and two other members of the "In the Footsteps of Scott" expedition decided to travel across the sea ice from their base at Cape Evans to Cape Royds before the winter darkness closed in. In the twilight of an April day in 1986, they were crossing a refrozen crack in Backdoor Bay with Gareth in the lead. Gareth "tapped his boot on the thin sea-ice to test its strength" and then, recounted expedition member Steve Broni, a leopard seal burst through the new ice. "The next thing I knew he was flat on his back. I just heard him screaming, and then I saw this huge creature had him by the leg."[41]

"The seal must have been tracking us [from under the ice, as they do with penguins] for some time. I remember this head with huge jaws, like a giant snake, appearing in front of me," said Gareth in a written account of the event. "I fell over backwards because I could feel myself being pulled in . . . It was like something out of a Japanese horror movie. I knew that if I hadn't had my left crampon dug into the ice, it would have had me in the icy water."[42]

Steve drove off the seal by kicking at it with his crampons, only to have it come back a second time, lunging out of the water and onto the ice to latch its jaws around Gareth's plastic boot, dragging him toward the crack once again. After a second round of kicks the seal retreated into the sea, shedding blood and water onto the ice as it went, and leaving Gareth with fearsome puncture wounds in his leg below the knee.

Then, tragically, in mid-2003, Kirsty Brown, a marine scientist at Rothera Station with the British Antarctic Survey, was snorkelling to check on her research equipment and was grabbed by a leopard seal, held underwater for several minutes, and drowned—the first recorded human fatality related to these animals.

But polar photographer Paul Nicklen made leopard seals famous for a different kind of encounter, through intimate images of an individual seal taken while scuba diving. Instead of attacking him, this large female killed gentoo penguins and tenderly proffered them, as if Paul were a potential mate or some novel marine creature incapable of catching its own food. Several times on the Antarctic Peninsula I have had a leopard seal follow my Zodiac, trailing the boat underwater just astern of the spinning propeller as if mesmerized by it, then propelling itself half out of the water to inspect the vessel whenever we stopped. The territoriality or prey-seeking nature of this behaviour was as unnerving as the unparalleled curiosity was fascinating. Nonetheless, whether leopard seals are more likely predatory or curious, I'm mildly relieved that at Cape Royds we're at a safe remove on the clifftop above the edge of the sea ice, instead of below on the ice edge or in the water with the seals: one less environmental hazard to navigate while working.

A small group of Kiwis is clustered in front of Shackleton's hut when I crest the rise on my way back for lunch, their dark green Hägglunds tracked vehicle parked out on the sea ice at the foot of the slope at Backdoor Bay. I stop by to say hello and end up asking for a lift to the elusive Cape Barne so that I can ski back to Royds. There's a twenty-knot wind from the south and I don't fancy skiing into it all the way out, but a downwind ski back home, five kilometres or so, will be just the thing for a Sunday afternoon. They're out for a half-day escape from the station, and are happy to give me a ride.

Back at the colony, where David is working, he hems and haws about letting me go, clearly not wanting to but seemingly unwilling to come right out and say so. At issue isn't really the skiing but the fact that "town" will get to hear of my solo trip since people from base are involved. I suggest I address that problem by asking MacOps instead, and David says they won't give me permission to go alone.

"Look, I'm going to call MacOps and do a radio checkout with them," I finally tell him. "If they say no, then I won't go, but if they say yes then it's no longer your responsibility."

David appears moderately okay with this solution so I head back to the hut and radio in. I get a bemused-sounding Ted, who suggests I do a local check-in with David and wishes me a pleasant ski.

"Thanks Ted," I say. "Cape Royds out." And I start packing my gear.

The Kiwis are ready to go just as I finish stuffing my backpack with everything I might need: water, lots of chocolate and Bumper Bars, a Thermos of coffee, camera and lenses, several extra gloves and mitts, my balaclava and a spare hat, an extra down sweater, VHF radio and spare battery, goggles, sunscreen. I'm already wearing the usual multiple layers under my salopettes and jacket. We load my cross-country skis and poles into the back of the Hägglunds and set off down the flagged sea ice track toward the decaying volcanic plug of Cape Barne in the distance. This is the route taken by Gareth Wood's team the day he was attacked by the leopard seal, but the ice is much thicker at this point in the season, and impenetrable by a seal.

It is only a thirty-minute ride, and on the way we chat of things inconsequential and silly. One of the Kiwis, Euan, will be wintering over at Scott Base with another nine people and claims to hate all of them until pressed into admitting that actually they are a great bunch.

The Kiwis stop the Hägg at Cape Barne and even unload my skis for me. They wave goodbye and drive off southwards, and already I feel I know them better than our half hour together should have allowed. It's one of the things remoteness does for you.

How funny, I think, as I watch them chug off into the distance toward Cape Evans and Scott's Hut, leaving me five kilometres from camp and the one human being there, and a lot more than that—over thirty kilometres—from McMurdo: I'm in the middle of absolutely nowhere at Cape Royds, and yet I feel the need to get away and come out here for a little retreat.

This choice to spend an anxiety-free hour or two alone is a privileged one, here where men have been stranded and faced months of deprivation under the grimmest of circumstances. In 1935–36, for example, American Lincoln Ellsworth and his Canadian pilot, Herbert Hollick-Kenyon, spent six weeks awaiting rescue inside the ruins of Little America, the first US station on the continent, after they ran out of fuel while attempting a trans-Antarctic flight. They had sledged for eleven days from their downed plane to reach the abandoned base. As they waited for rescue, Ellsworth nursed a frostbitten foot, and, according to writer Jason Anthony, "found an old wad of gum stuck under his bunk and debated with himself for two days about whether Antarctica's natural refrigeration made it safe to chew."[43]

I pull off the big blue insulated moon boots and tie them to my pack, then lace up my ski boots, strap on the skis, and take off. It is snowing lightly despite a clear blue sky overhead; the edge of a snowstorm has been boiling down around Little Razorback Island to the south all morning, and its flakes are drifting lazily northward. I had mentioned to Euan that I would need to beat the weather.

"Don't worry," he'd said. "It's a slow one, it's been there for ages."

The snowstorm stays at my back and pushes me and the snowflakes along as I ski home. I feel tiny in this vast space, yet the feeling is comforting, the reality of my insignificance putting all my sorrows, worries, and fears into their proper perspective. If I am insignificant, so are they, and all I can do is to experience the wind and the cold and the strength of my muscles propelling me over the sea ice back toward my summer home on the edge of a penguin colony in the shadow of Erebus.

At the next point of land I stop to take photos of a fearless Weddell seal pup, congregated with others of its kind around the thinner ice caused by the tidal cracks. I remember the advice from Susan, our sea-ice safety instructor of six weeks ago, about using Weddell seals as indicators of weak spots in the ice, and keep my eyes peeled for their snow-covered breathing holes. The seals maintain these by gnawing at the holes' edges; hence their preference for the tidal crack areas—less chewing. At the Crary Lab in Mactown there's the skull of a Weddell seal in a display case, and it is immediately distinguishable from the skulls of the leopard and crabeater seals that keep it company because of the incredibly worn canines caused by all that ice chomping.

After the seal congregation I ski over a kilometre of snow-free ice. I am glad of the wind at my back as the storm grows incrementally closer; crossing this icy patch under my own momentum would have been a struggle. The skis clatter as the wind pushes me over all the bumps and protrusions formed when the surface of the ocean froze months ago, and my thighs ache with the effort of keeping the skis aligned. The ice is the colour of the sky after a spring storm, an incredibly pale milky blue.

Beyond the bare stretch the wind begins to pick up. Fine particles of snow are whipped past me over the sea ice surface, making a whispering sound, the only noise for many kilometres. I catch up with a group of tobogganing Adélie penguins, pass them, then stop to watch them pass me. Instead of doing this, they of course stop too, and several of them get up and waddle toward me, curious. A platoon of ten more toboggan in from the distance, the wind whisking them along on their bellies in a whirl of snow. These new birds also pause, and then all depart down the sea ice track toward Cape Royds with the spindrift blowing around their hurtling forms. I take off behind them and we all end up speeding the last kilometre into Royds together, they tobogganing on their bellies on one side of the flagged track and I skiing on the other, all of us whizzing over the snow with the wind at our backs and the fine powder swirling around us like a mist.

13

TODAY IS THE warmest day of the season so far, as befitting the day after the solstice. On a radio call with Cape Bird, David is told by one of our Kiwi collaborators that penguin nests that were hitherto high and dry are now in the middle of a stream of glacier melt, with the birds trying to incubate their eggs as water flows around them. This is partly because the Cape Bird colony has more than doubled in size over time, meaning that some penguins are being forced to choose unsuitable nest sites, too low on the mounds on which the subcolonies usually form.

It was recommended that recruits to this project read David's book, entitled *Adélie Penguin: Bellwether of Climate Change.* Today, more than ever, its title seems to have perfectly captured the birds and the place we are studying. Despite our isolation from the problems of the modern world, climate change is also making itself felt here, with the local Adélies experiencing warmer average temperatures over the breeding season. Over the short term, however, warming trends at the very high latitudes of the Ross Sea are projected to increase the amount of winter sea ice, something that may benefit Adélie penguins for a while: Adélies are pagophilic (literally, "ice-loving"), a term used for organisms that depend on ice for all or part of their life history. Too little sea ice—a situation seen on the opposite side of the continent on the rapidly warming Antarctic Peninsula—is problematic, because sea ice forms these birds' marine habitat, both physically, as a place to rest and avoid predators, and biologically, as a place to forage for the krill that inhabit the underside of the floes. But from a penguin point of view the relationship with ice is complex; at the local scale, Adélie penguin colonies form where the wind blows the sea ice away—something I have been learning about firsthand from the incessant wind here at Cape Royds. Penguins would rather swim than walk to and from where they find their food. Increasing winds, and the greater reliability of open-water presence near the colonies, have played a large role in why Adélie penguin populations have been increasing everywhere but the tip of the Antarctic Peninsula. There they are being replaced by the historically more northern gentoo penguin, a species that prefers minimal ice year-round. The Intergovernmental Panel on Climate Change predicts that the Ross Sea will be the last place in the Southern Ocean where sea ice persists, and this is where Adélie penguins will continue to occur.

Despite a hat and multiple applications of sunscreen, my nose feels red by early afternoon, though in the shade the temperature remains well below zero. On days like this I have to remind myself to put sunscreen on the unlikely parts of my exposed skin—bottom of my nose up into the nostrils; tops and insides of my ears in case I remove my hat—and wear polarized glacier glasses to avert snow blindness or longer-term corneal damage, a risk worsened because of the increased UV-B radiation associated with the annual ozone hole.* But even without ozone depletion, the sun's reflected glare from snow and ice is of course a risk. In his memoirs Mawson described the symptoms of snow blindness as a painful or gritty feeling in the eyes, to be medicated with the preferred treatment of the day: tiny soluble tablets of zinc sulphate and cocaine placed under the eyelids. From his time in Scott's Northern Party, Raymond Priestley (later Sir Raymond Priestley) described snow blindness as "excruciating," and of a particularly bad bout endured by their party he wrote that "of all our experiences in these two years [which included an unplanned winter-over in a snow cave, subsisting on seal and penguin meat] I think that we should least like to repeat this twenty-four hours."[44] The modern treatment involves eye rest and pain management with ibuprofen or acetaminophen. Given Priestley's description, I suspect this regimen is unequal to the task.

Cal leaves this afternoon, his three-day stay extended to four because helos were grounded last night by the wind. He's got to be the chattiest man I've ever met—the karmic antidote to David, perhaps. He also seemed to fart more than anyone I've ever spent time with. Not overtly, but at night, once he'd fallen asleep on the floor of the hut, I could hear a low rumble like that of a distant thunderstorm. After Cal's helicopter disappears in the direction of McMurdo, David and I turn back to the hut and our eyes meet briefly. I smile at him faintly and he nods before we both turn to go inside, once more finding solace in the silence.

---

* The Antarctic ozone hole—caused by human use of chlorine- and bromine-containing substances such as refrigerants—was discovered in 1985 by scientists working with the British Antarctic Survey. The international agreement to phase out these compounds, the Montreal Protocol, was agreed to in 1987 and is leading to the slow recovery of the ozone layer. The Montreal Protocol is often described as one of the world's most successful examples of global cooperation on an environmental threat.

—

With chick hatch upon us, we deploy the first time-depth recorder, or TDR, of the season. I hold the adult penguin, which lies still in my arms like a heavy football or a big feathered purse, while David attaches the lightweight domino-shaped recorder and a radio-transmitting tag to the feathers along its dorsal midline. He carefully affixes the compact devices using tiny strips of Tesa-brand duct tape torn from a roll, his fingers sure from many applications in previous years. We are doing this to find out where the birds are foraging as they raise their chicks, part of the study's work in characterizing the marine habitat used by penguins from the colonies at Capes Royd, Bird, and Crozier. Based on a few radio-tagged individuals, it looks like the Royds birds are feeding close by, in the water on the west side of Ross Island, while the Crozier birds are foraging on the eastern side in an ever-expanding arc with Cape Crozier more or less at its centre. As the colony's chicks grow, the food in the arc is being depleted, so the Crozier penguins are forced to go ever farther afield, while those from Capes Royds and Bird are either avoiding this depleted area or have no need to travel that far from home to find food.

There is a knack to holding a penguin. With the right touch there is little struggling by either bird or researcher. Without exerting too much pressure I clamp this one under my left arm and hold its feet firmly but gently in my right hand; its head protrudes behind me, past my armpit. Later we deploy a TDR and a satellite tag on another penguin, and inject a couple of PIT tags into newly arrived weighbridge colony birds, just under the loose skin between their shoulder blades. The TDR and satellite tag will only remain attached for a day or two; we'll retrieve them when the bird returns to its nest and then deploy them on other penguins in turn. The tiny PIT tags are permanent, and each tag's microchip, with its individual ID, will be read every time the penguin crosses the weighbridge with its embedded scanner. By the end of the season we will have data showing the mass of food each individual weighbridge colony penguin has brought to its chicks, and how its own weight has fluctuated over the summer as an indication of how hard the birds are working to find food.

My left side ends up covered in bruises. One of the birds had persisted in turning its head and pinching my flesh with its beak right through three layers of clothing, up high in the sensitive junction of back, side, and armpit, as if it knew instinctively that this was the spot to generate maximum pain. Funnily enough, for such a large bird the Adélies don't usually try to inflict much damage with their beaks. Their hard-edged flippers are the nastiest weapons they possess, and this afternoon, to add insult to the injury of my bruised side, I receive the worst flipper bashing of the season.

I am on our daily search for banded penguins after deploying the tags and evidently get too close to a lone bird on the outskirts of one of the subcolonies. He (I'm sure it is a he—there has to be plenty of testosterone fuelling all that aggression) charges up to me as is usual with these unpaired young birds, but instead of braying loudly up into my face and perhaps giving a token chest-butt to my shin, he proceeds to grab the bottom of my parka with his beak, hanging on so fiercely that he is lifted onto his toes when I lean backward, and then vigorously pummels my legs with the edges of his flippers. The pummelling I've received before, but never with such dedication, and never with such excellent aim for the edge of my kneecap and the front of my shin. It hurts so much that I just stand there, gasping and paralyzed, eyes watering, for what seems like the better part of a minute, deafened by his furious braying. I try to shake him off a couple of times, standing on one leg and brandishing the other, before he desists and returns to his territory in an angry huff, head feathers still raised indignantly and eyes wide with rage at my audacity. When evening rolls around the entire lower half of my right leg is still throbbing.

A charging Adélie penguin is a formidable thing. It draws itself up to full height—a good 50 percent taller than when it is squatting benignly upright on its nest—and erects its head feathers into a threatening crest while throwing its head back and emitting a screaming bray that would sound loud coming from a donkey. At the same time, it widens its eyes, which, as these are boldly ringed with white, gives a convincing impression of madness, as if you're being charged by some escapee from the miniature lunatic asylum. Add to this the fact that they can wield their flat and bony flippers hard enough to cause the blood to stream from them when they're fighting with other penguins, and they're disproportionately scary for their size.

James Murray, the Nimrod Expedition's biologist, wrote while living at Cape Royds that the Adélie penguin "is very brave in the breeding-season . . . When walking among the nests one is assailed on all sides by powerful bills. Most of the birds sit still on the nests, but the more pugnacious ones run at you from a distance and often take you unawares. We wore for protection long felt boots reaching well above the knee. Some of the clever ones knew that they were wasting their efforts on the felt boots, and would come up behind, hop up and seize the skin above the boot, and hang on tight, beating with their wings. One of these little furies, hanging to your flesh and flapping his strong flippers so fast that you can hardly see them move, is no joke. A man once stumbled and fell into a colony of Adélies, and before he could recover himself and scramble out they were upon him, and he bore the marks of their fury for some time."[45] Like some Antarctic version of Hitchcock's *The Birds*.

Later I see poor old 1091 again. She's left the reference colony and her nest, and is propped awkwardly upright in subcolony 3A over by the entrance to the ocean, sleeping. She's on her way back to sea; hopefully her injured leg will be less of a liability for her there.

14

TWO DAYS BEFORE Christmas. NSF Santa was scheduled to arrive here by helicopter today, but the weather deteriorated in the late morning. The helos are grounded and we are hut-bound. I wonder if we are going to mark the holiday in any way, and broach the topic with David.

Me: "Do we do anything special for Christmas here? Take the day off or anything?"

David: "Why? Do you believe in the baby Jesus or something?"

Me: "No."

David: "Then why do you want to do something to mark it? Why does Christmas mean anything to you?"

Me: "Well, for me it's a time to spend with friends and family, to relax and eat a lot, to reflect on the year that's gone by. A time to celebrate the days getting longer."

David: "We don't celebrate Christmas at Cape Royds."

The snow is now blowing across the frozen landscape and Delibes's "Flower Duet," from the first act of the opera *Lakmé*, is playing quietly on my laptop as I enter yesterday's data. The voices of the singers form an ethereal counterpoint to the swooping cadences of the calling wind, somehow rendering it tame. Once again I notice how this sort of music calms us both, with David ceasing the agitated knee-jiggling that is his standard response to bad weather and me able to work at my laptop without jumping up every few minutes to compulsively tidy the contents of the hut's shelves.

By early evening the wind has dropped enough for me to go down to the colony to collect today's B-REF data. Bird 1096 has returned to an eggless nest. He kicked out the usurping pair of young penguins that had been squatting there, but 1091 is now back at sea. He has settled down to await her return.

There is evidence of a leopard seal kill—skuas in the middle of the colony fighting over the soggy, severed head of a freshly killed penguin. The birds clearly have just pulled it out of the sea, looking like something transported here from the Spanish Inquisition. I get back to the hut to find David wrapping up our daily 8 p.m. radio check-in with MacOps and switching to a call with Crozier, where I hear Grant talking about a pre-dinner drink.

This morning when I wake up, I realize that it's Christmas Eve.

I put on my headphones to walk down to the colony after breakfast and morning chores, turning on the music as I go out the door: some Cuban hip-hop by the group Orishas, shared with me by Viola back in November. A hot little tune is playing, the kind that makes you feel like there's a soundtrack to your life. I crest the ridge on the way out of our hut's little hollow, and stop in my tracks. Something about the music makes me see this place as if for the first time, and I am stunned by its splendour—Mount Erebus towering up to touch the sky on my left, the snowy ground falling away at my feet, in front of me the glittering whiteness of frozen McMurdo Sound stretching out to meet the Barne Glacier and seamlessly blending into the icy mass of the continent near the horizon. The steely ultramarine of the open sea lies to my right, and all of this under a sky as blue as the wing of a tropical butterfly.

The panoramic beauty slams into me so hard that the sensation is physical, and I spread my arms wide and shout wordlessly to the world, with nobody there to hear. I am tempted to say that this beauty is indescribable, but it is not. It is possible to describe it in pieces: the stark, jagged edge of the volcanic landscape against a pale sky; an unruffled ocean the colour of milk and robins' eggs in amongst the white purity of the pack ice that floats suspended there; the sunlit perfection of the Royal Society Range towering above McMurdo Sound—all of these things. But each piece the eye lights upon requires its own litany of words, its moment of contemplation, its own relationship with the viewer, some sort of sacrament in order to carry away a tiny piece of its meaning and beauty. Perhaps the whole world is like this but it is only here in the uncluttered spaces of Antarctica that we can appreciate that it is so, each moment of life a tiny meditation. It's not that the English language lacks the words to render Antarctica on paper. There are so many words that apply here: hard ones like quartz, granite, and glare; soft words like whispering and susurration; rounded phrases like golden light and drops of melting water. The words are all there. Perhaps it is just so outside the realm of normal experience that one needs to try new linguistic combinations to make any of it work, and to describe it well would take so long that you might as well just come back here.

Something lets go inside of me. I resume my walk to the colony realizing that I have lost whatever reasons I had found to be frustrated with camp life. None of it matters any longer. All that I want is to rejoice in the good fortune that has placed me in this here and now. If I never come to Cape Royds again, do I want to remember petty differences, damp socks, and predictable anxieties? Or instead, the transcendental beauty of Antarctica?

Rumour via the VHF's nightly chatter says that the US Coast Guard icebreaker *Polar Star* will arrive this evening to begin crashing its way into the fast ice, eventually clearing a channel all the way down to McMurdo so that the annual supply ships can get in next month with goods and fuel for the station. As midnight approaches, and with it, Christmas Day, the ship still isn't anywhere in evidence. I finally finish band-searching for the day and make my way up to the height of land. From there I can see south all the way down to the miniature airplanes sitting on the sea ice runway out past McMurdo, thirty-five kilometres away, and beyond into the white void that is the start of the continent itself. I sit on the ground next to the primitive navigational cairn placed there decades ago, and wrap myself in the crushing silence, wishing myself and the world a Merry Christmas as my watch ticks over to midnight.

Just before I'm driven back to the hut by the cold I notice a repetitive plosive sound, faint as a whisper yet clear in the stillness. Perhaps it is small waves slapping the underside of the ice tongue that is still held fast to the shore below me, I think, but the sea is dead calm, the wind a Beaufort zero. I realize with a start that the sound is loud but somewhere very far away in the absolute quiet: I am hearing whales breathing. I scan the ocean with my binoculars but they are hidden in the distance amidst the floes, not even the vapour of their breaths in evidence.

As I'm getting ready to turn in, another noise gradually imposes itself on my consciousness, sounding like snowmobiles coming from McMurdo. It is one thirty in the morning but I go outside to investigate anyway and there is the *Polar Star*, distantly steaming toward its first bite of the McMurdo Sound fast ice. Between ship and shore lolls the source of the distant breaths I heard earlier: a group of ten or so killer whales, making their leisurely way through an open patch of water and waiting to enter the southern reaches of McMurdo Sound via the new channel. David had mentioned this behaviour earlier; these whales have learned from previous years that the icebreaker means a fresh pathway for them to enter an area that until now has been under ice, an expansion of the seasonal area where they can search for toothfish. It is so still here that I could hear the ship from inside the hut even though it is still ten kilometres offshore.

Christmas Day starts out like any other day here, with me banding a couple more birds in B-REF, then catching eleven penguins in the weighbridge subcolony and holding them while David injects PIT tags. By early afternoon my gloves, parka, and field trousers are covered in penguin shit, and the back of my left hand is puffy and bruised from being flipper-slapped when I handled a particularly feisty female earlier this morning. Both of my knees are still severely bruised from their beating a couple of days ago, and are now even more sore from crawling over rocky ground in stealth mode to capture sometimes unwilling parents on their nests. My hands sport several new scratches and peck marks. We apply a couple more TDRs, which adds to the number of pecks.

Just as we are finishing up the weighbridge subcolony work, I look up to see four McMurdo-type coats marching down the hill toward us. These turn out to be NSF Santa and his elves, stopping by with the delayed Christmas delivery.

"Merry Christmas!" shouts one of them when they get close enough, unaware of the Cape Royds holiday embargo. "Hello!"

Given the earlier weather-induced grounding of helos they are doing the Christmas run by snowmobile. They are a disparate group, consisting of a NASA satellite technician (Erik 1); a microbiologist studying soil yeasts out in the back of beyond in the Dry Valleys (Rusty); the McMurdo fire inspector (Erik 2); and Santa himself (James, who wears the Carhartt gear of a McMurdo outdoors worker, along with a natural grey Santa beard and a safety-orange head of hair, dyed for the occasion).

"We've brought you some parcels!" says James after we've all shaken hands. "They're up at the Rac-Tent. Can we come and see the penguins?" David and I oblige, escorting them to the edge of the ASPA with instructions about not crossing its boundary line, and leave them there to exclaim and take photographs while we go back to complete our work, collecting a few diet samples and searching for bands as we wrap up for the day.

By the time we've finished in the colony our visitors have temporarily had their fill of looking at the penguins, and I invite them back to the hut for a hot drink—snowmobiling long distances is a very cold business—where they crowd around the heater to get warm. I brew hot chocolate and James pulls a bottle of Armagnac from inside his parka, and I offer around the bottle of Jägermeister. I notice that although this is mocked ("Jägermeister! Seriously?"), everyone is happy to consume a shot of it. It is all very festive and jolly and, friendships forming quickly as they do here, ends up being as Christmassy a gathering as any I would have had at home. I now have a standing invitation to visit the NASA lab at Crary 205, and new friends to share a drink with at the bar when I'm next in town (tomorrow if the weather holds).

After they leave David and I unpack the three parcels they've brought us. Christmas Day delivery in Antarctica: better postal service than at home. One is a box from the McMurdo galley full of chocolate, baked goods, and other treats, including tinned eggnog, Pringles potato chips (a field camp favourite, their tin meaning that they don't get crushed in transit), and four very mashed and overripe avocados that are unfortunately fit only for the trash can. There's a mail-delivery parcel each for David and me—mine from my stepmother and consisting of more chocolates and baked goods, with a card and a letter tucked in. David opens his package slowly, with focused intent.

"More brownies?" I ask him.

"No, cookies," he says, offering me one. "Not mouldy this time."

For dinner I drag out the Coleman stovetop oven from the corner of the hut and slowly roast a couple of Cornish game hens at three hundred degrees—the hottest temperature the oven is able to maintain in our cold and draughty hut—cook the fresh potatoes I've been saving, and make up a delicious gravy. David seems indifferent about his game hen, and admittedly their months in a freezer, combined with weeks of slow defrosting in the snowbank and ultra-slow roasting, haven't done them any culinary favours, but we both savour the potatoes and gravy and an extra glass of red wine. It has been a Christmas after all.

15

ON BOXING DAY we head into McMurdo for another overnight visit and supply run. Our helicopter flight has us out of Royds shortly after eleven in the morning—a good time to go to town in terms of picking up supplies and generally getting things done—and when we land, Gifford, our helo-tech, tells me our return flight has been booked late and doesn't leave until the end of day tomorrow. This extra time (we generally have a twenty-four-hour turnaround) is excellent news as it will make the difference between a relaxing stay in town and the usual frantic stampede.

Mactown is just returning to life after its two-day Christmas holiday over the twenty-fourth and twenty-fifth, and the residents are bleary-eyed and slow-moving. It seems I've finally sorted out my situation with Housing—when I check in for a key they tell me I now have my own permanent room and bunk allocation, something I've been lobbying for since November. After having to hunt down a new room and key every time I arrive back in town this feels like the ultimate in stability. I'm in 220 with roommates Sarika and Marian, two solid-looking thirty-or forty-somethings from middle America. They're intrigued to have a roommate who's working on penguins, though that may change as the stench of my clothing begins to permeate the furniture. Regardless, I'm thrilled to know there's a place in town for me with a made-up bed and the opportunity to make in-town friends. It's like moving into a new apartment after being on the road for a while.

McMurdo is certainly looking a lot different than it did during the days of "warm" weather after the hurricane at the end of November. The building-sized mountains of ploughed snow and the lakes of meltwater have been replaced with empty spaces and constantly flowing drainage ditches that cut across roads, along the sides of buildings, and under makeshift plank bridges. Even the gulag-style accommodation buildings are managing to look almost cheery under these sunny skies.

Being in town is taking on a new feeling as I realize that I have gradually amassed something approaching a small social network here. Brien at *The Antarctic Sun* emails me saying he's heard I'm in town, and might I want to grab a beer later; he still wants to do that story on Cape Royds. On my way back to 155 from Crary I run into Erik Richards, the tall, dark-haired NASA engineer from yesterday's festive visit to Royds, and he offers to buy me a glass of wine after dinner. I accept and then call Paul Rogers over at Scott Base on the inter-station phone to request a tour and a couple of metric-sized buckles to replace the ones on my pack (field supplies being in imperial sizes at McMurdo), all of which have snapped from cold stress and UV exposure.

I end up eating dinner with Brien and some of his town friends. I ask him how he knew I was around, and he says they put out an All Call over the PA, a comment implying that my arrival was newsworthy enough to have earned a station-wide broadcast.

"Shut up!" I say, punching him on the arm as he grins.

Over dinner Brien tells me a bit about the history of *The Antarctic Sun*. It's the descendant of a volunteer publication that was sporadically put out by US Navy radiomen starting in 1960, back in the days of Operation Deep Freeze when the military ran all of McMurdo. It was then called *The McMurdo Sometimez*, later *The McMurdo Sometimes*, then *The Antarctica Sun Times*, now *The Antarctic Sun*. In its early days it was composed on teletype and printed by the hundreds on a spirit duplicator, technologies that virtually nobody alive can remember. In Antarctica, expeditions and stations have a long history of producing their own periodicals, some of which were printed only once, while others were produced over a year or more. Among them were *The South Polar Times* (1902–03) of Scott's British National Antarctic Expedition, edited by Ernest Shackleton and illustrated by Bill Wilson; *The Adélie Blizzard*, of Mawson's 1911–14 Australasian Antarctic Expedition; and *The Hallett Daily Hangover* (1965) from Hallett Station in the Australian sector of Antarctica.

While I scrape clean my dinner plate at the dish pit, I chat to the woman working there. It's Sandwich, whom I first met in the lineup for Ivan the Terra Bus on my first day here.

"How's your season going?" I ask her.

"It's going great," she says. "There were a couple of penguins on the ice in front of town the other day and I went out to see them along with the crowds."

From talking with others on station I know that a penguin sighting is a seasonal highlight and I'm reminded again how fortunate I am to be working at Cape Royds. As I'm sliding my dirty cutlery into the soaking tray Erik walks by, so we head straight over to the wine bar. Over drinks at a corner table he tells me a bit about his life. It turns out he'll be spending his fourth winter here this season.

I look at him incredulously, but for him it's just a job, with the winter of total darkness not too different from what he'd experience at his hometown in Alaska. I learn that the year-round NASA team here recovers data from polar-orbiting science and weather satellites; one of their less frequent tasks is to provide satellite support for launches shot straight out to sea from California's Vandenberg Air Force Base,* which don't cross land until they reach Antarctica. I am interested to find out that the radome visible on Arrival Heights above McMurdo contains the local NASA space-to-ground station, MG1, but it doesn't take long for the space-related conversation to reach the limits of my interest and understanding. We nonetheless hang out and chat about life on and off station until 10 p.m., at which time Erik, who is on an office-based work schedule, needs to head off to bed.

After saying goodnight I head over to Scott Base, a thirty-minute walk along the three-kilometre dirt road that joins the two stations. I call the Firehouse before setting out on my trek to find out whether I need to check out of town and then back in again on my return, but am reminded that both the road itself and Scott Base are within bounds.

It's a stunning walk, despite beginning in the bowels of McMurdo Station's industrial storage area at the back end of town. The only vehicle that passes me at this hour is a passenger van on its way back from the snow runway at Williams Field, on the Ross Ice Shelf, where much of the air traffic from the sea ice runway is currently being relocated in preparation for the icebreaker's arrival (and related seasonal loss of that runway). Williams Field, known as Willy Field to the locals, is named for Richard T. Williams, a US Navy Seabee equipment operator who drowned when his tractor went through the ice during the first Operation Deep Freeze back in January of 1956. Williams died at the start of a new era in Antarctic exploration; the role of the first Deep Freeze was to build a permanent research station at McMurdo in advance of the 1957–58 IGY.

Willy Field is for ski-equipped aircraft only—LC-130s and Twin

* Now Vandenberg Space Force Base.

Otters—and so once the sea ice runway closes, wheeled aircraft will relocate to Pegasus, the blue ice runway still farther inland.* I've heard we'll depart from there when it's time to leave, but I don't want to think about leaving right now. Past the outskirts of McMurdo, the outlook at the end of the road unfolds to reveal the best vista in McMurdo Sound, with sweeping views of Mount Erebus on one side and Mount Discovery and the jagged faces of the Transantarctic Mountains on the other, all funnelling down to Herbie Alley, dead ahead at the pinch point between Black and White Islands. "Herbie" is local slang for the dangerously powerful storms that funnel through this gap from the south, from the US Navy term for combined hurricane-blizzard conditions, Hurr B. Beyond the two islands the blankness of the continent itself recedes away past the edge of the sea ice and into the vanishing horizon, a misty nothingness in the place where the earth meets the sky: nothing here but sculpted whiteness, splashed with black volcanic striations for visual relief.

At the top of the track down to the New Zealand station sits a large sign decorated with the silhouettes of a couple of keas—an endemic New Zealand parrot—that reads "Welcome to Scott Base. Capital of the Ross Dependency. Population 85," with the population count changeable. This sign apparently strikes a negative chord with some American officials, territorial claims being officially in abeyance in the context of the Antarctic Treaty. But given that McMurdo's sprawling presence is at its essence a claim of some prominence, I have to cheer on the Kiwis for their cheekiness.

I veer off just before the offending sign and cut across the slope and down a footpath to the station. It's a small huddle of buildings painted an ugly 1970s avocado green that looks grim on a miserable

---

* Pegasus was closed at the end of 2016 and replaced by Phoenix.

day but rather cheery in the sun. The buildings' modesty seems much more sensible than the excess of their US counterparts back down the road, and against its impressive backdrop, the Kiwi station appears a far friendlier place. When you get to Scott Base, you think, "Now *this* is Antarctica!" while on arrival at McMurdo you are tempted to plagiarize Scott himself and think, "Great God! this is an awful place . . ."[46]

I come across Paul in the station lounge, a well-appointed and spacious area with a stainless steel galley and self-serve hot drinks area at one end, and a cozy reading nook at the other. The nook is lined with floor-to-ceiling bookshelves and overlooks a panoramic view of the ice shelf and the mountains. Directly below the windows the Ross Ice Shelf crashes into Ross Island at about one-tenth of a kilometre per hour, or a couple of metres per day, rearing up into a fantastic welter of massive crinkled and broken shapes as it does so. Down by the sea-ice cracks formed by all this slow-motion violence lie the black shapes of Weddell seals, hauled out to rest and give birth on the ice, as usual taking advantage of the weak spots in the frozen ocean caused by its upheaval.

The Kiwis are just at the end of their own two-day Christmas break, which fell on the twenty-fifth and twenty-sixth. Paul shows me the hot drinks area (a real espresso maker and decent tea), where I make a hot chocolate, and then he tours me around the base. The place is so snugly laid out that it reminds me of the inside of a ship. The buildings are well sealed (unlike draughty McMurdo) and the air extremely dry as a result. So much so that everyone drags a hand along the wall as they walk, running fingers past the metal studs to prevent a massively painful electrostatic shock the next time they touch something solid. Static electricity is problematic at McMurdo, but it is far worse here, where people can kill an electronic device if they forget to ground themselves before touching it. The station is so tiny that a tour doesn't take long, so we play Scrabble and eat mincemeat tarts until the wee hours, Paul from time to time amusing himself by grounding his personal buildup of static electricity on my arm.

Late the following afternoon David and I fly back out to Royds in one of the Bell 212 helicopters.

"How was your time in town?" I ask him over the headset as we clatter along.

"Um, good," he says, without elaborating. Then a minute later, "I bought another bottle of Scotch."

A couple of kilometres away from the ocean's edge, we can see the *Polar Star* embedded in the sea ice and making slow progress toward Mactown. This is how far the ship has come since I saw it start breaking into the ice edge at Cape Royds early on Christmas Day. Seeing the vessel there gives me a new sense of McMurdo Sound's proportions—against the expanse of the vast plain of sea ice and the backdrop of the improbably large mountains, this big ship is a mere speck below us, and the sound suddenly looks immense. It pains me to see the smooth white canvas of the frozen ocean rent with the dark line that the icebreaker trails behind it. I feel as if Antarctica's purity is being besmirched, its wholeness assailed and violated. On a more prosaic level, I hope it won't speed up the breaking out of the sea ice that currently holds the road to Royds from Mactown and Scott Base, our link with weekend visitors and the rest of the world.

I think of the emails from Grahame Sydney I downloaded today. He too is infatuated with this place, and has been describing it in several articles written for New Zealand newspapers. He modestly says that they're not much—but I think that in these and subsequent writings he has captured it exactly:

> You look at your watch and it says four o'clock and you have no idea if it's four o'clock in the morning or four o'clock in the afternoon, except if the sun's over White Island it's night-time,[47]

and

> Nature makes it abundantly plain that this is no place for humankind, and that our presence on the sterile frozen continent is a temporary pass, as unwelcome and inappropriate as on the moon.[48]

Back at Cape Royds, it is a breathless summer evening. At ten o'clock at night I'm sitting in a chair out on our little deck, overlooking one of the most gorgeous vistas of the season and trying to decide whether I should crawl into my sleeping bag or take advantage of the fabulous light and go down to the colony with my camera. When the nights are like this, bed seems superfluous, and with all of the daylight the lack of sleep never seems to catch you up—you can just keep going, wired on adrenaline and serotonin.

The air is still, but cold. I'm comfortable, not overheating, in my fleece pants and long johns, two polypro undershirts, a mid-weight shirt, a wind jacket, a down vest, and a hat. I sit here, not moving, and enumerate the sounds that I can hear piercing the stillness, a sort of meditation. The noise of the penguin colony drifts faintly over the ridge. Behind me, in the hut, our battery bank hums as it's recharged by the solar panels. David makes the occasional noise as he shuffles papers or brushes his teeth. Other than that, a skua cry pierces the air every few minutes, and I can hear my body make tiny ticking sounds as it digests its dinner. And that is it—birds, batteries, and bodies form the sum total of everything that I can hear tonight, anywhere. It's as if Antarctica is holding its breath.

Below me, the ocean is the milky bluish-white of a cataract, its waters as smooth as the surface of an eye. Sleep seems a sacrilege in the face of the sublime. A broad band of sea ice sits offshore, the evening sun tinting it the subtle pink of a rosefinch's breast, a faultless counterpoint to the shimmering blue wash suffusing the sea, the sky, and the mountains of the Royal Society Range that soar beyond the water. Colour here is understated in its beauty, in a delicate balance with the harsh black and white of the glacier-clad volcanic landscape. It's hard to reconcile this place with the one that nurtured such a savage set of weather conditions at the end of November.

16

THE WEATHER HAS been erratic, with the gorgeous but cold evening of our holiday trip to Mactown followed by temperatures that have again been above zero, too warm for the penguins. Yesterday the temperature reached 2°C at Cape Royds, and it was probably higher in the sheltered corners of the colony. Penguins crouched above their chicks, beaks open and panting, cooling off both themselves and their offspring. Today the skies are grey and sullen. The air is still calm here, but we hear from Crozier on the radio that there are big winds up on the slopes of Mount Terror (like Mount Erebus, named in 1841 by James Clark Ross after the two ships in his expedition, which were subsequently taken to the Arctic by Sir John Franklin and lost on his disastrous search for the Northwest Passage) and so we may be in for a blow. It would be nice if the temperature dropped. Sub-zero cold is not a problem for growing penguin chicks, with their thick coats of woolly grey down and hefty layers of fat. It's this heat they have trouble coping with. And once again our frozen food is going soft in the cooler in the snowbank. It is now too warm in the hut to keep perishable foods indoors. Contrast this with the beginning of the season, when any corner not immediately above the propane heater was cold enough to freeze things.

As David and I walk down to the colony together this afternoon, I realize we are now past the midpoint of our study season. We talk about what the penguins have been eating—or rather I make observations and he responds with his typically economical use of words, but by now I'm used to it and can follow the thread of the conversation. The current quick turnaround times of birds exchanging nest duties with their mates, and the almost fluorescent colour of their excrement, means that the penguins are feeding close to the colony and gathering crystal krill—*Euphausia crystallorophias,* small, shrimp-like crustaceans—from the waters beneath the nearby pack ice. The krill cluster there in great swarms, grazing on the algae blooms beneath the frozen waves. Our diet data protocol has had us observing chick feedings, and these show that parents are finding plenty of the tiny red invertebrates for their hungry offspring. Throughout the colony, scarlet poop and crimson breast and belly feathers are the norm, as the penguins' krill-based guano gets everywhere. We're also recording the stomach contents of dead chicks for a more detailed assessment of what the young birds have been eating.

Today I surprised a pair of skuas eating a freshly killed Adélie chick (from our B-REF colony, so another data point on chick survival). They drag it out of my path and continue their meal, but the first thing skuas go for is the stomach contents, and now these spill out and trail in the birds' wake—sure enough, these are mostly krill, but a few fleshy, semi-digested pieces of Antarctic silverfish are also present, gleaming palely amongst the mash of persimmon-coloured euphausiids.

While we are retrieving a TDR from a penguin I tell David about the PhD fellowship application I had been working on before heading south on this trip.

"What's your research question?" he asks.

"I'm interested in the sorts of questions you're reading about in *In a Perfect Ocean*," I tell him. "What the world's oceans looked like before we started hoovering up everything edible." Over the years I have worked there, Antarctica has shown me some facsimile of what those oceans could have looked like.

"Huh," says David. "Good choice." And then he talks about the historical demise of seals, whales, finfish, and penguins at the hands of the commercial outfits that operated around much of the continent (including in the subantarctic region) from the late eighteenth century onward. Nonetheless, much of Antarctica is still—or again—home to populations of marine birds and mammals in the sort of immense numbers no longer seen across most of the rest of the planet. The fact that this could be changing, given growing fishing efforts for toothfish and krill in Antarctic waters, is behind the campaign by Antarctic scientists and many others to protect the Ross Sea.

The non-breeding Adélies are presently swarming into the colony in ever-increasing numbers, and the subcolonies are burgeoning, spilling over their previously defined edges and swelling to create completely new ones. It's a tide of penguins, filling the nooks and crannies of Cape Royds like a river in full flood. I saw nearly a hundred banded birds today, my seasonal record to date. Each day brings more penguins than the day before. The original breeding birds, those that started off the season in November or even October, quietly brood their chicks or put the finishing touches on incubating their eggs, but all around them is noisy penguin activity as these midsummer arrivals find mates, defend territories, build nests, and steal nest-building stones from their neighbours. None of these birds will raise a chick or even lay an egg: They're here far too late, their hormones out of sync with the egg-laying portion of the breeding season and the externalities of krill swarming, ice break-out, and eventual refreeze. But it's crucial to their annual cycle that they be here anyway, establishing a territory, perfecting the rituals of penguin courtship, renewing a bond with a late-appearing mate from a previous year, or, for the younger birds, just being in the colony and increasing their comfort with the place so that they might enjoy a successful breeding season in a future year.

But this spillover of newcomers is causing trouble for the skuas. The reference colony is expanding into the flats where two skua pairs have been incubating their eggs in little scrapes in the gravel. A couple of days ago I watched three penguins—obviously thinking about claiming this area as new territory—repeatedly charge one skua and drive it off its nest. The penguins eventually wandered off, but today the shell of the skuas' single egg (a lovely rich khaki-green background with deep lilac and chocolate splotches) is lying broken in two pieces nearby, the near-to-hatching contents gone, presumably eaten by yet another skua after the parents had been driven too far away to defend it. I feel a pang of sadness for the pair—a futile summer of effort come to naught. I admire these fierce birds, eking out an existence in this harsh environment. Most years their breeding appears to fail—conditions are hard—but the oldest banded skua in the Antarctic is about thirty-five years old, and demographic analysis predicts that they live much longer, so they have many years in which to reproduce successfully and replace themselves. These remarkable birds are the only wildlife ever to show up at the South Pole, occasionally stopping in for a quick visit at the base there as they fly over the continent.

Despite this small setback for the skua population, though, the adjacent nest is persevering. Yesterday I heard a chick peeping from under its fiercely protective parent (this is the nest where I photographed a bird buried in snow, but still incubating, right after the hurricane), and today I saw it, very small and fuzzy, the first chick of its kind of the season, sitting near a rock as its parents battled yet another squad of juvenile delinquent penguins. In this instance, I'm rooting for the skua chick. These parents were certainly more aggressive than any I've yet seen, whether motivated by their chick's hatching or just being better parents, and they were dive-bombing the penguins and actually driving them back from their chick. This is no small feat for a skua; they are heavily outweighed by an adult Adélie, which is why all their egg- and chick-theft is that of the grab-and-snatch variety. The majority of skua depredations on eggs and chicks are opportunistic, taking place when nesting penguins are fighting and distracted or have begun paying less attention to the second egg after the first has hatched.

I have more flipper-generated injuries today. I think one of the bones in the fingers of my right hand is bruised. This afternoon, I had to pluck a female off her nest for PIT-tag implantation. Her mate was there too, and as he had just gone through the same rigamarole a couple of days ago he was not happy to see me skulking toward his nest again. He charged at me in full rage mode, beak agape and screaming, flippers beating in a blur. He went for my hands—extended to grab his mate off the nest—and I briefly felt nauseous with pain as the solid bone of the flipper's leading edge cracked across my fingers like a slamming door or the edge of a thick wooden ruler. Then I grabbed my attacker and shoved him behind me, from where he beat a tattoo on my kidneys before running forward to brood the chicks that I'd briefly exposed to the light of day.

Picking up unaccompanied penguins from the nest is much easier—one hand on the back of the neck, the other around the tail, then lift up smoothly to avoid the bird inadvertently kicking chicks or eggs in the struggle. Drop a fleecy hat over the chicks, who snuggle into its soft folds, and carefully hold the parent while it endures whatever indignities we have in store for it. The adults usually manage to get in a retaliatory squirt of fishy-smelling guano at some point in this process, adding to the general filth on my outerwear. The field trousers are the worst as the knees are also encrusted with everything I've crawled through—including regurgitated food and the occasional dead chick from previous seasons—on my way to what is now dozens of nests. My gear is definitely beginning to smell a lot like penguin.

17

WE'RE UP EARLY. By 7:45 a.m. we are ready and waiting for the Coast Guard helicopter that's going to take us out to the icebreaker *Polar Sea,* loser in the race to be the first of the two US Coast Guard vessels to break ice here this season. The winner, *Polar Star,* was the ship that bashed its way into McMurdo Sound in the early hours of Christmas Day, and the same one we flew over on our way back from town the other day. Now the *Polar Sea* is hove to and waiting for us at Beaufort Island, out in the middle of the Ross Sea, way past the ice shelf edge. I am drinking coffee and trying to wake up, groggy after the usual 3 a.m. bedtime. The scanner is blipping in the corner, listening for the complement of radio transmitters we currently have deployed on the backs of several penguins. Temperature is right around zero and the sun is out on a crisp, clear, cold morning that is somehow, bizarrely, reminiscent of late fall at home. The wind is from the north, which should mean decent weather for our day at the Beaufort penguin colony.

I go outside and climb up onto the ridge behind the hut to listen for the helicopter, which is late. In the still Antarctic air, you hear things long before they come into sight. At first the noise will be so faint that it might be the beating of your heart but then it will materialize into something more tangible, the beating of a helicopter's blades or a surfacing whale perhaps, and then, many minutes after that, the distant source of sound will be visible somewhere against the frozen white spaces.

The sea ice sweeps in a breathtaking expanse from Cape Royds toward the distant mountains and the start of the Ross Ice Shelf. Today the frozen sea looks as satiny as shaved sealskin under the morning sun, and the snowfields up on Mount Erebus gleam with an intense purity. True to form, the Coast Guard helicopter is audible long before it comes into view, and when it does it's a dark fleck like a dust mote against the silver flanks of Erebus.

At 8:30 a.m. the helicopter touches down in the melting snowfield below our hut. Unlike the rather deluxe machines flying out of McMurdo Station, sleek A-Stars and huge Bell 212s, this helicopter, a Dauphin, is all about work and is clearly made for serious operations such as rescues at sea. To prove this, the tail rotor is not gaily whirring around out in the open but instead is enclosed within a businesslike casing set into the tail fuselage, impact-proof.

A crew member jumps out of the back and trudges methodically over to us in his big insulated boots and padded clothing, bearing our flight helmets and lifejackets. We'll be flying over the open ocean, where for safety reasons McMurdo helicopters are not allowed to go.

"Make sure you follow right behind me," he shouts in our ears over the chopping of the blades. These "hot" landings—done without shutting down the engine—are the norm down here, where pilots are anxious to get in, pick up people and cargo, and be out and on their way again before the weather changes or the wind picks up, as it is wont to do in the blink of an eye.

We follow the crew member back through the snow. He points inside toward what appears to be the rear cargo area and yells "Sit there!"

at me before going to stow our telemetry gear in the tail compartment. "There" is a barely discernible little jump seat, looking like a hard cushion tossed into the corner of the helicopter's aft area but with seatbelt and shoulder harness sprouting around it from floor and bulkhead. I wedge myself into this minimal space and struggle through fastening all the buckles, hampered by my bulky parka and the vice-like grip that the flight helmet has on my head. Too late, I discover that the bulkhead's electrical connection for the headset is out of my reach once I'm pinioned in the corner, so I have to undo half the buckles and then start again.

David's seat is even more minimal—the floor of the cargo area itself, with a webbing strap and clip as his seatbelt. Our remaining gear—cameras, daypacks, the bags of ever-necessary ECW clothing—is slung in after us and wedged around our feet. Our helo-tech climbs in through the side doorway, and we're airborne as soon as he gives the pilot the all-clear signal over his headset. His seat slides on tracks across the width of the helicopter like that of an airplane gunner, which allows him to see everything that's going on during the flight; he can even hang bodily out the side door while still strapped into place (and does so, to view our clearance as we lift off). This feature is apparently most needed when they are hoisting rescues from the sea or the decks of sinking ships.

Happily, there's a big window next to where I sit pinned motionless in the corner; I can watch the coast of Ross Island flash by beneath us without needing to move my immobilized head. Our helicopter has one more stop before arriving at the *Polar Sea,* on the northernmost tip of the island at Cape Bird to pick up Kerry (the researcher who replaced Katie when she left for Christmas) and Willie, our current collaborators from the Kiwi research hut. There beneath us lies Wohlschlag Bay, just north of Cape Royds, where the sea is as flat and still as the Ancient Mariner's painted ocean. Entire glacier-clad mountains are perfectly replicated in the surface of the water and these vast silvery reflections creep shyly up to meet their solid cousins at the interstices between land and sea. The reflections are perhaps even more serenely beautiful than their real-world counterparts, enlivened by the geometric white shapes of broken sea ice drifting about the bay like surreal clouds floating in a marine-blue sky.

The Adélie colony at Cape Bird appears below and the crew member barks out a pre-landing checklist at the pilot before shooting his chair sideways to roll back the side door and hang out the side of the machine, firing off landing site conditions over his headset while the ground rushes up to meet us. We drop below the top of the cape, which towers up just behind the narrow landing beach, and my view is cut off as suddenly as if someone has pulled a curtain over the window. Then we're down on the beach and several penguins are scurrying away from us at full speed; we're well away from the colony here, but these hapless individuals had been taking a rest on the makeshift helipad.

Kerry and Willie run in a crouch to the helo door, slinging on their helmets and life vests and jumping straight on board while the helicopter rotors turn at full speed. Their gear joins ours on top of our feet and we're off again, out toward Beaufort Island, seventeen nautical miles away. It looms large in the distance, an ice-capped volcanic crag rearing straight out of the Ross Sea. On our way out we see the massive iceberg B-15A in the distance, where it has been grounded for the past couple of years. All season long I have been hearing comparisons with its size—three-quarters the size of Crete, the size of the US state of Delaware, bigger than Prince Edward Island . . . These all make it sound very large, but it has been hard to envision what this might mean in real life. When I finally see the iceberg, it is awe-inspiring. It fills our field of view to the northeast; it is hard to tell where it ends and the horizon begins against the blinding white of the sky.

Everything about this flight—radio communications, pre-landing checks, passenger loading—is precise and efficient, executed with minimalist military precision. The Helo Ops crew at McMurdo runs things as professionally as if they were operating in any aerodrome back home, but this Coast Guard operation makes them look like Boy Scouts. When we finally land on the aft deck of the *Polar Sea,* after much circling and reporting of wind speed, wind direction, ship's heading, angle of list, and similar crucial pieces of arcana, a choreographed team of four purple-suited crew run out on each side of the helicopter, lines at the ready, and lash the pontoons to the deck before retreating as one. They remind me of schooling fish or a herd of gazelles, so intuitively coordinated are their movements. This time the helicopter shuts down, and we're released from the shackles of our helmets and harnesses and set free onto the broad expanse of the ship's flight deck.

Our Cape Crozier colleagues are supposed to be meeting us on board, but there's now an estimated hour and a half delay because the helicopter that went out to pick them up was unable to sight their hut and its landing pad amongst the sea of half a million penguins nesting at the Crozier colony, and so it has flown off to do something else. We get taken on a ship tour and fed a cup of coffee and a fresh muffin while we're waiting for the morning to unfold. We all comment on the presence of a fruit fly drifting about the mess—for the past couple of months none of us have encountered any sort of insect.

Eventually the helicopter with Grant, Viola, and Rachael arrives. It has been six weeks since we've seen them and they've not had a shower or used a washing machine in that time. At least we've been heading into McMurdo Station every ten or fourteen days. Kerry and Willie haven't bathed in three or four weeks either, and even David and I look weather-worn and scruffy, despite our recent McMurdo trip. Next to the neatly clad women and close-shaven men of the Coast Guard crew, we're a ragtag bunch with our dirty hair and sunburned faces, our coats and trousers stained with a colourful accumulation of penguin shit. The crew, out on deck for a smoke break, eye us covertly and presumably give thanks for their daily showers.

After the usual sort of milling about that presages these sorts of operations, we step through the ship's rail onto the Jacob's ladder and climb down into an enclosed aluminum boat that is waiting to take us and our gear ashore to Beaufort Island, only a couple of minutes away. Kerry can barely bend her knee after blowing it out in a recent fall at Cape Bird, so after some discussion the bosun gives her a safety harness and uses one of the lifeboat derricks to lower her ignominiously over the side to the boat below.

Beaufort is surrounded by a tall fortress of sea ice stuck fast to the shore, a remnant of the winter's thickly frozen ocean. The landing craft's driver somehow finds a low entry point in the barrier and runs us into it, grounding the hull on a frozen ledge. On either side of our landing spot, sculpted fast ice towers well over our heads, higher than the boat's cabin, and we disembark over the bow to follow a group of Adélie penguins through a small crack that opens ahead of us. This leads to a broad, flat ice bank, which leads in turn to a narrow, twisting corridor through the frozen wall. It's a surreal, fairy-like entryway, with massive icicles suspended from overhanging ice walls and a clear, shallow pool of aquamarine meltwater lining its frozen floor, like a lesser-used entrance to the Ice Queen's palace.

Instead, though, it's an entrance to the wild and raucous world of the Beaufort Island Adélie colony, thirty-five thousand pairs strong. The birds are serried before us in seemingly endless ranks along a series of raised beaches that sit like a set of curved blades around the southern point of the island. Imposing volcanic cliffs rear above the flats, overhanging at impossible angles and carved by wind and ice and gravity into fantastic silhouettes against the sky. Colours here are as rich as some expensive tapestry—ochre, rust, and chocolate volcanic rock against the cobalt blue of the summer sky, and mats of the plant-like terrestrial alga *Prasiola crispa,* glowing vivid chartreuse against the upper slopes of the colony, thriving where they are fertilized by wind-blown penguin guano. In the distance the ubiquitous glaciers of Ross Island form a silver backdrop to the day.

For two hours we walk about the flats searching for banded penguins, and then weigh chicks selected at random from thirty nests throughout the colony. Some are small and a velvety dove grey, newly hatched from their eggs. Others are big and floppy and fat-bellied, like big dark downy pears. All of them regard us fearlessly with slate-coloured eyes as we measure their wings and put them into canvas bags to be suspended from a balance and weighed before we return them to the irritable parents at their nests. In contrast to the volcanic stones at Cape Royds, nests here are built with rounded beach pebbles, attesting to the geological history of this place and the fact that the sea level has changed with the coming and going of the ice ages (hence the raised beaches). At the top of the uppermost beach is an original hand-lettered sign documenting a more recent history, the landing of a New Zealand party in 1959, including all the names of the party. Like us, they came ashore in a small boat launched from their larger ship, but to have come here through the icy waters on a vessel from one of the rustic Ross Island camps must have been an uncomfortable trip indeed. This place is wild and remote and fantastic, but all too soon we must leave and head back to the landing craft that is waiting to transport us back to the ship.

Back on board, we make our way to the crew mess, where we sit and warm up and gradually become aware of the gamey penguin odour emanating from our clothing. We seem to have been assigned a multitude of crew members to take care of our various needs—from lowly ordinary seamen to the executive officer, or XO, one of the most senior people on board. One of the sailors locates us while we're drinking juice and swapping field camp stories in the mess. She tells us that the weather at McMurdo has been deteriorating all afternoon and everything there has ground to a standstill. Since the ship's helicopters took a load of crew to town, they too are grounded there, and our minder informs us that we'll be spending the night on board.

So much for this morning's northerly wind presaging good weather. We greet the news with various degrees of excitement or dismay, depending on our individual reactions to the chance of a shower vs. missing a day or more of our work. Other crew periodically appear with things like towels and toiletries and a request for our vital statistics. One set of toiletries arrives in a compact travel kit, complete with miniature containers of toothpaste, hand lotion, hair conditioner, and a complimentary sticker reading "God Bless America" underneath a US flag. The non-Americans among us snicker at this unwholesome mélange of religion and nationalism, while our American colleagues roll their eyes unpatriotically.

We're led down to the cabins where we'll spend the night, lower deck aft, with lots of time before dinner to enjoy long, hot showers. I'm sharing a cabin with Rachael. While we're scrubbing up, two new minders appear to let us know they will be escorting us to dinner and doing our laundry for us. We protest, uncomfortable with the idea of valet service, but they politely insist, and after they leave we voice our suspicion that the removal of penguin odour from our beings has been ordered from the highest officer level, given the miasma that has followed us as we've warmed ourselves on board.

We pass the evening eating and then hanging out on the bridge. David talks with Viola not far from where I stand to watch the ship push through the sea ice. It's hypnotic to stare at the ever-advancing dark crack spreading ahead of the bow, languorously gushing water as it opens. I recognize David's by-now familiar chattiness with fresh faces, realizing that I must do the same thing given how little the two of us talk in camp, and how much I talk when strangers are around.

"How's your wife doing?" I hear Viola ask him.

I stare at Grant, who is standing beside me.

"His wife?" I hiss incredulously. "His *wife*?! I had no idea that David is married. We've been in camp together for six weeks and he hasn't mentioned her once."

Grant grins cheekily. "Yeah, well, that's David for you," he says. "Not exactly a talker."

Dinner on board is served at approximately the time most of us are used to eating lunch. By 10 p.m. Rachael and I are starving, and we hang about the galley chatting to the crew while waiting for midrats to start at 11 p.m. It's of course far too early for either of us to fall asleep afterward; Crozier too is on the backsliding field schedule brought on by twenty-four hours of daylight, and Rachael confesses that she never falls asleep before two in the morning either.

After midrats we pass the time in our cabin reading the lengthy list of rules and regulations on the back of the door. Among other things, it proscribes the number of pairs of shoes allowed to be stored under each "rack," or bunk, and the number of garments and laundry bags allowed to hang external to the lockers; it states how to make the bed and where to stow televisions and guitars or keyboards; forbids personal visits by males to female cabins, and vice versa; and reminds crew members that no more than one stuffed animal is allowed per bunk. The stiff penalties imposed for infractions of these rules are also listed. It all seems a lot more uptight than the Canadian and European vessels that I've worked on. We were told earlier that it's a dry ship, meaning no alcohol, anywhere. Harsh conditions I've never experienced at sea. On the other hand, many of the crew are not yet of legal drinking age in their home states so perhaps this keeps things simple. And sometimes a dry ship wouldn't be such a bad thing, I muse, thinking of the stories my father told me while working as chief engineer on ships in the Canadian Arctic, where more than once he had to order people off watch for showing up drunk.

Shortly after we tuck into our bunks, the ship starts to break thick ice off Cape Royds, broadening the channel started by the *Polar Star* on Christmas Day. The grinding noise against the hull stays with us all night long, breaking into my sleep. It's like being inside a car that is scraping along the side of a building.

We're rudely awakened by some sort of electronic buzzer ringing in the passageway and a muffled announcement over the PA system. The windowless cabin is completely dark, but when I look at my watch I'm surprised to see it's already 7:15 a.m. The only words I can make out through the door are a repeated "flooding, flooding, flooding." I'm sitting up in my bunk wondering groggily whether this is a drill when the XO, our minder from the evening before, bangs loudly on our door and yells at us to get up, get dressed, we've got to get out and he'll be back to collect us in one minute.

Rachael and I jump out of bed and fling on warm clothes. She grabs her parka and I grab my bag of spare clothing—"Just carry your shoes with you, let's go!" shouts the XO, who's back and hovering in the doorway—and we're hustled up to the upper decks. Hurrying crew are slamming and sealing hatches and fire doors behind us as we pass. We're led to the helicopter hangar on the main deck, where we hang out with the bosun and his mate, who update us while they stand by their radios. Apparently the seal on the port propeller shaft has blown. The bosun is surprisingly blasé about the fact that there's now a sizeable hole in our hull and somewhere down below us water is pouring into one of the engine compartments.

"Happens a couple of times a season," he says dryly. "All this ice-breaking shakes the seals and pipes loose and sometimes they break."

Reportedly the crew are right now engaged in inserting an inflatable seal into place, which they'll use as a stopgap measure (literally) until the ship's divers can go down and put in a new permanent seal.

"It's basically got to be glued and stapled together once it's put in," the bosun informs me. "It's a piece of shit, really."

I tell him that's not a terribly encouraging thing to hear about such an important part of the vessel's structure, and he just shrugs.

But soon enough the alarm is over, and we can go back down to our cabins and collect our gear. The storm that delayed our departure is blowing itself out, or at least moving north. There's not even enough time to eat breakfast as our helicopter is due to land back at the ship within the next thirty minutes, so we quickly pack and make our way back to the hangar. It's a reverse of yesterday's drill and once we're up in the air we can see that the *Polar Sea* is now just a few minutes away from Cape Royds, despite the fact that being on board has made it seem like we're a world away. The helo lands in front of the hut and we disembark quickly, and despite my newly awakened awareness of the stink of the place, I am glad to be back home at the penguin colony and our humble abode above it. As I drag our gear up to the door of the hut, I realize that tonight will be New Year's Eve.

18

ON NEW YEAR'S Day I can feel a bad mood building. The last few nights haven't allowed for much rest, given my general inability to fall asleep before 2 a.m. and the need to be up early during the Beaufort trip. And the wind is blowing the successor to the gale that kept us on board the *Polar Sea* overnight. Days like this are a pain at the best of times—too windy to get much done but not windy enough to be forced to stay in the hut, where at least we can catch up on hut chores.

At the colony I try to read flipper bands but it's hopeless in this sort of weather. With wind vibration affecting the binoculars' acuity, we have to get so close to the birds that they become nervous and pirouette in circles to keep us in sight, while we in turn try to circle back behind them to see the numbers on the bands. It's an annoying dance that, as always, finishes with me giving up and waiting for the wind to drop.

Last night we had a clear sky but today its promise of better weather has disappeared. Along with the wind, grey and heavy clouds now press down upon us menacingly—the ugliest day we've had in a while, though it's not particularly cold. I realize that I'm experiencing some mid-season blahs, as far in time from the freshness of the beginning of the season as I am from going home. Mostly I am fine with the solitude of the hut and the rough realities of our fieldwork, but it has all been gnawing at me these past couple of days, as I feed on thoughts of the parties that friends will be throwing at home (a day behind us here, where we operate on New Zealand time). I have a strong desire to go out dancing and drinking and socializing and generally behaving for a few hours like someone without a twenty-four-hour-a-day job in the middle of nowhere. Basically, I need a day off, and not a day off in Mactown spent running around doing errands. Since that's not an option I hope we have a really big blow tomorrow: It's time for a hut day.

Chick condition check number one today—the first of our weekly chick weighings. This means extracting chicks, randomly, from the nests in a designated section of the colony to get their weights and wing chord measurements, with these two metrics an index of how well they are being fed and how quickly they are growing. We did the same thing at Beaufort Island. A new collection of bruises is blooming on my hands and forearms: A couple of the neighbours of our target nests took real umbrage at my gently pushing them out of the way, as did a couple of the parents of the study chicks. I have a nasty puffy swelling between the thumb and forefinger of my left hand due to the excellent flipper aim of one particularly angry bird.

Later in the day the *Nathaniel B. Palmer*, the US research icebreaker, sails past on her way south, following the *Polar Sea* and the *Polar Star* down the channel. Soon the tourist ships will also be here on their annual pilgrimage, the very few that make it this far south. I look forward to their arrival but it has its downside. The day before yesterday, on the ship, Kerry was telling us that when she was working here a few years ago she was sitting on the shit bucket at two in the morning, admiring the view, when a group of red-coated tourists strode over the crest of the hill in front of her.

"Now *that's* where I draw the line!" she said indignantly.

It looks like I may get my wish for a big blow—I just went outside for a visit to the vile and noisome toilet bucket myself and nearly got blown around the corner of the hut. A few tiny flakes of snow are falling.

After dinner I use the satellite phone to call home and put in a virtual appearance at the New Year's party of a couple of friends. Everyone shows alcohol-fuelled overexcitement at my call, and all are complaining about the midwinter cold. It is about the same temperature in their northern winter, a couple of degrees below zero, as it has been here this week; in fact, it's a little bit warmer there. How funny that what feels freezing to them seems relatively warm here, especially when compared to our early season storms.

It is closing in on midnight, and I have the headphones plugged into my laptop, listening to Yo-Yo Ma playing the cello again, Bach Suite No. 1. It is heart-stoppingly beautiful music, and the notes soar swiftly upward like birds taking flight, then drift deliberately down again like autumn leaves. Last time I listened to this piece the wind was screaming outside, rattling the walls of the hut, and the instrument echoed the wind, calling to it from inside our canvas walls. I turned it up loud, to shout back at the Antarctic storm. Tonight the wind is gusty and can't make up its mind, and the evening sun is turning the Transantarctic Mountains purple. The music echoes the changing colours of the mountains; it tells a tale of the dying hours of the day, the drifting clouds, the passing of the season, and the cycling of the sun.

For the second time today I am feeling low, and this music, a celebration of life, sends tears running down my cheeks. Something about the new year coming in without having friends here to mark the passage of the old one, perhaps, and David sleeping soundly on his mat in the corner of the hut, each day to him simply another opportunity to learn more about the Ross Sea. Or perhaps it's because the date always reminds me, now, that my sister will never again experience the passage of time. Sometimes I wonder that I can ever even attempt to write about this place. When I feel this desolate I sometimes wonder whether it's just an internal manifestation of the incomparable, bleak beauty of Antarctica, intense enough to burn like a wound.

At ten minutes past midnight I tell myself that I've indulged this melancholy mood enough, and take a glass of whisky out to our little deck to toast the day. Miles Davis is playing "So What" on my headphones. Stacks of big lenticular clouds hover over Mount Erebus like giant spaceships while across McMurdo Sound some altocumulus is doing funny things with the sun, dimming the sea beneath it but setting the glacial slopes of Mount Discovery and the adjacent peaks on fire. To the south the sky is almost clear, promising another serene summer morning, but at the moment it is bitterly cold and the energetic snapping of my tent fly suggests another noisy night.

The wind has indeed kept up and so I've got my wish for a hut day. A good thing too, as I'm fighting off a cold after our visit to the ship. I went to bed shortly after my midnight excursion last night and still don't wake until ten thirty this morning. Coffee and breakfast don't help much and I am still groggy at noon.

The wind is blasting us from the south again today, bringing with it a spectacular ever-changing sky. Altostratus and altocumulus are torn into fantastic shapes as they speed past overhead against a backdrop that changes from overcast dove grey to clear periwinkle blue. And I have never seen such lenticular clouds, last night's notwithstanding. One hovers now between Mount Bird and Mount Erebus, a massive dark grey structure with a cyclonic dimple punched into its middle so that it looks like a giant red blood cell under an electron microscope. Out of the wind, the temperature is still what passes for midsummer warm, but with these forty-five-knot gusts it has felt frigid for much of the day.

On going out the back door to get some icy snow for our melt-water container, I realize that for the first time our snowbank, which towered over camp at the start of the season, is now low enough that the lower slopes of Mount Bird are visible over the top of it. Another sign that midsummer is here, despite today's inhospitable weather. Even so, last night was a cold one in the tent, the first time in a while that I've needed to do vigorous sit-ups in my sleeping bag to warm my feet before going to sleep. Also the first one in a while when I've had to wear earplugs in order to muffle the staccato rattle of the tent fly. Though David has mentioned to me that he too uses earplugs to block the noise of the flapping, I never see a hint of him resorting to such crutches as hand-warmers or sit-ups in his sleeping bag; there is no doubt that he is more stoic and hardier than I.

Later in the week half a dozen people come out from McMurdo to remove the flags marking the sea ice road to Royds. With the warmer temperatures of midsummer (and the radiating cracks from the channel that was cut by the icebreakers), base has decided to limit over-ice travel out to our part of the sound, though the ice is certainly still traversable and should be for a while yet, especially as tracked vehicles carry boards they can use to drive over the narrower leads. The main potential barrier is the crack at the Barne Glacier to our south, between here and Cape Evans. The ice there was a metre thick at its thinnest point when it was drilled by Scott Base a couple of weeks ago, but this is the route's weakest spot, the place where the ice is likely to start to break up.

I feel a pang upon hearing of the flags' imminent removal, as it means an end to the unexpected visitors we've so far received every week or so. Now they'll mostly be restricted to those important enough to come by helicopter—although the Kiwis reportedly use an overland route around the edge of Mount Erebus once the ice breaks out, so I'm hoping we'll continue to see them out here. They seem a more adventuresome lot than the Americans—or perhaps it is just their less litigious culture. Participants in the Scott Base field safety training reportedly get to rappel down a crevasse, something that no one in the US program would ever even think of doing. An example of these two disparate cultures of safety is described in American author Nicholas Johnson's book *Big Dead Place*, in which he writes about a midwinter medevac flight into McMurdo. A medical flight is always something of great interest to winter-overs because in principle, if there's room on board, it provides a chance to obtain things like freshies (the local term for fresh fruits and vegetables). Whether or not there's actually room on board to bring them depends who's flying.

"If the [US Air National Guard] flew down, they would bring a complete extra crew, extra rotors, and extra parts, leaving little room for freshies or mail," he noted. "If a Kiwi plane flew down . . . there would be plenty of room . . . because the only things the Kiwis would need for themselves are the Sports section and a pint of milk."[49] So I suspect we will indeed see a few Scott Base residents out here via the overland route once the flagged sea ice track is out of commission.

It's the fifth of January. Sir Ernest Shackleton died suddenly on this day in 1922, still in Antarctica but on board his ship *Quest* at the island of South Georgia, far from the place where he and his men constructed their Cape Royds hut. He was only forty-seven years old. South Georgia lies on the other side of the continent just south of the Antarctic Polar Front, the marine barrier that separates Antarctica from the rest of the world. Sometimes I imagine dying in some misadventure here on Ross Island, surrounded by the calls of penguins and with Erebus in my eyes, and the thought fills me equally with terror and with joy. I wonder if Shackleton regretted being so far from home as he fell, or if he knew that he was already there.

"A wonderful evening. In the darkening twilight I saw a lone star hover, gem-like above the bay," reads his final journal entry, written on the evening of the fourth of January.[50] Arrangements were made to return his body to Lady Shackleton and to England, but in Montevideo, word reached the accompanying party that she wished him to be buried on South Georgia—and there he still lies, in the tiny graveyard at the old whaling station of Grytviken, his grave pointing south toward the Antarctic continent.

Down at the colony the birds have passed peak hatch—it is now apparent that this occurred a day or two after Christmas—and most of the chicks are getting big enough that we can spot downy heads, flippers, or bums poking out from underneath the brooding parents. Chicks that hatch much later than this will run the risk of not fledging before the end of the summer, or fledging at a weight low enough that they won't make it through their first winter. But not all of the earlier birds are doing well either—for example, the penguins at nest number 37 in B-REF, one of the first pairs to lay eggs and hatch chicks, have already lost both of their fat offspring to a resident pair of skuas. The worst parents in B-REF this year, the pair at nest 13, also hatched their chicks early but had one chick die right after hatching while the second was squashed in its shell while halfway out of it. This in contrast to the exemplary parenting of the penguins at nest number 4, where their two chicks are thriving at the edge of the subcolony, in an exposed location frequented by the skuas.

When the weather is as fine as it is this evening, it's my favourite time to be at the colony. Work is done for the day, and the long shadows brought on by the sun's daily dip toward the horizon somehow make the colony look peaceful, even though the raucous calls and fights over territories and mates continue unabated throughout what we loosely call "the night." Pony Lake—half of which is now a bona fide body of liquid water—is a deep, slaty indigo under a cloudless sky, and its surface is ruffled by the wind that is just beginning to pick up. That same wind is blowing hard at the top of the Erebus crater, shredding the ever-present plume of smoke and steam that issues forth. As it does on these clear and golden summer evenings, Erebus itself dominates the entire eastern sky above us, looking almost impossibly high. Far offshore from Cape Royds a huge tabular iceberg is drifting. Well, "huge" doesn't quite do it justice; though it is nothing like B-15A, it nonetheless looks to be the size of a habitable island, or the downtown of some large city. It is so far distant that even here in this land of crystal-clear air it looks blurred, as if only half real. Despite all my time here I'm still not used to seeing things this large that aren't anchored to a continent or the ocean floor.

On my way up the hill I stop at the Kiwi hut, the little green wanigan, to warm up out of the wind with a drink of tea from my Thermos. I thumb through the dog-eared logbook, looking at more entries from years ago. Some of them catch my eye and I jot down passages in my field notebook.

> 26/1/97. Mike Single, Sir Ed Hillary, Tom Scott, John Carlow, Davie Mess, Wax Buck and Al — . . . . Light snow;

According to a couple of logbook entries, this place has been cleaned up considerably since the 1980s or '90s. Paul Broady of the University of Canterbury (one of the scientists based at Cape Royds to study the algae of Pony Lake, Green Lake, and the other small water bodies in the area) describes the local litter as consisting of "wood, cans, wire mesh, nylon rope, old smoke canisters, rope, rags, broken thermometers, shovels, chimneys, stakes, tent poles, knives, forks, spoons, shotgun cartridges, bamboo sticks, paint cans, jerry cans, etc. etc."

Sounds like there was quite the mess around the Shackleton hut. In the same vein I'll be giving Scott Base a call on the radio this week with a message for the Antarctic Heritage Trust about the hut's "historical" tins of food. Quite a number of them were scattered about the landscape by this year's winter storms (with the rusting empty shells of other cans doubtless having been scattered by previous years' wind events), and the skuas are getting into them. Earlier today I saw what appeared to be—if my memory of the labels of some of the intact tins inside the hut is correct—some slices of parsnip scattered around the rotting remains of a cuboid can. Imagine that, I thought—those parsnips were pulled out of the ground one hundred years ago and some of those slices still look fresh, both on the ground and when flying past in the beak of a skua. Of course, other slices were an almost unrecognizable, disintegrating mess. I hope the skuas aren't actually eating them. The entire situation seems bizarre to me, almost obscene—root vegetables lying about on the ground of Antarctica.

Apparently His Highness the Duke of Halswell has visited here as well, though I only know this from his calling card (signed for authenticity) stuck on a nail high on the wall, and from the seal that he's stamped in black into one of the shelf supports. I briefly wonder what some minor member of the British nobility was doing down here.

"You'll meet him later this season," David tells me enigmatically when I mention this to him later. I look at him quizzically but he doesn't elaborate, so I leave it.

And the most recent logbook entry is less than a month old: "Paul Rogers and Grahame Sydney. Two memorable nights, one Scrabble defeat, one day tranquil and mirror-calm, the next wilder and cutting. Emperors graced our final hours, Adélies were our constant music. Unforgettable."

—

At one in the morning I return and step silently into the hut, where David is sleeping in the corner. I shed a couple of layers of clothing and place my gear under the desk, but as I'm quietly readying myself for bed I hear the sound of whales blowing somewhere in the distance. I again pull on a hat and gloves and a couple of coats and grab my camera, and set off down the hill in the direction of the sound, toward the ridge that hides Green Lake just to the north of camp.

I haven't been down here since this actually became a lake as opposed to a huge snowbank. It is now a disgustingly murky body of soupy water with a number of vile-looking red algal mats floating on its surface. Green Lake is one of the interesting local water bodies mentioned in the wanigan's logbook, from which Shackleton's expedition took the first samples used to describe these Antarctic algae species. It's a surreal little corner of the Cape Royds neighbourhood, concealed behind volcanic ridges in the midst of a lunar landscape that's presided over by several pairs of skuas. It's far enough from our hut that we never get over here and so the skuas are much more aggressive than the ones that are used to us down at the penguin colony. Getting past these new birds in order to reach a good vantage point above the sea is like passing some Homeric test.

Numerous plumes of breath are still vaporizing out over the water when I get to the viewpoint. I see a very large pod of killer whales, forty or fifty of them—probably Type C again, known for their often large pod sizes and for inhabiting the thick pack ice of the Ross Sea—swimming quickly toward the south and the edge of the sea ice. The closest ones are a good nautical mile offshore, and the hut is about a kilometre from the shoreline—it still amazes me that we can hear them breathing so clearly from so far away.

I take a few photos of them as I sit on the ridge, not because they'll be great whale shots but because they help to bring a sense of perspective to this vista. All those enormous animals, relatively close to shore, look as tiny as mites against the broad reach of McMurdo Sound and its corrugated coating of drifting pack ice. Against this foreground the mountains of Victoria Land seem impossibly tall, like the peaks that might lead to Valhalla.

On the way back I photograph our hut. I've just come over the ridge from Green Lake and see something white peep through the clouds; for a brief second I think it's a daylight glimpse of the moon, like the one I had a couple of weeks ago when she was riding high in the sky like a ghost. But it is the peak of Mount Erebus, wreathed in a low belt of pale grey cloud. The whole thing—volcanic peak, clouds, sky, endless vista—makes our hut look utterly insignificant. It is a day for feeling tiny in this immeasurable landscape.

19

THE NEXT AFTERNOON we fly into McMurdo aboard a Bell 212, one of the big cargo helicopters. Taking advantage of its size we retrograde several bags of trash, Human Waste Bucket number 3, and a sizeable pile of excess gear that David wants us to get rid of—including an extra pair of skis, a couple of spare penguin nets, a coil of rope, and the pole-mounted PIT tag reader. The penguins hate this particular device, their reaction to it a marked contrast to their blithe lack of concern when scanned for their ID chips by its hand-held counterpart, so we haven't been using it. Perhaps the pole-mounted reader looks too much like a skua as it hovers over them. I'm not sure why we can't just ship all this stuff out at the end of the season—it's not as if sending it out now so it can sit in the lab is saving us any work, and it's not like we really need the room out here either, in our camp of limitless horizons. Anyway, it's gone now. Sure hope we don't need that electric drill . . .

The weather is beautiful for the flight, and the pilot flies us out to the ice edge and then in to Mactown along the channel being created by the icebreakers. The channel is now impressively wide and, as I feared a few days ago, is having a definite impact on the integrity of the sea ice between here and McMurdo. At Cape Barne to the south of our camp, a big lead now runs in from the new channel almost to the tidal crack that runs along the shore, and a couple of other large cracks are forming in the vicinity. There goes the sea ice route.

At the store I run into some of the Beardmore Glacier crew buying T-shirts in preparation for heading home, their field season now over. They left Beardmore at the same time as did all the sunburned, wild-haired people I'd seen in the Crary Lab shortly before Christmas, but this smaller group had subsequently moved on to another field site for a final couple of weeks.

"How was it?" I ask one of them. It's Zelenda, the grad student I first met at Snow School. Her short blonde hair is tousled and her complexion wind-burned.

"It was absolutely amazing!" she says in quiet awe. "I didn't want to leave there. I was supposed to head back north to Christchurch with the others yesterday, but I gave my seat on the flight to someone else."

I am suddenly reminded of a passenger on an Antarctic Peninsula cruise on which I worked; one day she slyly turned her ship's passenger number back to "on board" as she disembarked into a Zodiac heading for shore. She was caught in her deception and found striding over a nearby ice-capped ridge, but she had wanted to stay forever.

The last time I had seen Zelenda and her friends Nicole and Simon was a day or two after Snow School. Viola and I were getting our food orders at BFC, and the three of them were putting together sleds for hauling gear out at the glacier. They are as cheerful now as they were then, nary a sign of burnout. Despite the various ups and downs of camp life I imagine I'll be the same at the end of our own field season—reluctant to leave and looking for ways to hang on for another few precious days. Our own season's end is coming up all too quickly and is now just a month away.

—

From my room I call Scott Base hoping to talk to Paul Rogers to see if he wants to get together for another game of Scrabble after dinner, but I get an unpleasant shock when I ask for him: He's gone back home for a couple of weeks to attend the funerals of three guiding friends killed with a client in a mountaineering accident the previous week on Mount Tasman, the second-highest peak in New Zealand. One of the three guides, Dave Gardner, worked in Antarctica as a field safety trainer. The other two, Paul Scaife and David Hiddleston, were directors of a professional mountain guiding company.

"Perhaps it's the reminder that sometimes being the best-trained person in the world isn't enough to avert disaster, there or here," I write later to Grahame in an email, logged on to one of the computers in the evening silence of the Crary Lab library, the mountains of the Royal Society Range filling the sky. "Or the realization that even down here, The Real World has the ability to intrude."

In our tiny community of like-minded souls the loss of a friend of a friend has a deeper impact than it would back home. In this environment every emotion has the room to expand and to threaten to overwhelm. But I am unsure how to grieve: They weren't my friends, after all. I feel slammed by some floating, disassociated feeling of loss, more so after reading the details in a news article online: The avalanche was likely triggered by the guides themselves. It was a very small one, only a few cubic metres of snow. Just a case of wrong place, wrong time.

"Come to the Coffee House later," says NASA Erik when I see him at dinner and tell him the news. "I'll buy you a drink."

On Monday nights the Coffee House is supposedly closed, but despite this the doors are unlocked and there are coffees and lots of chocolatey desserts and it is BYOB. Erik has brought along a very nice Chianti and entertains me with stories about overwintering at McMurdo. Apparently the first year that the company Raytheon had the US Antarctic Program contract to manage McMurdo—the US National Science Foundation manages research through its Antarctic Program, which outsources logistical support to a private contractor—they were lax on reference checks and desperate for overwintering construction workers and so ended up hiring a bunch of hardened ex-cons. They had names like "Tiny" or "Butch" and a propensity to pick up pool cues by the wrong end and use them in a fight. Needless to say, this made the winter on station rather tense, although also at times entertaining.

Before going to the Coffee House I had stopped by the ice pier to watch the newly arrived *Polar Star* hard at work smashing its final few hundred metres through the frozen ocean toward McMurdo. The ice pier is at the foot of a huge embankment, and it was to the spot alongside this slope that the ship was heading. The vessel would pull back into the open channel and then speed forward like a charging bull, the round icebreaker bow sliding up onto the ice near the pier, then breaking down through it by force of sheer weight. With two engines and two turbines revving it would accelerate forward onto the ice as far as possible, churning the sea astern into a foaming maelstrom of ice chunks and frigid water. As much of the ice in the bay is covered in wind-blown sand and gravel, it looked as if the ship was repeatedly ploughing ashore like a whale intent on beaching itself. The vessel was being manoeuvred as if it were a small boat rather than a large ship and it was all very impressive—though I did think whoever was at the helm was getting a little too gung-ho. Someone's boyhood big-truck dream come true.

Sure enough, Erik the fire inspector comes by our table later and shows us his fresh video footage of the vessel ramming the ice pier itself—a big no-no, as it could well mean the pier will be unsafe to use for offloading supplies, or at least that it won't last as long. The pier is a heavy-duty piece of construction built of ice reinforced with steel cables that's supposed to last several years, so destroying it is not something that would look particularly flattering on the CV of the ship's captain.

In the morning I catch the shuttle over to Scott Base. The usual passenger van has been replaced by a lumbering leviathan Delta now that the sea ice runway has a crack in it and air operations have been shifted over to Williams Field, meaning far more people are heading out there every day.

The Delta does a drive-by drop-off at Scott Base on its way out to the planes; as it leaves McMurdo every thirty minutes all day long, it's very convenient. I stop by the Kiwi base shop to buy a new pair of merino long johns. I've been living twenty-four hours a day in the pair I brought with me and would happily make a commercial for their brand. The US Antarctic Program–issue gear is all polypro and so I never use it—like most field workers, I hate the stuff because it stinks so horrendously after just a few hours of wear. The Scott Base purchase will be my souvenir of the season too as its logo is modest and tasteful; I've come to realize that much as I like the McMurdo crowd, I'm not keen on going home with a T-shirt decorated with surfing penguins. McMurdo is a loud and brash place, suited to the American way.

It turns out my timing at the Scott Base store is good as they're expecting to be cleaned out by tourists on Thursday—the icebreaker *Kapitan Khlebnikov* is reportedly approaching McMurdo Sound with a load of them, and will be helicoptering passengers in for their Antarctic station experience. (This is the ship, incidentally, on which the Australian author Thomas Keneally had journeyed to Antarctica to return his pilfered portion of Scott's biscuit.) Eventually vessels such as this one will be banned from operating in Antarctica under the

Polar Code of the International Maritime Organization, but for now they are still here. I guess this means we can expect the ship at Cape Royds in the next day or two as well; I feel a frisson of excitement at the possibility of interesting new visitors, alongside a stab of annoyance that work will likely be interrupted again. At least we won't have to sell them souvenirs.

Before leaving Scott Base I stop by the office of the station manager, who is also from Canada, and tell him about the decaying tin cans down at Shackleton's hut.

"Oh right," he says. "Thanks for letting us know. The Antarctic Heritage Trust will be staying out at Royds later this month for their annual cleanup, so I'll add that to their list." Yet more visitors, apparently.

After lunch, I run into Rusty in the hallway at 155. Rusty of Christmas Day at Royds fame. They've just got back from the Dry Valleys, where they were stranded over the holiday weekend by the same weather that kept us on the *Polar Sea,* thus missing Icestock, the Mactown New Year's festival. Worse than that, they ran out of booze and were dry for three days over the holiday; they'd only brought enough to last them until their scheduled date back in, and drank accordingly.

"What a debacle," he says. "We managed to put the 'Dry' into Dry Valleys."

Rusty talks with infectious enthusiasm about his work out there. He and his wife Regina call their research team the Yeastie Boyz, because they are looking at the reproductive rates of fungal life forms—yeasts and a few filamentous fungi—in the soil of the Dry Valleys, and at the density of soil bacteria. These are very stable systems, with populations of these organisms, and their upper-trophic-level counterparts like nematodes and rotifers, remaining highly invariant despite fluctuations in moisture and temperature. I ask Rusty if he is looking at food web dynamics, and he laughs and says the communities are so stable that there isn't going to be much change in them over the course of his entire career, let alone a couple of years, so it's not a long-term project. This turns out to be prophetic as I find out later that he and Regina have put their backgrounds in microbiology to good use and started a winery near Seattle. Based on the number of hellos and nods coming his way while we're talking he knows a lot of people down here, and after experiencing his enthusiasm for their arcane research topics and everything else, I can understand why so many are drawn to him.

Today McMurdo is full of beefy types in tight T-shirts. The Coast Guard is here and I'm glad I'm not sticking around town to witness the excitement of their shore leave from a dry ship. The McMurdo store has closed for "inventory," conveniently timed to avoid the onslaught of alcohol-seeking sailors, male and female alike. At this time of year the rumour is always that this closure is really to prevent some alcohol-deprived sailor from drinking himself into a stupor, passing out in a snowbank, and dying of exposure, something that is rumoured to have happened in an earlier era.

On our way back out to Royds today we fly the land route, over Scott Base and up toward Mount Terror and Castle Rock. It is beautiful, all white ice fields and glaciated peaks and immense crags sticking up through the whiteness like broken stubs of brown teeth.

But when we get back to camp this afternoon, the momentum of a whirlwind trip to town wears off and the bad news of yesterday settles in. To make things worse, I'm feeling ill and crampy. I can usually set my clock by my monthly cycle but it is now completely off schedule, probably because of the complete lack of darkness and interrupted circadian rhythms. I unpack gear and food supplies and then leave David a note that I am feeling lousy and taking the evening off and to please give me a shout when dinner is ready. I come out of my tent to eat a small meal and David stares at me in absolute amazement when I wave goodnight to him at 8:30 p.m. I am now back in my sleeping bag again, writing and sipping a glass poured from the fresh bottle of Jägermeister I picked up at the station store. I'm sure that by morning some of this uncharacteristic funk will have subsided, but I expect to be a bit subdued for the next couple of days.

20

THE SKY IS overcast and the pack ice has once again drifted in, ghost-like, with the slight north wind. The sun is dimmed by thick slate clouds, and in this muted light the entire world is coloured in shades of ivory and grey, mauve and indigo. I feel the first chill in my bones that I've felt for a couple of weeks, not due to the weather in particular—I'm used to it by now—but because David and I have skied out to the *Kapitan Khlebnikov* for dinner this evening, and my sweaty clothes have dried against my skin.

The *Khlebnikov* once was a Russian research icebreaker, and it stayed afloat in the decades following the demise of the Soviet Union by chartering itself out to the adventure tourism industry in the West. Now the ship and her load of tourists are visiting Cape Royds, arriving early this morning after making a landing across McMurdo Sound in the Dry Valleys at 2 a.m. I woke to the unexpected noise of helicopters flying back and forth in the stillness, and crawled out of my tent to see the ship wedged fast into the sea ice a kilometre to the south of us, a black-and-cream leviathan beached on a frozen shore. Already a snake-like tendril of tourists was extending from the vessel's bow and making its way across the ice toward Shackleton's camp.

So it has been a day of work interspersed with talking with a keen group of tourists and ship's expedition staff. In the early afternoon I finished banding the last of my assigned quota of thirty penguins in the reference colony; I perfected the technique a couple of weeks ago and can now squeeze the bands closed with my fingers and with a minimum of struggling from the birds. Instead they lie heavy and still in my arms, feeling rotund and muscular under their sleek coating of feathers.

Passengers and crew are a mix of nationalities—Kiwis, Australians, Americans, Germans, Brits, and more. On my way back to camp for a late lunch I stopped by Shackleton's hut and met Mick, expedition staffer and Tasmanian, who was showing an enthusiastic crowd of tourists around the exterior with its historic piles of rusty hundred-year-old cans of food, desiccated dogsledding gear, and weathered wooden packing cases, all still remarkably well preserved by Antarctica's extreme cold and dry. In the course of our conversation I mentioned I'd be skiing out to the ship later to take some photographs, and Mick—a tall and muscular fellow with a big shock of sun-bleached hair—ended up radioing the expedition leader to invite us for dinner on board.

Outside Shackleton's hut I chatted with the ship's Kiwi geologist, Barrie McKelvey, who first came down to Antarctica in the 1957–58 International Geophysical Year, while still at university. Initially rejected by the New Zealand program, he and fellow undergraduate Peter Webb eventually talked their way onto both it and the US mission. Victoria Valley, one of the Dry Valleys, is named after his alma mater, the Victoria University of Wellington, which sponsored the expedition. He tells me that when he was working here in the field in the 1950s, the Heroic Age of Exploration was still fresh in everyone's mind. That the historic huts were still in use, some of the men from those expeditions were still alive, and that McKelvey and his cohort knew them. "We slept in their bunks," McKelvey tells me.

His first visit had been at an inflection point in polar history. It was as part of the IGY that Sir Edmund Hillary led the construction of Scott Base in support of the Commonwealth Trans-Antarctic Expedition, which was to be the first overland crossing of Antarctica via the Pole. Hillary—already knighted in 1953 for having been the first climber (with Tibetan-born mountaineer Tenzing Norgay) to have reached the summit of Everest—was leader of the support party to the expedition, while the Briton Vivian Fuchs (knighted by the young Queen Elizabeth following this expedition) led the main party. Fuchs was to traverse the continent via the South Pole, starting from the temporary Shackleton Base on Vahsel Bay at the southern end of the Weddell Sea, on the far side of Antarctica from Ross Island. The expedition's route was a re-creation of the one proposed by Shackleton himself in 1914 but thwarted when the *Endurance* was beset and then sunk in the Weddell Sea ice. Under Fuchs, the British finally hoped to have their Antarctic crossing.

After constructing Scott Base, Hillary's party was to lay fuel and food depots along a seven-hundred-mile route toward the South Pole—depots containing supplies for Fuchs's party to use on the final leg of their crossing—before themselves returning to Scott Base. Taking advantage of the half century of technological advances realized since the Pole was first attained, the Hillary-Fuchs parties travelled entirely with tracked vehicles rather than with sled dogs, and carried their own fuel (twenty-two tons of it in the case of Hillary's group). Rather cheekily, after laying all of the depots Hillary's party realized that they had both the time and the fuel to reach the South Pole ahead of Fuchs, and did so, arriving about two weeks before him. This was the first overland trek to reach the Pole since Scott followed Amundsen in 1911–12 (although in 1956, the USA's Amundsen-Scott South Pole Station had been established by air, also in preparation for the IGY). Fuchs and eleven other men did the entire crossing, from Shackleton

Base to Scott Base, in just ninety-nine days. Though they may not have known it at the time, these men were giants astride a divide, standing with a foot in each era. With the IGY, and Fuchs's successful crossing of the continent using machines, the modern age of Antarctic exploration and occupation had begun.

David and I ski out to the ship at 7 p.m., passing up the offer of a lift in one of their helicopters. This year, Helicopters New Zealand is flying for them and this is reportedly a vast improvement over previous years with the ship's own dilapidated Russian machines and allegedly drunken Russian pilots.

But we've done so much shuttling around in helicopters this season that the offer of a two-minute lift to the ship has far less appeal than a ski across the sea ice, so David and I set off down the slope together. The near-shore ice is continually influenced by tidal motion offshore and by the nearby tidal cracks, and it seems even more hummocky than when I went out on it a few days ago. Out near the ship much of the snow has blown away and the surface has been thawing when the sun is out and later refreezing, so it is slick and treacherous. My legs ache from the effort of skiing across the bumpy ice without crashing. Not the best ski of the season, but I take a photograph of David looking small underneath the massive ship's bow with the coruscated pack ice in the distance, and it is dramatic to traverse around the hull to where the gangway unfolds down from the upper decks to rest on the frozen sea.

We come aboard and are immediately escorted to a warm and cozy bar where crew and tourists alike hang out when not ashore, and where the expedition staff and helicopter pilots eat dinner. The bar is wood-panelled and well stocked, and we're offered our choice of beer, wine, or cocktails. I choose a glass of Australian red, poured for me by a smiling and uniformed bartender, then we're shown to our tables, which are set with pristine white tablecloths, gleaming glassware, and polished cutlery. I sit with Mick the Tasmanian, one of the pilots, and Ian, the ship's physician, who's on board as a volunteer in exchange for a free trip for himself and his wife. Though he's Australian, it turns out his wife is from Vancouver and one of their daughters is attending Canada's University of Victoria, my undergraduate alma mater. He is also in a slight state of shock, it transpires, as Mick explains *sotto voce* over the main course, looking over his shoulder for guests.

"Bit of a drag, we had a death on board this trip, first one ever," he whispers in his broad Australian accent. "Just before we crossed the Antarctic Circle, his heart gave out. We have to be quiet about it though; the passengers are still getting used to the idea of losing one of their own."

"Yes," whispers Ian. "We actually had to stand him upright to get him down in the elevator."

The corpse, now in post-rigor-mortis phase, is apparently still on board, down below on the second deck in one of the walk-in coolers, awaiting removal tomorrow with the assistance of the ever-helpful personnel at Scott Base.

I put a forkful of mahi mahi into my mouth and contemplate the fact that there is a body a couple of decks below the dining area.

"It was all right that he missed seeing the Antarctic Circle though," continues Mick, with hearty Australian pragmatism. "He was with a whole group of old folks and they'd just had a good few days in the Campbell Islands. He had heart problems and they all knew he was on his way out."

I find it hard to believe that his group would be quite that blasé about their travelling companion's demise, but perhaps they too are Australians.

The best things about the food are the strong tastes of fresh cilantro and tomatoes, and the cooked fresh vegetables. After dinner, a passenger from Tofino—a remote community of a couple of thousand residents that is nearly as far west as one can live in Canada—buys me a brandy and we chat about some acquaintances in common. Just before starting my MSc program I had spent two field seasons based in Tofino while studying marbled murrelets, seabirds noteworthy for their habit of nesting not on rocky islands but on mossy tree limbs in the old-growth temperate rainforests that stand in that part of the world.

At a few minutes to ten, Mick hustles David and me out to the gangway just in time for the ship's ten o'clock departure. We're only halfway down the steps when a grumpy-looking officer up on the bridge deck high above us shouts down orders in Russian and a be-capped crew member runs down behind us to ready the gangway for raising. We stop and look back at the ship five minutes into our return ski trip and already the *Khlebnikov* is sliding in reverse out of its icy berth, the bow swinging south toward McMurdo Station and Scott Base. We are once again left to the frigid stillness punctuated by the distant braying of the penguins calling to their chicks, and the swishing sounds of our skis on the surface of the frozen ocean.

David and I reach the shoreline and unclip our ski boots from their bindings. As we trudge silently up the slope together I reflect on the contrast posed by the warm, well-appointed ship full of lively passengers and crew—a bright and shiny bubble of civilization slipping away from us through this wild landscape—and the draughty canvas-sided tent with no toilet that awaits us.

"That was nice, but I'm glad to be heading home," I say to David.

"Me too," he replies.

21

THE KIWI WANIGAN has become like a friend to me. Or at least it feels like a haven in the way that friends sometimes do, here in this land with few human friends. I'm down here now after dinner, writing, and have the door flung wide open to let in the air and the evening sun. Tonight I've come here to get some solitude. Solitude! How can anyone need it in this place, which is sometimes loneliness itself? But I love the quiet and contemplative air of this cozy little space, the knowledge that so many others before me have stayed here and looked out the window or sat on the doorstep in the sun and listened to the distant music of the penguins. It is tied to the history of Antarctica in a way that we, up in our temporary Rac-Tent, are not. In the logbook are the names of the visitors who have been here over the years for purposes as diverse as studying the local invertebrates, or taking a break from base, or doing a shakedown trip, or cleaning up the Shackleton hut site, or counting the penguins at the colony. We up the hill are such a small part of this whole procession of people who have visited and worked at Cape Royds.

This hut has a much better view than ours. Through the open door I can see penguins at the colony, Pony Lake and the huge snowbank that still covers half of it even at this stage of the season, and the ice-clad expanse of McMurdo Sound, where water and ice alike are sparkling in the sun. Out there the luminous white of the pack is broken by shadows in mauve and dove grey, and the incandescent turquoise of old ice glows deep in the hollows of the biggest chunks of bergs. The jagged peaks of the Royal Society Range sit wreathed in drifting banks of mist and form a hazy backdrop to all of this splendour. Through the side window I can catch a glimpse of the grey metal-clad roof of Shackleton's hut. Even though the wanigan has a more open view than we do up at the Rac-Tent, the Kiwi refuge is in a more sheltered spot—down low, and in the lee of a bluff that blocks the worst of the southerly winds.

But Shackleton picked the best spot. His hut is even closer to sea level, and has a sheltering slope on three sides—not to mention a view as good as the one from here. I've walked past his hut so many times now that sometimes I don't even notice it's there. But every couple of days its presence strikes me, timeless against the backdrop of Erebus, and I can sense the presence of Shackleton and his men. They are starting to seem nearly as real to me as all the friends and family I've left at home, looming large in my imagination, closer in space than home is in time. Some days I stand across Pony Lake and look at the closed doors and shuttered windows and am just a blink away from seeing Shackleton himself, leaning out the door and calling to someone or laughing at a joke that's just been made. Tonight I nod a good evening to him as I pass and murmur a hello out loud, back in a child's fantasy land of expecting dreams to be suddenly clad in the flesh of reality, slightly surprised when he doesn't appear to greet me. In the timeless air of this place his men have only just left the hut, and at any moment I expect to see them reappear over a hill or around the corner of a grounded berg.

—

There is a brief detente in the ceaseless hostility shown to us by the skuas. I am up at the ridgetop on the north edge of the colony, traversing from one side to the other of subcolony 11/12, and the older bird of the skua pair there gets up from where it is guarding its chick and flies straight at my head. I prepare to duck and fling up my arm in self-defence as usual, but instead of going for my face in an attack the skua abruptly brakes in midair and drops to the ground a couple of metres in front of me, where it sits regarding me and bobbing its head expectantly. When we sample the stomach contents of dead penguin chicks some of the skuas forage on the remains when we're done; this must be one of them. I drop down to the far side of 11/12 and look back; sure enough, the bird has followed me to the crest of the ridge and stands there watching my progress.

I see a dead two-and-a-half-week-old penguin chick beside its former nest, and pick it up. The skua is on the ground beside me before I've even finished getting out my knife, and it watches avidly from a metre away as I open the dead chick's stomach, empty but for a number of small stones. No wonder it died, presumably starving to death. I make a note of the contents in my field notebook and clean my knife on my field trousers, by now so disgusting they are impervious to yet another layer of sundry filth. When I drop the carcass and move away it is immediately pounced on by the waiting skua. I'm a bit perturbed—is this akin to feeding the local wildlife?—but dead penguin chicks abound here. The skuas like to open the stomach first and go for the fishy digesta when they take or scavenge a chick so it's possible they are just taking advantage of us doing this for them; the abdominal wall of even a small chick is tough. When I turn back in the direction of the bird and its nest, it raises its wings and screeches a warning at me, immediately back in full aggressive skua mode and far from pacified by my accidental offering.

It has been a good marine mammal day, even though over the past week or two there has been a notable drop in the number of Weddell seals that haul out on the fast ice in front of the colony. This morning David reported seeing a leopard seal devouring a penguin, while this evening during shoreline watch I observe two minke whales foraging in front of the colony for ten minutes, only to see them disappear when a pod of four killer whales rounds the cape. Below my clifftop vantage point the ocean has taken on a greenish tinge from a summer algae bloom, and thin pancakes of translucent new ice float on water so still it is as if they are suspended in a pool of absinthe. Just beyond these delicate pieces of frozen summer sea are thick white slices of winter ice, where penguins periodically land after shooting upright out of the water in standard penguin fashion, as if they are spring-loaded or shot out of the water from a cannon. Each time they alight they look wide-eyed and shocked to find that they have transitioned from sea to land, and then they get over it, shaking the drops of water from their feathers and self-importantly trotting shoreward or else settling down to do some immediate preening. The foot of the fast ice currently extends underwater for a metre or two from shore and so it forms a subsurface backdrop against which the underwater movement of arriving and departing penguins may be seen. From up on the clifftop they look like giant water beetles as their wings flap rhythmically open and closed and they fly along in their undersea world of clear green.

Penguin 1091, she who was crippled by a leopard seal attack a month ago, is back at the B-REF colony today, limping badly but otherwise looking healthy and fine. Her mate, 1096, is still at their territory despite the empty nest, and the two greet each other and settle down together as I watch; as unsuccessful breeders they will soon be returning to sea for the rest of the season, readying to return to the colony next year.

I recall David's words when I first told him about her: "Prepare to be amazed." I am indeed amazed. These are tough birds, and, if we need one, a metaphor for living life fully while we're still alive.

The weather today has been quixotic. Moody and overcast and cold. Sunny and peerlessly calm with the pack ice drifting back in from the north. And now there is a halo around the sun and the south wind has started up once more. It has blown out most of the pack ice again and under a thin, high layer of cloud the sea looks sombre, like a giant plate of burnished sheet metal. It appears we may be in for a bit of weather. Bands of altocumulus are being pushed northward over the ocean and the leviathan shapes of icebergs loom in the sound, rough white islands in the pale, undulating mass of the pack. When I went in for dinner earlier all but the lowest slopes of Erebus were shrouded in a smooth cape of cloud; now that the wind has sprung up, it is free and clear again, its aloof presence once more felt. I am struck by the magnificence of Mount Bird's glaciated peak, a radiant white mound against a slate-grey backdrop of cloud-ridden sky. As I walk back to our hut it's −4°C outside despite the sun, and my hands are frozen. It seems that the halcyon days of summer may already be drawing to a close.

My tent is warm when I turn in. Going to sleep fully zipped up in my bag and wearing two layers of long underwear is still a thing of the past; I am soon sweating in my single layer of long johns, and leave both bag and liner halfway open as I go to sleep. But then in the early hours I wake up shivering and zip it all up again, pulling my fleece snood over my head so I'm entirely cocooned. We'll have more warm days, I'm sure, but the timeless passage of summer is indeed over.

I'm awoken mid-morning by the noise of a helicopter. Sound is so odd here. The rumbling and clattering in the sky seems very close, but for all I know the helo could be over on the far side of McMurdo

Sound, kilometres away. Last night one went past as I was cooking dinner, transporting Pete Wilson, David's counterpart at Cape Bird, for his two-week stint there. Inside the hut it sounded so loud that I thought it was coming in to our makeshift landing pad, and I stepped outside to watch for it. Instead it was a tiny dot over the lower slopes of Mount Erebus behind us.

It is still nearly –5°C when I get up and stumble into the hut from my tent, and there's again a stiff breeze blowing from the south, bringing with it a few flakes of snow. This is the first morning in weeks that I've turned the propane heater up to high. During band-search before lunch I am thankful for the hand-warmers that I tucked inside my gloves before stepping outside. Keeping hands elevated and holding tightly to binoculars soon becomes unbearable in this wind. When I see David down at the colony and stop to say good morning, he says, "Fall is on its way." I think it's already here.

Another New Zealand Artists and Writers Programme group arrive today, bringing an absolute mountain of gear—tents and stoves and emergency survival gear and crates of food—even though they are only staying for three days. There is no such thing as travelling light in Antarctica, but even so, this seems like overkill. On the way back for lunch I stop by to say hello and introduce myself. Aaron, their AFT escort, is tall and lanky, with what sounds to me like an Aussie accent. He tells me he is off to tackle some of the major South American peaks in the early fall. "After that, maybe somewhere in the northern hemisphere," he says, another mountaineer following the seasons like a migratory bird.

Laurence is the only woman of the group. She is writing a novel about pioneering biologists Euan Young and Rowley Taylor, and their time here in the 1960s studying skuas and penguins. I don't understand how one can transpose a unique factual event into fiction but then I'm not a fiction writer, and perhaps I'll soon find out as I've invited myself and my second-last bottle of wine down for a visit tomorrow night. The third member of their group is Patrick, a composer, who intends to write music inspired by the rather non-musical calls of the Adélies, Grahame's farewell logbook entry notwithstanding. Still, he comes back from having stood above the colony talking about call and response and other musical terms whose meaning I can only dimly guess at, so it seems he's getting material already.

David and I will be attaching a TDR to a penguin later this afternoon, in a part of the colony where the Kiwis will be able to see us from their watching post; if they later ask what we were up to I'll tell them that we were holding down the bird and reading it Coleridge as part of our own Artists and Writers Program, and that it responded favourably. And who knows what stories a penguin could tell . . .

When I walk back down to the colony after lunch, Aaron is standing outside the wanigan, smoking a cigarette. A cigarette. I'd quite forgotten about them. It's the first time I've seen someone putting fingers to lips and exhaling smoke since I've been down here, and it looks very alien and vaguely sexual. I stop for a chat, of course.

In town at Scott Base it's apparently freezing cold with a nasty wind. He tells me about their AFT course for Scott Base personnel, confirming that it's a lot more fun than the one put on at McMurdo. Not only do the Kiwis get lowered down a crevasse, they also get to walk through an icefall. I learn that the training used to be joint with McMurdo until, presumably, some risk manager at the US Antarctic Program nixed it. And it turns out that all the AFT guys knew the mountaineers killed back in New Zealand in that avalanche a couple of weeks ago.

"There are only, what, just over a hundred of us mountain guides in New Zealand?" said Aaron, looking suddenly strained. "We all know each other."

—

It has been snowing off and on all evening, small dry flakes that make a whispering noise as they blow across the canvas roof of the hut. I go out before dinner to fill the snowmelt container. With the recent warm weather and now the sudden dip in air temperature, our mushy snowbank has solidified into ice, making it hard on shoulders and wrists to hack out chunks with the shovel. Despite the grim feel of this weather, in some ways I'm glad it's here given the recent consequences of warmer temperatures: the snowbank slowly melting down the hill; the difficulty of keeping perishables fresh; penguins and chicks panting in the colony.

By the time we have finished our meal it is heavily overcast outside, with a thick, uniform blanket of woolly grey cloud that's making the hut the darkest it's been all season. If we had a light I'd turn it on. After last night's splendid McMurdo Sound concerto of ice and sun and sky, it's as if Antarctica has gone into some big post-performance sulk. During our semi-regular evening chat with Cape Crozier, Grant reported it was snowing and very cold there too. But there's still a lot left to do before the season ends—more chick condition weighings, chick banding, another trip to Beaufort.

As I enter data on my laptop in the gloom, I feast my eyes on a collection of clothing I've gathered on my nearby shelf. I have deliberately stacked hats and scarves and neck gaiters so that their colours play off one another—mulberry against royal blue against scarlet against powder blue against turquoise against lilac and salmon. On my desk lie the colourful fruits of a couple of months of hoarding. There I have arranged brilliantly hued Christmas envelopes and bits of coloured writing paper, even the bright blue foil wrapping of a Belgian chocolate bar, gathering them together like a bowerbird, talismans against the monochromatic landscape outside. A full palette of colours will be one of the things I'll revel in when I return to The Other World. But I am not ready to leave, not yet.

—

Cape Royds has taken on a festive air. Yet another helicopter-load of Kiwis arrived today, joining the group already camped out at the wanigan—this time it's the inimitable David Harrowfield and his Antarctic Heritage Trust gang coming here via Cape Evans, with eighteen hundred kilos of gear. During their brief visit they'll be cleaning up the hut site (including the decaying heritage parsnips, I hope), inventorying Shackleton's hut itself, and doing other prep work for future restoration efforts. I'm almost sorry that David and I are going into town tomorrow as we'll miss some prime Antarctic socializing here. I traipse down the hill after dinner and data entry, taking with me the bottle of Jägermeister, still three-quarters full. Three Scott tents and a couple of mountaineering tents have been erected around the wanigan, and it has mushroomed into a village of nine inhabitants, complete with a plywood screen for the biffy, which now sports an occupied/unoccupied flag.

Most of the Kiwis are hanging out around the door of the hut when I arrive, swapping stories and telling jokes. The Jägermeister is met with the usual insults and derision ("Oh, a *herbal* beverage!") but is soon dispatched to comments like "Not bad after all!" and "More, please!" I am reminded of our Christmas Day Santa party. I've noticed a remarkable consistency in responses to the Jägermeister bottle since I've been offering it to camp visitors.

At 9:30 p.m. Aaron hangs the hand-held VHF on a hook on the outer wall of the hut and we listen to the nightly Scott Base news digest, read out over the airwaves by a laconic comms operative with a lapsing Irish accent. He drones through a monotone account of the recent increase in oil prices, an outdoor concert of Elvis impersonators back in New Zealand ("the Elvis lookalike wiped the rain from his hairy chest"), and a human-interest story about a ninety-year-old who drove off a burglar with a carving knife. Next are the sports, and, as always, a couple of the radio operator's risqué jokes to wrap it all up.

We all stand around in the cold and drink wine and laugh at silly things. It has turned into a fine evening, with plenty of big flakes of snow falling to add to the atmosphere, and no breeze. Aaron very kindly loans me his overcoat and spare gloves, seeing as how I went down to the wanigan attired for several-people-in-the-hut coziness rather than open-air partying with cold beverages. The people include Fiona Wills, trust administrator of the Antarctic Heritage Trust, who is lovely and who has invited me back down for a meal while they're here. Julian is a restoration expert of some sort who is originally from the UK but has lived in Sydney for twenty years, a stay that has not softened his upper-class accent, or the accompanying horsey look, but has slightly softened his approach to life, and he is jovially relaxed among us commoners, although I notice he's retained an annoying habit of asking a barrage of clever questions without stopping to listen to their answers. It turns out that his father is the former Bishop of Bath and Wells, so I mention an old scandal surrounding my uncle, former head verger at a famous English cathedral, who was forced to resign following revelation of his affair with the organist's wife. His resignation was newsworthy at the time, coming as it did on the heels of a series of sex scandals in the Church. When I mention it Julian looks pained and says nothing, so I assume he's heard of it, and it still rankles.

Someone else starts talking about the group's work here. Much of what they've been doing during their brief visit is inventories and site assessment in preparation for the preservation work proposed to begin next year. It sounds as if the majority of the artifact conservation, as well as hut repair, will take place on site at Cape Royds. This will involve huge logistical hurdles, so one member of their party is here to look at camp deployment and management issues while Julian and another team member are assessing the heritage conservation work itself. Conversation inevitably drifts to the topic of the local wildlife, and Julian tells me that earlier today he fled headlong from an attack by the fierce skua pair over the ridge to the north, stumbling, falling, and breaking the lens off his new and expensive camera. He is perversely grateful when I tell him that skuas have drawn human blood as recently as last month and as close by as Cape Bird (I heard this one night during a radio sked), clearly feeling that his flight was prudent after all, camera or no camera.

David Harrowfield grows progressively more wasted ("Wasted! Do you know that word in Canada?" he asks repeatedly) as the evening progresses. He has the visage of a happy drunk, though, with apple cheeks, a ready grin, and a twinkle in his eye. I tell him I've read about him in British author Sara Wheeler's beautiful book *Terra Incognita,* and he exclaims that he could have sued her for the portrayal of him as "an eccentric *bon viveur,*" and would have, except for the fact that he knew her "quite well."

"She didn't even get it right," he says indignantly. "It's *bon vivant*!"

As people gradually drift off to their tents, I go into the wanigan to get warm and hide from the big drifting flakes of snow that are now coming down heavily. Visibility is worsening and the weather socking in, and I am starting to wonder about our flight tomorrow. David Harrowfield plies me with hot liquids and more stories, and then Patrick and Aaron come in from where they've been lurking by the door, finally shutting it on the biting cold.

"About fucking time!" I say, which we all end up deciding, probably with unoriginal insight, is what AFT really stands for. This inevitably descends into a semi-inebriated conversation about other things it could stand for, and the sharing of a chilly can of Guinness; then Patrick and I teach Aaron some Spanish swear words for his upcoming trip to South America. The Antarctic Heritage Trust crew is only here until Saturday and I think most of the gear they've brought with them is comestibles; this includes a case of wine and an entire raft of beer, all to last them about three days. It turns out that this David is the self-styled "Duke of Halswell" whose business card I found a couple of weeks ago on a solo visit to the wanigan.

"I thought you were some British tosser," I tell him. He laughs, eyes twinkling, although wickedly this time.

After the Guinness we go outside again and the snow has stopped. Through a rent in the clouds the sun casts down light on the splendour of the landscape, dusted as it now is with a fine coating of snow. Patrick stretches and announces he's about to turn in.

"You can't go to bed!" exclaims Harrowfield loudly. "You have too much work to do!"

The truth spoken through the overstated words of the drunken man. I know what he means; I feel the same way every night now. Last week I looked at a calendar for maybe the first time since arriving over seven weeks ago. The endless days make this feel like a timeless place. But today marks two months that I've been here. I have felt as if Cape Royds, and me with it, has stood still in the middle of a stream, with time flowing on past us like water. Now, however, time is catching up with us again.

I say my farewells and return to our hut, then get my camera and go back down again—something about the soft dusting of snow running down the sides of the Scott tents against the freshly coated landscape draws me back. Patrick is still outside, taking notes and photographs and about to fetch his recording equipment to take advantage of the penguin calls echoing in the utter stillness of this post-blizzard air. Apparently he's realized that Harrowfield was absolutely right.

At nine thirty the next morning I stop by the wanigan to say goodbye to the Kiwi Artists and Writers gang, as they are leaving early for Scott Base.

"What are *you* doing up?!" exclaims Aaron, as if it were 5 a.m. Good question, but it's a town day. Patrick is looking a little worse for wear.

We do our third chick weighing of the season this morning. Many of the chicks are now big enough (and annoyed enough by previous weighings) to flee when they see us approaching and so we use a soft fish-landing net to catch the older ones. For the first three or four weeks of their lives, Adélie chicks are always attended by one or both parents, but after this "guard stage" the chicks are left to fend for themselves, and they begin to gather in multi-chick groups called crèches. By the time these young penguins leave the nest, they and their parents can recognize each other, mostly by voice; thus a crèched chick can find its parent, and vice versa, despite being away from the original nest site. The older Cape Royds chicks have just started to crèche over the past day or two and now they can be seen in the subcolonies lying asleep in piles of threes and fours, floppy dark grey bundles of guano-streaked down with beaks and bellies and fat pink feet protruding.

Satellite data from our tagged birds, downloaded via a satellite phone link and rendered into an email from CLS Argos, show that the parents are foraging not far north, probably just up around Wohlschlag Bay between here and Cape Bird. These short foraging trips mean the chicks are getting plenty of food, and they're continuing to grow apace. Mean mass of chicks from today's weigh is 1,790 grams, up from 1,141 grams a week ago. They are pooping apace too. During the weighing I was wearing my parka to ward off the chill wind, and the front of it is now absolutely drenched in fishy-smelling pink and white and green guano. My clothing is getting to the state where its smell regularly permeates my consciousness as I'm walking around, even though I'm inured to it by weeks in the field.

At 2 p.m. the helicopter arrives to transport us to McMurdo for what may be our last in-town break of the season. It is a big Bell 212, already loaded with some other passengers, including Coast Guard liaison officer April Brown out to view the tanker in the sea ice channel (or out on a boondoggle, depending on one's level of cynicism). We pile a substantial load of garbage and surplus gear on board and then climb in ourselves and promptly fill the helicopter with the stink of penguin. The other passengers are perfectly polite about it, I must say, but if I find the smell strong, they must find it overwhelming.

Our flight takes us overland along the shore: Since the helicopters can't fly over open water, we can't follow the route of the old sea ice road any longer. More of the ice has broken out between the Barne Glacier and the edge of Backdoor Bay, and a couple of polynyas are forming near Cape Evans. The sky is clear today and in the afternoon light the whole world gleams, polished by the wind. The glacial slopes of Mount Erebus roll away beneath us, undulating and perfect as the giant sand dunes of the Sahara until they reach the frozen sea and cascade downward like soft icing slumping down the side of a cake. Behind Scott Base and McMurdo, Castle Rock looms up to meet us, ochre and craggy, and then we're swooping out over the white ocean at the junction where the ice shelf meets the ice-covered sea, and huge swells stand frozen in time as they crash slow-motion into each other and into the shore. We round Pram Point, where the ugly scar of McMurdo comes into view, and land at Helo Ops, removing our flight helmets as we wait for the blades of the helicopter to stop turning.

Our trip to Mactown is okay, but the thought of Cape Royds and the work awaiting us tugs at me the whole time I'm there. I go over to American Night at Scott Base with my in-town roommate Sarika, her friend Jen, and Jen's extroverted boyfriend Gary. Gary calls Jen his "ice wife" and tells me, "Yep, back at home I've got the wife, the kids, the mortgage, the whole disaster." The term "ice wives" (and husbands) refers to long-term relationships that endure season after season among the McMurdo Station workers, kept secret—one presumes—from their legal families back in the USA. They are a common enough occurrence down here that there's a name for them. We go out to the parking lot outside 155 and wait for the Scott Base shuttle, which duly arrives. Gary stands around gossiping to a friend until well after the shuttle van's scheduled departure time, prominently displayed to all on a post adjacent to his head, until finally the driver honks and yells at him to get on board. "Clearly not ready to go back to The Real World," remarks the passenger sitting beside me.

Entering Scott Base is always a pleasure, its warm and homey feeling like an embrace after the barracks-like anonymity of McMurdo. The door to the Kiwi bar sports a sign telling those who enter that if you wear a hat you've got to buy the bar a drink, but the punch line is that the sign is in Japanese. There's a novel system of drinks payment on American Night, a longstanding Thursday tradition where the Scott Base bar hosts McMurdoites: A basket sits on the corner of the bar and you throw a few dollars into it when you enter. Then when you order your drinks the bartender takes the amount due from the basket; as as long as there's money in there the drinks keep flowing for whoever cares to order them. Rumour has it that there's usually a heap of money left at the end of the night and so the Kiwis drink for free on Friday evenings—which is why American Night is on a Thursday.

We end up hanging out with a group of four Kiwi military personnel who have just got back from a month out at Cape Adare far to the north, cleaning up the debris remaining at the old station huts. They tell us that New Zealand military personnel compete to volunteer for trips to Antarctica, and the competition is intense despite the fact that most of them spend their stay chipping ice out from underneath the old base buildings while enduring horrible weather—another example of the difference between Kiwi and US attitudes to the Antarctic. These four feel they've hit the jackpot and are a delight to talk to, still raving with overflowing enthusiasm about Cape Adare and the penguins. They and four base staff lived for thirty days at a site far more remote than Cape Royds, and they unreservedly loved it.

I stay at the Scott Base bar for a couple of drinks, hop the shuttle back to McMurdo and end up in Crary, reading and sending emails. Received are a couple from Grahame, to which he's appended letters he had written to friends while still down here. They are full of his trademark wisdom, and droll and incisive observations about Antarctica and its human residents.

Just after midnight I take a break and go over to the Galley, where they are serving crab legs at midrats. In the cafeteria lineup I run into one of the crew of the helicopter that picked us up at Royds to take us out to the *Polar Sea*. He keeps rabbiting on about how they landed in the wrong place and had screwed up but wanted to do the best they could and how they did it right the second time, and he keeps it up to the point where I wonder whether there is something wrong with him. After a couple of minutes I clue in to the fact that he is merely drunk, but it's been so long since I've seen anyone shitfaced (with the exception of David Harrowfield last night) that it takes me ages to realize the guy isn't just a simpleton. I eat a solitary meal while reading the *Times Digest* "newspaper," a Mactown wire service compilation of mostly missable news, and then go back to Crary for more emailing until 3:30 a.m. I am so tired by the time I finish that I am starting to go cross-eyed, and when I stand up my knees are wobbly. Funny thing, all this sunlight. It makes you feel like you can just keep staying awake, but eventually your body disagrees.

So back out to Royds at noon, on an A-Star this time, and I am happy to return. The smaller A-Stars leap into the air in a sprightly way, in contrast to the big Bell 212s, which take off with a powerful surge like an elephant getting to its feet. I already miss the tranquility of our camp, as usual, and am looking forward to visiting with our new

Kiwi neighbours. On the way out we see a pod of twenty-five killer whales cavorting amongst the brash ice and bergy bits in the middle of the icebreakers' channel. Today has seen nothing but clear blue skies and little wind, but the weather continues its gradual descent into autumn and the sea surface in the channel is already beginning to refreeze, bits of frozen surface water growing in extent until they touch each other, bumping in circles to form pancake ice. For the past couple of days the mercury has not climbed above zero.

In the afternoon I do the daily shoreline watch, looking out for the elusive leopard seal, while the sun hangs in a clear sky and is reflected from the ocean with a tropical glare. It renders the remnant fast ice beach-like, white sands instead of wave-lapped frozen shore, and the black rocks poking up through the pale submerged foot of the ice look as dark as coral heads under the turquoise waters. I squint at the scene and fancy the waiting penguins to be standing on an equatorial beach like their relatives in the Galapagos, though this is a vision that is hard to sustain in the frigid breezes drifting down across the frozen sea to our south.

Before dinner I sit outdoors on our little makeshift deck, writing with the laptop balanced on my lap; periodically I look up to be mesmerized by the pack ice drifting about the bay, doing a hypnotically slow ballet that's lit by the evening sun as it traces its slow dip toward the horizon. The air is utterly still under a blue watercolour wash of a sky. Countless bergy bits float lazily amongst the corrugated surface of the pack, and the way the light falls on them is worthy of endless study. Their folds and crevices are stained with smoke-coloured shadows while the sun illuminates their angular exposed faces with a sort of oceanic alpenglow. In the leads between the floes, the mirror-still surface of the sea is a pastel blue that is more sublime than the sky. Every so often one skua chases another up the gully toward the hut, and the rush of their wings through the unmoving evening air breaks the silence like an approaching jet. Occasionally I can hear the slow, measured breaths of a minke whale as it surfaces a kilometre or more offshore amongst the ice floes.

David and I dine with the Antarctic Heritage Trust gang since they're leaving tomorrow. I'm sad about their departure, as I've immensely enjoyed having neighbours again; one's neighbours in Antarctica are always interesting. Mike, one of the logistics guys, is Welsh and ex–British Antarctic Survey; he has stunning blue eyes in a tanned face under dark hair. He talks about working at Rothera Base for a number of seasons so I ask him if he was there when Sara Wheeler spent the time she describes in her book.

"Sara bloody Wheeler?" growls the normally sanguine Mike. "She was a royal pain in the arse!" He goes on to tell me that all the men at Rothera had bent over backward to be nice to her but despite that, all she did in her book was complain about how unfriendly everyone was.

David Harrowfield chimes in and demands to know who really cared whether or not she had been able to find a place to throw away her used tampons, and asks rhetorically why she'd had to put that in a book.

This is the most impassioned speech I have heard since arriving on the continent and I no longer have the social skills to say anything in the face of such vehemence, so remain silent. I do wonder about the other side of this story. It wouldn't surprise me if Wheeler had encountered hostility—the British Antarctic Survey's policies didn't allow women to overwinter until sometime in the 1990s. I could see it as having evolved into the kind of place that was friendly to women as long as they didn't do unpleasant things like draw attention to the fact that they menstruated, or to the reality of tampons.

The conversation meanders, and midway through the evening David Harrowfield puts on a hat from Kyrgyzstan; it is made from black-and-white felt and is in the shape of a large morel mushroom. With the hat perched above his wickedly twinkling eyes and ruddy cheeks, he looks like a jolly gnome. We all talk of hut restoration and penguins and politics and the arts, and work our way through cheese and biscuits and wine, then curry and beer and coffee, perching on food boxes and packing crates outside the open door of the green wanigan, all of us bundled up snugly against the autumnal Antarctic air. I translate Kiwi English for the Americans in the group ("chutney" is a bit of a challenge but after some thought becomes "relish"), and have my own translation problem when a request for black tea (instead of herbal) results in the arrival of orange pekoe tea without milk. The evening light is pure and golden and so is our meal together. Another minke whale surfaces to breathe in front of the colony just before dinner and I take photographs of everyone because the light is so beautiful, and, accordingly, so are they. It is only the second night of the season to have been this calm and clear, and it has been wonderful to share it with others.

Sometime during the evening I realize that I am truly happy here. At Cape Royds, I have found peace and tranquility.

22

MOST OF THE Antarctic Heritage Trust gang leave Royds first thing the next morning, departing in a Scott Base helicopter. Their helo arrives full of people and gear and deposits these new visitors to replace those leaving. The new group is here through Antarctica New Zealand: a staff member from the Canterbury Museum; an entrepreneur based in New Zealand and London who has invented some sort of aquatic car or terrestrial boat; and Bonnie Burnham, head of the World Monuments Fund and based in New York. Apparently Shackleton's hut is on their list of the world's one hundred most endangered monuments, and this ties in with the conservation work that the heritage group has been here to assess all week. Despite the fact that it has started to feel crowded out here with all these visitors, I have come to realize that I'm not quite as anti-social as I believed myself to be at the start of the season. Just before they got here I had periodically been hearing helicopters flying by, on their way to the Dry Valleys or some other remote spot, and willing them to land.

David Harrowfield and Julian have stayed on for the day to show the new visitors around the hut site, and so at the end of the afternoon I find myself at the helipad, sprawled on the ground amidst a mountain of gear and crates of empties, talking to Harrowfield and a woman from the Christchurch Antarctic Centre while they all wait for their helicopter to return. A thick layer of freezing mist hovers above the sea ice at Cape Evans, obscuring the lower half of Inaccessible Island and turning into a dense white band of cloud closer to McMurdo, where all aircraft are doubtless grounded as a result.

"Bloody helicopter's two hours late," grumbles David Harrowfield lazily as he lounges against some luggage. But the sky is clear and in the shelter of the pile of gear it is warm, so it's a good day for a delay.

"So, you ready to go home?" he asks me.

"I don't know," I say. "I'll really miss this place."

"Well, it can't go on forever," he barks in his no-nonsense way. "Don't you want to go home and clean up a bit?" And he goes on to talk about being barred from his local for the week before Christmas.

At the colony's seasonal peak a few days ago there were more penguins here than David has ever seen at Royds. This despite the fact that only half as many pairs were counted during the New Zealand flyover in early December as at that time the previous year. It's apparent that for many of the pairs, this season's breeding was delayed or missed because of asynchronous returns of mated individuals, presumably a result of the heavy spring ice conditions caused by the giant iceberg. Now the number of banded adults we're seeing on our daily search is suddenly decreasing and the colony is quietening as the non-breeders start to give up their territories and return to sea. The seasonal and hormonal ties that have bound them together are already weakening, and I haven't been flipper-slapped in several days: Summer is beginning to draw to a close for the penguins too. This morning I saw the season's first two fully moulted Adélie chicks, sleek in their new plumage, though they're still sporting mangy-looking tufts of down on various parts of their heads and faces, like victims of a bad shave. The chicks first start to resemble adults from the bottom up, with some requiring a second look to confirm their age if only the feet and tail are glimpsed in the melee of the colony. Eye colour and beak shape still remain unmistakably babyish even in the largest chicks, and a foppish topknot of downy feathers will stay with most of them until fledging time, the unreachable (for the chick) top of the head always being the last place that any young bird loses its down.

And although I saw the skuas take a large chick today, the majority of the young penguins who are still being fed by their harassed-looking parents will now survive to go to sea: They are mostly too big for the skuas and there appears to be plenty of food around Cape Royds to feed them through to fledging. The wide-eyed chicks are bursting with life and eager for the next phase of it. In the next couple of weeks they will leave the colony and enter the ocean for the first time in their young lives, at only about fifty to sixty days of age.

I do my shoreline watch in the afternoon, sitting up on the bluff with my back to the cold southerly wind as I munch through my last chocolate-banana Bumper Bar while scanning for leopard seals. Where it meanders down to the open water of McMurdo Sound, the Pony Lake meltwater stream has carved a deep channel through the remaining fast ice, now thickly algae-lined from a summer of being fertilized by guano, and the penguins are using this watercourse as an approach to the colony. From my perch high on the bluff they remind me exactly of salmon swimming upstream, quick dark torpedo shapes against a murky moss-green river bottom.

The Antarctic Heritage Trust and its affiliated individuals have been replaced by the Historic Hut Deterioration Assessment Project, a New Zealand and US team led by Roberta Farrell of the University of

Waikato and Bob Blanchette at the University of Minnesota, and an even larger village is surrounding the wanigan. This particular group is here on Ross Island to look at biological agents of deterioration in the historic huts. These are the people who found anthrax spores at the Cape Evans hut; but not being content with that they're now sampling the meat from some of the tins of food here at Shackleton's abode to see if they can come up with some botulism. What a fun bunch. They've also found a new species of fungus amongst the ones attacking the wood at the Cape Evans hut. Main threats to that hut: fungi. Main threat here: ablation of wood by wind-driven gravel and snow.

These people are among the best in the world in their respective sub-fields and it's been fascinating to have these two groups here, focused as they are on a different sort of conservation than the biological kind that David and I are immersed in. Over evening drinks and the occasional afternoon cup of tea at the wanigan I've been party to lots of discussion about the pros and cons of preserving the hut and its contents versus just letting it meet its natural end through collapse and decay and eventual oneness with the environment, and about on-site versus off-site artifact conservation, with the hut conservation groups containing representatives of both sides of each debate.

I find myself solidly in the "just let it fall down" camp. Though the hut is a comforting presence here, I see nothing wrong with leaving it to meet its maker just like the rest of us will have to do. But the hut preservationists have already won the debate, of course; that is why they are all here, in preparation for the work that is to come. I can't help wishing that society would focus its preservationist efforts on the need to ensure that penguins and other seabirds—and their ecosystems—persist far into the future. Historically, penguins were hunted en masse for their blubber just like whales and seals—herded alive into trypots or bludgeoned to death and then rendered into oil—on remote islands such as South Georgia and the Falklands. In the late 1800s and early

1900s more than three million king and royal penguins were killed on Australia's subantarctic Macquarie Island alone. So extreme was the slaughter that it formed a focus for bird conservation efforts worldwide, led by the likes of Lord Rothschild and Bill Wilson, famous by then for his voyages with Shackleton and Scott (with whom he was later to die on the return journey from the Pole). That slaughter was stopped, but today seabird species are disappearing in a slow act of attrition; penguins as a group face modern threats such as competition with humans for the krill and fish that form the mainstay of their diet, bycatch in net fisheries, introduction of terrestrial predators to islands, and of course climate change and its effects on marine food webs.

Though we don't have to contend with botulism, our own food situation is worsening. The cooler-in-the-snowbank substitute for a freezer has continued to be inadequate since the first warmish spell a month ago. Ambient temperatures have remained just cold enough to preserve frozen goods for a couple of weeks at a time, but not cold enough to keep them fully frozen for more than a couple of days. Frozen foods progress from solidity to being shot through with a few ice crystals in the space of about a week, like something at the back of an overly cold fridge. This means that the fish I pick up on our biweekly trips to Mactown remains safe to eat but tastes old by the time we get around to eating it. And by now our bread has been sitting outside for two and a half months, slowly desiccating in its semi-frozen state. Amazingly, it's still edible, but it is far from a gastronomic delight.

The variety of our meals is also diminishing as we run out of our favourite foods; with departure looming before the end of January, now only about ten days away, we no longer have enough time left out here to make it worthwhile to replace them. No more baked beans, canned tuna, bagels, or English muffins, and not much point in making more yoghurt once this batch is gone. But I am so fed up with eating canned and dried food that I don't have much appetite for our dwindling supplies anyway. What I crave are salads, and spicy Thai curries. At this stage of the season ingredients for these aren't much in evidence at McMurdo either, where incoming freshies are being bumped in favour of higher-priority supplies for the overwinterers and extra crew for the supply ship offload. Personnel from field camps and town alike are thinking fondly of Christchurch, with its balmy air and restaurants.

David and I move the weighbridge today. All season it has been collecting data from the penguins that traverse it. Corralled as they are by the orange snow fencing around their subcolony, the bridge has formed their only path to and from the sea. We've slowly been extending a fence around the adjacent subcolony, getting its occupants used to seeing the low-slung orange mesh nearby. Today it's time to close the gap in the fencing extension and immediately double the number of penguins that will be shuttling back and forth across our sophisticated scale. For an hour or so during our manoeuvres, all of the fencing is down and the weighbridge sits unfettered in its new location. But by now the birds from the original subcolony are so used to its forming part of their daily route that they seek out the unfenced bridge and walk up and over it as they enter and exit the colony, as bound to their daily routine as commuters everywhere.

The weather as we work is gloomy, overcast, and cold—another hand-warmer day, with a few hard flakes of snow falling. After dinner I go outside and use a hammer to break the ice on the ground outside our back door, something I've had to do for the past two days as the seepage from our huge drinking water snowdrift has begun refreezing in the shade right behind the hut, creating a hazard whenever we venture out to the malodorous toilet bucket. As I did back in November, I stand in front of the propane heater to warm up before going out to my tent—no longer as cozy a prospect as it was a couple of weeks ago.

With the external shift in the weather I begin to feel an internal shift too. My farewell conversation with David Harrowfield has been on a playback loop in my mind, and I realize that he was right in saying I have to go home at some point. I love it here but it can't go on forever, and neither would I want it to. My fingernails are chronically dirty, my skin is breaking out from the infrequent washing, and my hair needs a cut. I'm getting tired of smelling like penguin and eating frozen and dehydrated foods. On top of that I'm now succumbing to the particularly nasty cold I've been fighting off since just after Aaron and the others got here, the dreaded lurgy that's been going around Scott Base. I will miss Cape Royds profoundly, but my mind is almost ready to turn toward home. After the purgatory of a one-room hut at the edge of the world, I am feeling lighter, pared down, my layers of grief sloughing away like the skin of a snake.

In *H Is for Hawk*, Helen Macdonald writes of fleeing to the wild on a "quest . . . inspired by grief or sadness"[51] in the tradition of the Scottish American naturalist John Muir, a desire she later decides is misguided because what she really needed was the company of other people. But I have found that Muir was right: "Nature in her green, tranquil woods heals and soothes all afflictions . . . Earth has no sorrows that earth cannot heal."[52] In the Antarctic wilderness I have found the solace that had been denied to me in the company of others. In the cycling of the penguins' breeding seasons, year after year, decade after decade, I see parallels to our own lives. I have come to see how human life and death cycle too with the wheeling of the sun, that the penguins live and die, and that, like my sister, one day I will too. Yet life will go on, irrepressible. The knowledge of life's persistence beyond our own is one of the comforts that nature offers us.

23

IT'S THE NINETEENTH of January. A couple of big tabular bergs between five and ten kilometres in length have been wheeling about in front of Cape Royds all day, drifting in lazy circles with the pack ice and the lesser bergs. The light has been gorgeous, turning the world the colour of pale liquid amber, and I am planning to go out right after dinner to photograph the landscape and perhaps a couple of the skuas. But just after I arrive back at the hut to do our daily weather report (cloud cover 30 percent), a big front of thick, woolly-looking clouds, reminiscent of penguin chick down, rolls in like a steam train from the south. It's got to be the quickest weather change I've seen since we've been here: I'd just photographed the view from the ridge on my way back to the hut twenty minutes ago and the sky was clear for tens of kilometres to the south.

The Historic Hut Deterioration Assessment Project (they've certainly summarized their mission in a name) pulled out this afternoon. After a week of Kiwi visitors the place felt empty when the second helicopter finally lifted off. It took two full loads in a Bell 212 to get them out of here, which is pretty impressive given that they were here for only two and a half days. We have been here for two and a half months, and I think we brought less gear than they did. But if the weather doesn't continue to pick up we'll have more visitors tomorrow. The battery for the weighbridge computer is not charging properly, despite our various recent injections of replacement bits such as extra solar panels, so Solar Joe is due out from town to fix it.

Down at the colony, the number of penguins continues to drop daily, and the local ambience is gradually changing from that of a teeming metropolis to that of a busy small town. Only 74 banded birds sighted today, down from 115 last week. And following on the first few fully moulted chicks three days ago, moulting chicks are suddenly everywhere with their bare chins and bellies, their emerging backs clad in sleek new plumage the colour of a ripe blackberry. Most of the young birds in the colony now appear to be sporting dashing little masks as the fuzzy down around their eyes is some of the first to go, leaving the dark new plumage visible. The air is adrift with pale, weightless tufts of grey, reminding me irresistibly of late springtime in the foothills of the Rockies, when the cottonwood trees are shedding their fluffy seeds to drift upon the breeze like thistledown.

During our group check-in with MacOps tonight, I hear Grant mention to the radio operator that he and Viola and Rachael are entering their last week at Cape Crozier. They are pulling out on the twenty-sixth of January, and Cape Bird will be done on the twenty-fifth, before which we'll go to Crozier to help with chick banding. I don't know yet when we're leaving, but it too will likely be within the week. It feels surreal to contemplate leaving here, almost as if I have never known anything other than ice and penguins, sea and sky, black and white.

After the call I ask David if he's decided yet when we'll be going. Hard to be here and not know. "I need some time to say goodbye," I tell him.

"Start saying goodbye," he replies.

We will nonetheless be leaving camp a bit later than the other two penguin crews, as the timing of the penguins at Royds has been a week behind Crozier—although lately "our" chicks nearly seem to have caught up, given the plentiful food resources we've been seeing nearby in the sound. It's hard to believe, but there aren't many days left at Cape Royds before the penguins start to swim away northward for the season, and we too pack up our bags to leave. Then it will be back to The Other World, The Real World, The World, as it is variously known here. Back to the petty obligations of mowing the lawn, washing the car, paying the bills for the things we don't really need. Back to banks and blacktop, to darkness and door locks, to politicians and to war.

In the International Geophysical Year of 1957–58, the Antarctic Treaty was signed, designating this continent as a place of science and of international cooperation. It is still that. It's not just the incredible beauty of Antarctica that people miss when they leave. It's being somewhere that shows us what the world could be, a saner and more peaceable place. I have not missed home much since I've been here. It all seems so far away, not quite a dream, but not quite tangible either. In these few short weeks I seem to have shed much of my desire for civilization and all its distractions—the constant busyness, the half-alive hours spent online, possessions beyond the daily necessities of life. Instead of all that, a sure sense of purpose fills our days, our daily rhythms melded with those of the penguins. Cape Royds feels more like home than most homes ever have.

Geologist Raymond Priestley, who with the other five members of Scott's Northern Party survived an unplanned seven-month winter-over at Terra Nova Bay by living in an ice cave and subsisting on meagre rations of seal and penguin, wrote afterwards that "the luxuries of civilisation only fulfill the wants they create."[53] The cave was a meagre hole excavated when they realized their ship was not returning, kept away by an impenetrable ice pack; its ceiling was so low that standing upright was impossible; their clothes and sleeping bags were filthy with grease from blubber-oil spills; unrelentingly bad weather kept them confined inside; and they suffered food poisoning and diarrhea from tainted meat while living on starvation rations. At the start of the winter a hurricane stranded three of the men in a collapsed tent away from the cave: "We had had nothing to eat for twelve hours and were becoming very hungry. As there was a large lump of raw seal-meat handy, we gnawed at this, but it was so cold that it froze to our lips, and so hard that after we had eaten off the angles we could no longer make any impression upon it."[54] Yet in his memoirs Priestley wrote of the acute happiness afforded by their simple days, saying that this hardship interspersed with sweetness formed part of the "Call of the Antarctic."[55]

Solar Joe comes out at lunchtime to fix the charging system for the weighbridge, and it powers up all afternoon. Virtually all the banded penguins I see today are on their own, their mates absent, a departure from previous weeks when plentiful food nearby meant that pairs could lounge at the colony together. In an eventful season it has been an uneventful day—one of denouement. Even the weather was blasé—cloudy and sunny by turn; frigid, but not unbearably so. The barometer has been rising all day, however, and here, on the far side of the Looking Glass, rising barometric pressure often heralds bad weather: Perhaps we are in for a blow. I could almost welcome it before our stay ends—like a fond farewell from the harsh continent. It wouldn't do to have our departure marked by something as inconsequential as a mediocre day.

—

Tonight during shoreline watch the slight Antarctic tide is high and flooding more of the decaying fast ice than usual, like a flood plain to the diminishing Pony Lake stream. A couple of days ago the underwater ice was green with algae, rendering the penguins into fish in a mossy stream. This evening the upper portion of the submerged ice foot has turned the inshore water above it a brilliant turquoise like an illuminated swimming pool, or like the shallows of a tropical sea. The penguins swim in and out of the depths, leaving and entering the colony, flying under the water and over the sunken ice as swiftly as swallows darting about in an azure summer sky.

24

PLENTY OF VISITORS again this morning. I'm trying to convince myself to leave the cozy interior of my sleeping bag when I hear the whir of one of the US Coast Guard Dauphin helicopters. Their noise is distinctive, presumably because of that enclosed tail rotor. It quickly becomes apparent that the helo is heading in for a landing here at the hut, and so I drag on some extra clothes and squeeze out of the tent while the helicopter is still airborne and assessing the landing site. Last night's bad weather has blown itself out, but it is cold, −7°C or so. I stand in the door of the hut to watch the helo come in, then retreat indoors as it hovers just over the ground nearby and sends gravel flying everywhere. As usual during these landings, the canvas sides of the hut vibrate like a flag in a hurricane and I can hear my tent flapping madly, straining at its ropes outside.

Soon enough the helicopter shuts down and the passengers alight—a surprise visit from oceanographer Walker O. Smith, who has been doing plankton work out in the Ross Sea on the US research vessel *Nathaniel B. Palmer*. Today he is tagging along with NSF program manager Marie Bundy as she travels around McMurdo Sound to inspect some of the projects being funded this cycle before the season ends.

It is now the twenty-first of January and it's not just the penguin study that is wrapping up for the season. David appears over the ridge from the colony and escorts them off for a tour. The two helicopter crew members appear to be thrilled to have some Antarctic shore time and so they wander off too. Before parting ways we have a brief discussion about the fact that there's a tourist ship down in Backdoor Bay. I jog up to the ridge for a quick look and sure enough there's a small vessel parked in the sea ice, up fast against the side of the V-shaped gouge made there by the much larger *Kapitan Khlebnikov* a couple of weeks ago. The passengers are black upright figures travelling slowly over the sea in single file. At this middling distance they look like penguins.

After a face wash and a quick fried breakfast—last night's reconstituted dried potato slices with an ancient egg from our dwindling stores, and a cup of tea—it is time to go down to the colony. By now the tourists are milling about Shackleton's hut like expectant cattle, obediently respecting the occupancy limits and awaiting their turn to go inside. The ship, it transpires, is the *Akademik Shokalskiy*, an Australian-run vessel operated out of New Zealand, passengers primarily Kiwis and Aussies. It all seems a little less snappy, a little more worn around the edges, than the *Khlebnikov* group. Not sure what it is—less glitz and no helicopters, or just a burned-out end-of-season crew in the lowering grey morning. None of the staff or passengers go up to the lookout to watch the penguins, in marked contrast to the enthusiasm and solicitous regard shown by crew and passengers on the *Khlebnikov*. I don't linger long with them. End of a long and isolated field season or not, I feel a bit burned out on people after our week of visitors. And they all seem intent on Shackleton's hut in a way that suggests it's merely something to check off on their trip list.

I do chew out one of the visitors later, however, a passenger who has wandered south along the line of ASPA markers, traversing three skua territories as he does so. Since informing passengers about the

Antarctic Treaty and its Environmental Protocol protection measures—and the obligation of every visitor to adhere to these—is a condition of every tour ship's permit, it is inconceivable that he has not heard several times by now of the requirement to maintain a minimum distance from wildlife. None of the cruise staff is in sight to provide the necessary reminder. The skua chick in one of the territories has just been chasing after its parents and soliciting food (some nice regurgitated fish), taking it well within the protected area boundary, but the other two chicks, still too young to move, happen to be right in Mr. Tourist's path. So intent is he on photographing the dramatic image of a territorial and protective skua that he doesn't notice the small chick it is defending, a couple of metres from his right boot, though the chick is fortunately off to one side of his route. I watch with supreme irritation as he advances further on the parent, takes some more photos, and then backtracks to the first nest. He starts to repeat the process there, stepping closer to the adult with camera raised, until I stomp over and tell him he's disturbing the bird on its nest and needs to back off.

"Yes, I could tell I was disturbing it and that's why I backed off," he says, avoiding my eyes.

He shoulders his camera and scuttles back to the hut, where his shipmates are still congregated, ignoring the penguins. Presumably they have already ticked the Adélie penguin box at some previous stop. I glare after him, adrenaline slowly subsiding, sharing a sidelong glance with the still-ruffled skua as it settles back down near its chick.

I go for a walk up to the old navigational cairn just before dinner. From the lookout the sea is as flat as a polished silver tray, and to the north, where the clouds sit thick and low, the water shows the faded mauves and yellows of an aging bruise. From time to time the sun's ghost appears, a pale platinum disc in the overcast sky. The clouds are heavy and I can almost feel them pressing down on my head; the weather seems pensive and watchful, summer contemplating its own demise.

It starts snowing as I leave the cairn. On the way back I find the ruined remnants of some previous field worker's standard-issue ski goggles and am reminded of one of David Harrowfield's stories, a parody of the compulsion to call everything old here a historical artifact. On a trip to the Larsemann Hills he reportedly found some junky piece of old wood someone had stashed near their supplies cache there. "Artefact no. 434, Larsemann Hills," they'd written on one side of it, and "Read other side" on the other.

We do our fourth chick weighing of the season, and the nestlings, now much larger and more vigorous, aren't as easy to hold as last time. Nonetheless, when I gently handle their downy bodies it remains a profound connection with another being. I ease their fat little bums into the weighing sack (a geological samples bag of a utilitarian bleached cotton), which gets suspended from the hook on our spring balance. And the chicks are very fat! Average weight today is 2,882 grams (more than 1,000 grams above last week's mean) but a couple of the twenty individuals we randomly select to represent the colony are nearly 4,500 grams—possibly even heavier than some of the busy parents at this point, though with so much food around perhaps not. Even these very large chicks still retain their typical pear shape, barely, though the round bellies are now dirty white, with only a few disreputable little tufts of down remaining. And most of them still have typical chick flippers, which appear oversized, floppy, boneless, and quiver like aspic as the chicks shake themselves. After the weigh I am covered in the filamentous grey plumes of chick down that are now ubiquitous in the colony, and I smell like krill-scented chick shit. They are cranking out a lot of the stuff if they're eating enough to gain a kilogram in a week—about a 50 percent increase over last week's body weight.

A chill and overcast morning has turned into a clear and brilliant evening, a view of white pack ice and tabular bergs the perfect counterpoint to indigo sea and periwinkle sky, each colour somewhere on the spectrum of purity: virginal white, eternal blue. Erebus has emerged from its attendant wreath of clouds, and I am glad because I want to feast my eyes on its gleaming slopes at least once more before we leave. I go out after dinner to take some photos and am screeched at by the neighbourhood skua pair as I pass their chick at a safe distance. I finish by photographing a penguin and then lying on my stomach nearby to watch it from bird's eye level. Two other penguins approach from different directions, curious about this large object lying in the middle of their path to the sea. One goes around me, but the other stretches forward, unafraid, looking. It disappears for a moment and then reappears in my field of vision to drop a stone in my general direction. Apart from the emperors serenading me, it is the most romantic thing I have had happen in nearly three months, and I am profoundly moved. Such is the act of taking a photograph, taking an image that you can carry away with you forever, allowing it to be imprinted on your memory as you view it numerous times later on, that I know I will remember this particular penguin years later: what he looked like as he bowed to me, and the shape of the ridge between hut and colony where our tentative courtship took place. Eventually and inevitably the two of us part ways, the penguin drawn by the pull of the ocean, and I driven by tiredness back to the hut, a pre-bed cocoa, and my sleeping bag.

I leave my tent at one in the morning to pee. The sky is completely clear and the sun is now low in the sky, the light almost tangible. Out on the water the ice does its endless dance and looks as if it is all on fire, lit from within.

25

WE'VE HAD AN hour and a half's notice over the radio that we're flying to Cape Crozier to assist with penguin banding today instead of tomorrow as scheduled. I'm grumpy about having to rush up from the penguin colony, where I was in the middle of the day's work. When I get back to the hut I throw clothes, bedding, and field equipment hurriedly into bags and bolt down some lunch. But it's a perfect day for the flight, a cloudless sky and unlimited visibility; later tomorrow there's bad weather coming in. The helicopter's clatter can be heard approaching just as I'm finishing my mug of tea out on the deck, leaning against our pile of waiting bags.

We load our gear on board and take off into a peerless sky, then turn and make for Mount Erebus. We fly past its northern flank at nine thousand feet; away to the north in the open waters of the Ross Sea, the massive berg B-15A stretches to the horizon, there to bend with the curvature of the Earth. Past Erebus lie Mounts Terror and Terra Nova, rearing up out of the glacial sheet that's covering Ross Island like a voluptuous sheet of marzipan or a drapery of royal icing. Ross Island's glaciers flow away below us to the south and east, to join the white expanse of the Ross Ice Shelf. The shelf itself stretches toward the south, where eventually, out of sight, it rises up to meet the glaciated continental land mass. There, everything disappears into a white haze that obscures the horizon, and Antarctica vanishes into the blank nothingness of the icy mists that shroud it like mystery. We chase the shadow of our helicopter toward our destination, an insignificant dot fleeing across the monochrome landscape beneath us.

Ahead is Cape Crozier with its vast Adélie penguin colony of hundreds of thousands of birds, but first we fly over the peak named after David last year; in Antarctica, it is still possible for non-politicians to be immortalized in geography. Like many aspects of human life in Antarctica, place-naming is managed under the Antarctic Treaty, and in this case David's name was proposed by the US to recognize his colossal contribution to Antarctic research.

"How does it feel?" I ask him.

He inspects the mountain through his window, and over my headset I hear him mumble something in modest tones. Even for someone who has spent as many years in Antarctica as he has, I imagine this to be a rather overwhelming honour. As we approach the landing site I can see far below us where the Cape Crozier emperor penguin colony had formed in the lee of a deep crack in the ice shelf, the colony site now just visible as a dark guano stain on the fast ice there—most of the penguins departed around the beginning of January. Few birds are more isolated from humanity than emperor penguins, which only occur in Antarctica, but seeing them here serves as a reminder that even the most remote corners of the world are vulnerable to climate change. As one of the species' most southerly colonies this feels as if it should be inviolate, but reliant as they are on the presence of fast ice for chick rearing, emperor penguins are going to be affected by a warming world.

Below us the Crozier research hut appears, a small orange cube on the black volcanic landscape below, with a Scott tent erected alongside as sleeping quarters. The Scott tent is indeed named after Scott the explorer, and although its design has been modernized in the hundred years since he died inside one of them on the Ross Ice Shelf, its essential features remain the same: double-sided canvas walls, pyramidal in shape, with a drawstring closure on a tunnel-like opening that keeps out wind and drifting snow. Today, as then, these structures are known for their extraordinary resistance to being blown apart in a storm. This was the same kind of tent used by Apsley Cherry-Garrard, Birdie Bowers, and Bill Wilson on their overland trek, the so-called Worst Journey in the World.

I think of these men as we fly in to land; our trip has been a mere thirty-minute helicopter ride past the ridged and crevassed terrain that they crossed on foot, wearing frozen suits made of caribou hide. It took them nineteen misery-filled days, man-hauling nearly eight hundred pounds of gear in temperatures as low as −77°F ("We began to look upon minus fifties as a luxury which we did not often get," wrote Cherry-Garrard[56]). Despite the tent's reputation, on that midwinter trip theirs was torn away during a hurricane, leaving the three men huddled in reindeer skin sleeping bags under deepening drifts of snow within the walls of the roofless stone igloo they had constructed, singing hymns to keep up their spirits and pass the time. After the hurricane subsided they went searching, and notwithstanding the near-perpetual darkness and the force of the winds that had taken it, they found the tent wedged in a hollow half a mile away—averting the death sentence they knew awaited them without it.

We land downhill from the Crozier field camp. Solar Joe and his assistant are here from McMurdo for the afternoon, winterizing the solar panel and the wind generator (currently whizzing along at a fierce pace), and after we disembark they help us haul our small mountain of gear up the hill from the helicopter landing site. We aren't carrying the eight hundred pounds of gear hauled by Cherry-Garrard's expedition, but as usual we are not exactly travelling light either. Along with sundry personal supplies we've brought our bulky sleeping kits, the mandatory duffels of Extreme Cold Weather gear, crates of extra food and water to augment the dwindling end-of-season Crozier provisions, our cameras and laptops, and all the other Cape Royds electronics so that they don't freeze there overnight.

Soon after we finish moving our supplies, Grant, Viola, and Rachael appear as black dots hauling a sledge on the snowfields far below the hut, coming toward us around the corner of a huge cinder cone at the edge of the penguin colony where they've been working all day. They are tiny against the towering hundred-metre cliffs of ice welded to the shore, left there by B-15A when it literally crashed into Ross Island on some earlier perambulation brought about by wind and tide—likely the one we heard about over the VHF radio during one of our skeds, when it was making the Crozier hut shake like an earthquake. Later, when I'm back at McMurdo, I view a satellite image and realize that B-15A's other end is actually jammed up against Franklin Island, 160 kilometres away, with the whole berg being held in place by the fierce winds of the Ross Sea polynya. The fact that against the face of the broken ice cliffs our Crozier colleagues look like ants, or distant penguins, emphasizes the massive features of this landscape, its immensity hard to comprehend. I'm reminded of David's comment when we first arrived in McMurdo, nearly three months ago now, about Crozier being one of the power spots of the world. I'm still not sure what that meant to him exactly, but I have a sense of it: The forces at play here—volcanoes, ice sheets, hurricane-force winds—are beyond normal human contemplation, and it's undeniable that Cape Crozier feels . . . different. Aloof, untouchable, dispassionate, even hostile. To be honest I'm a bit intimidated by this landscape. It would be easy to die here, I think. Much more so than at Cape Royds.

Inside, Cape Crozier's research hut is cozy and permanent-looking, unlike our Royds abode. There's an accumulation of foodstuffs and gear that have the weathered look of having wintered over several times; a permanent biffy with one of the ever-popular hand-carved Styrofoam seats (warm!); built-in bunks; a foyer-cum-storage-area-cum-washroom, including a "sink" that consists of a wide-mouthed funnel that is set into a plywood counter and attached to a hose leading to a fifty-gallon grey-water drum outside. Paintings and cartoons of penguins adorn the walls, taped there or drawn on directly by field biologists from previous seasons. The cured skin of an emperor penguin that was found dead in an earlier year by David and another seabird ecologist, Larry Spear, hangs on the back of the door. Its feathers are short, slick, and very dense; running a hand over it is more akin to stroking a thickly-pelted seal than it is to touching a bird.

Rachael and I go for a long walk before a late-evening dinner, first up to nearby Pat's Peak so that we can see the hut looking tiny below us against a backdrop of snowfields. Beyond it the top of Mount Terror is visible, towering behind the lesser peaks that rear up to meet its lower slopes. On our way back we cut along the edge of an icy snowfield where the blasting wind whirls eddies of spindrift across the talus slopes and flings it into our faces. Ahead of me, backlit by the dropping sun, Rachael looks as if she is caught up in a brilliant cloud of swirling gold. "Dramatic, spectacular, powerful, huge" are what I write in the camp logbook as my first impressions of Cape Crozier, but those words are dwarfed by the reality in the same way that the place dwarfs its visitors.

After we eat I go outside to a spectacle: The vertical face of B-15A has been turned by the light of the evening sun into a wall of flame dancing across the frigid waters of the Ross Sea. Now that it's past midsummer the sun has recently started "setting" at Crozier, which means that it dips behind the towering mass of Mount Terror for a couple of hours each night and the shadows lengthen. Even so, tonight I can't sleep until after 3 a.m., kept awake by the colour of the light and the ending of the book I'm reading—Margaret Atwood's *The Blind Assassin,* passed on to me by Rachael back on the *Polar Sea*—as well as the noise of the wind hooting in a vent hole in the hut's eastern wall. It sounds just like the call of a screech-owl.

After four hours of sleep it's time to get up again: A helicopter is due to take David and me back to Cape Royds mid-afternoon, and there's lots to do before we can leave. The occupants of the hut and adjacent Scott tent stir exceedingly slowly as most of us are on the late-to-bed, late-to-rise work schedule, compounded by late-season fatigue. We procrastinate over multiple cups of very strong coffee as we slowly pull on layers of cold-weather gear in between eating mouthfuls of breakfast cobbled together from a diminishing food supply. Efforts to get ready are also hindered by the presence of four people (David, as the group's early bird, has long since left) in a hut that would be cramped even with three.

Today will be hectic, with one thousand penguin chicks to band. Much of what we've been spending our days doing at Cape Royds and on our visit to Beaufort Island—slowly walking through the colony, searching for banded birds, and recording band numbers—has its origins in days such as these in earlier years. At Cape Crozier on this particular morning, banding is a production line of moving across the landscape and slowly herding groups of chicks into portable "chick corrals" (fashioned from PVC piping and plastic mesh fencing), then gently extracting those too young to hold a band plus the adults and shooing them away before banding the rest in what feels like a whirlwind of flying feathers, wide-eyed chicks peeping and crapping, agitated parents, floppy young flippers. We all start out closing the metal flipper bands with our thumbs, and then as thumbs become sore we progress to the pliers on our Leatherman tools. The bands have to be closed completely to limit drag when the penguin swims through the water once it fledges and goes to sea. Like a metal bracelet on a human, the painless bands fit closely but don't bind (they can't slip over the penguin's "elbow"). As soon as the chicks are released from the corral they rush to their original corner of the subcolony, quickly forgetting their recent experience as they await the next meal from a parent.

On a short break I go for a walk. I'm munching on an energy bar when I drop a piece of it onto the frozen ground, an icy sheet of solid guano. Without thinking I stoop to pick it up and pop it in my mouth, realizing too late what I've done—then mentally shrug, well past caring about such niceties. Out over the frozen sea, this morning's white haze still obscures the horizon. I notice two dark and upright figures far out on the sea ice and start uneasily. Who else is out here, and what are they doing on the ice?

Then I laugh at myself. With the lack of horizon there is no sense of perspective, and instead of being human-sized figures I realize they are in fact two emperor penguins—at over a metre in height, the size of a human child at least—shuffling toward shore. I stand there watching them as they make their way along, periodically looking around. One of the birds suddenly stops and seems to do the penguin version of a double take, staring toward where I am standing up the hill. I realize that it is having the same experience I have just had, but in reverse: It thinks I am an emperor penguin, standing where no emperor should be. Like me, it quickly seems to realize its mistake and turns to continue its walk, trundling past the shapes of the Weddell seals that lie resting on the ice. The above-water vocalizations of these seals sometimes sound eerily human, and now I can hear them calling to each other.

"Hey!" I hear them shouting. "Heeeeyyy!"

—

We finish the banding just in time to head back to the hut to meet our helicopter. David and I each take one half of the corral contraption, now looking very much the worse for wear after a summer of exposure to UV radiation and today's wear and tear, including someone falling on it. There are lots of skua territories on our return route across the talus slopes; we even step right over one little chick in the middle of the rough path, crouched motionless amongst the stones in response to its parents' angry calls. Grant walks beside me and we chat as we make our way slowly uphill.

"I was walking through here one day and heard a commotion from the skuas," says Grant. "One had just grabbed an unguarded chick from another pair, and the chick was shrieking out distress calls as the adult flew off with it."

"Oh," I reply. "I haven't seen that yet." Skuas are known conspecific nest predators, so this is not an unexpected tale.

"But this is the crazy part," Grant continues. "One of the parents obviously heard the calls, because it suddenly materialized out of nowhere at full speed, caught up with the adult that was flying off with its chick and started dive-bombing it." He pauses for a moment while we navigate a steep section of scree and I try not to drop my end of the chick corral, then he continues. "The parent's attack was so vicious that the first skua dropped the chick in mid-air and flew off. And at the same time the parent swooped down, actually caught the chick in its beak as it was falling, and flew back to their nest to brood it for a while."

Grant's story literally stops me in my tracks. I am continuously awe-struck by the way Adélie penguins have adapted to life in the harshest environment in the world, seamlessly moving from land to ice to sea. But this skua's demonstration of offspring recognition, aerial agility, and advanced parental care fills me with a sort of reverence. There is still so much for humans to learn about the diversity of ways there are to be in the world. I think of Dutch-American primatologist and biologist Frans de Waal's remarkable book *Are We Smart Enough to Know How Smart Animals Are?* with its message that the intelligence of nonhuman animals is shaped by their need to respond to their *Umwelt,* their surrounding world. That to grasp these different manifestations of intellect, we must consider how a species navigates the challenges of its daily life, rather than asking how it stacks up against human characteristics like language or tool use (neither of which is the sole province of humans). The skua knew from a distance that the chick in danger was its own, used its aerial skills to effect a complex and successful rescue it had most likely never done before, and then tenderly cared for its traumatized young: Surely all this shows a highly successful form of intelligence, one that is worthy of our deep respect. My thoughts turn to the injured penguin 1091, expertly navigating her world despite a crippling injury. I hope that she and her mate are now growing fat again, far out at sea, and wonder whether they'll succeed in returning to raise another brood in another year.

Back at the hut we carry our gear down to the landing site. Our helicopter turns out to be an hour late, so we laze in the sun until it is time to go. David suspects that one of his fingernails will be black and blue tomorrow; he used pliers for the banding least of all. I mostly used my Leatherman—now utterly caked with penguin shit—but even so my thumbs are now useless for anything requiring pressure; even something as simple as opening a box of crackers to snack on as we wait is excruciating.

On the way back our flight takes us past the south side of Erebus, in behind McMurdo Station and Cape Evans. The smooth whiteness of the glaciated landscape below is broken only by the sharp azure angles of multiple crevasses, and the occasional russet volcanic outcrop thrusting free of ice and snow. In front of us the icebreaker's channel spreads down the white surface of McMurdo Sound like a scar; and to the south, Black and White Islands are like minimalist paintings of themselves, rising faintly out of the sea ice past the frozen, featureless plain of Windless Bight just before the horizon disappears into the hazy white nothingness that marks the start of the continent.

We get back to Royds shortly after 5 p.m., touching down in a swirl of blowing snow. The wind is gusting and the pilot isn't used to this site so it takes him four tries to land. There's a rush to shut down and offload before the helicopter blasts off again, with the pilot nervous about the weather. A local gale is blowing but it is uncharacteristically coming from the north, so the water in front of Cape Royds is choked with pack ice, bergy bits, and huge wrecked icebergs that have come in on the wind, the regular seasonal ice clear-out in the wider Ross Sea also having been affected by B-15A. On days like this the penguins struggle, floundering for miles over the ice looking for enough open water to enter and find food for their chicks. A reminder, if we still need it, that life is harsh here at the extreme edge of the world.

26

THE PENGUINS ARE leaving. Our Crozier trip meant a forty-eight-hour break between visits to the Royds colony, and the difference in the number remaining here is noticeable. Today I see fewer than forty banded adults, down from twice as many last week. The subcolonies of non-breeders are now all but gone too, and there are big gaps on the ground where a month ago all was noisy chaos. In some of the subcolonies the crèched chicks now almost outnumber adult birds, and most of the youngsters have grown large enough that they no longer need the anti-skua patrol provided by the aggressive non-breeding penguins. In the last two days most of the chicks have also shed the bulk of their down, rapidly following the onset of moult at the colony just a week to ten days ago. The chicks at Cape Royds are noticeably fat in relation to those at Crozier. It's apparent from the colour and quantity of their guano that fish (white poop) and krill (orange) are still hyper-abundant here. Our satellite-tagged birds continue to forage close by—we are still getting data downloads via satellite phone link—in contrast to the ever-increasing distances being travelled by the Crozier parents on the other side of Ross Island as a halo of food depletion grows around that colony.

I do my final count of adults and chicks in the B-REF subcolony and realize that I've nearly come full circle with these birds: opening, crescendo, and denouement. I watch a pair bow courteously to each other, and in this gesture see the timelessness of all that has passed this season, part of a great endless cycle as summer fades into fall. Next spring the bowing will begin anew to herald the start of another year. I've been but a short event in their busy lives, and that is as it should be. This week I'll leave here, but the penguins will go on swimming and feeding and courting and bowing without me through the months and years to come.

The conditions have turned harsh again today. Our weather station showed that the temperature dropped below −10°C overnight. Now there are southerly winds up to forty knots and the wind chill sits at about −20. The first thing I saw when I opened my eyes this morning was a thick buildup of hoarfrost on the inside of the tent, my body moisture trapped and frozen to coat the ripstop nylon for the first time since late November. It was also the first morning in a couple of months that I've awoken to find my water bottle frozen.

Paradoxically, when I walk down to the colony late in the afternoon a big chunk of the sea ice is blowing out from Cape Barne, leaving only a fringe of frozen sea clinging fast to the shoreline. Now there's a wide gap of open ocean between Backdoor Bay and the Barne Glacier, so our road south to McMurdo really is cut off, the sea ice at its most minimal extent of the season. But it will be frozen over again soon enough. Throughout the summer the melting ocean has continued to refreeze in areas that are sheltered from the action of wind and waves, and in the next few weeks the sun will begin to set and the cold will begin again in earnest, with the loss of daylight like an insulated door closing on a giant freezer.

Kerry and Pete are due to leave Cape Bird for Scott Base tomorrow. Maybe it'll happen according to schedule, though on our radio chat before dinner Pete reports that it is overcast and snowing there. The gang at Cape Crozier are supposed to be pulling out tomorrow afternoon too, with an overnight at McMurdo followed by a day here with us before we all pull out of Cape Royds on Wednesday. It feels like an abrupt end to the season, though I suppose I'm now ready for it. But it's going to be very odd to go home.

Two mornings later there's no sign of the helicopter that's supposed to be bringing out the Crozier crew. I walk to the ridge with a steaming coffee in my gloved hand and see why—a thick bank of ice fog is squatting low on the ground to the south, heavy as a big toad. The top of Inaccessible Island is visible above a fluffy skirt of whiteness that makes it look as if the sea ice has dissolved and risen several hundred metres into the air. I spend part of the morning prepping a pile of gear and trash to be sent back with the helo, should it make it out here. I flatten and bundle our stash of cardboard boxes and pile them in the shelter of the leeward side of the hut, then hammer a lid on the full Human Waste Bucket. Those lids are a tight fit—something for which somebody somewhere will be grateful, I am sure—and so require a lot of hammering.

Shortly after noon, the weather clears abruptly and Grant, Viola, and Rachael arrive to join me and David. All of us load the pile of trash into the helicopter and wave it goodbye. We spend the afternoon in a flurried repeat of last week's chick-banding escapade at Crozier, though it takes us less time because we are banding far fewer chicks here at the tiny Royds colony. We also deploy a dozen miniature GLS tags, which each recipient will wear on a snug-fitting tie on its leg until it returns to the colony in the spring; in the meantime each tag will be soaking up more information about where Adélie penguins spend the winter, on a round trip that averages over twelve thousand kilometres. Then next year David and my replacement will spend the days looking for these birds until they find them, remove the tags, and download the data, and the research season will have begun all over again.

I vacate my mountaineering tent so Grant and Viola can occupy it; I'll spend the night down at the Kiwi hut so the rest of us don't all need to squeeze our sleeping bags onto the floor of the Rac-Tent. Descending the ridge on my way to bed, I am once more stopped in my tracks by the view. The ocean is breathlessly still, and to the south Cape Barne's decaying volcanic plug is reflected in its mirrored surface like some gothic chimney. Across McMurdo Sound, Mount Discovery is but a dim shadow through an evening haze, a backlit misty silhouette of itself. Beneath Discovery floats a huge and angular chunk of tabular berg, which sits placidly in a calm sea that so perfectly reflects the white of the overcast sky that it might be the sky itself, and the berg a drifting cloud of cumulus.

It is wonderful to be alone in the peace of the wanigan, my only company the sound of the wind and the music of the penguins. I was wrong to think that there was nothing for Patrick, the Kiwi music composer, in their raucous cries. The calls combine to form a melody that will see me through the night. It occurs to me as I unpack that I'll be one of only a few people ever to have spent the night here alone. Some of my warmest memories of Cape Royds will be of the times I've spent at this hut with visitors, yet on my own here I feel completely at peace. I almost wish for a day or two of whiteout conditions to arrive tonight so that I could spend the time quietly alone and extend this period of meditative solitude.

Grant and David go to McMurdo in the morning, slinging out the fifty-gallon U-barrel with their helicopter. It is more than three-quarters full, an entire season's worth of urine from our two often-dehydrated bodies. Viola, Rachael, and I stay behind to pack up the remainder of camp. After the helicopter leaves we do the penultimate chick condition weighing of the season, a companionable task at the end of a sunny late-January afternoon. We laugh and talk a lot, about anything and everything, feeling lighter, liberated by our impending departure despite the weight of it. Viola scavenges the ingredients for a burrito dinner out of the remains of our food supplies, and we drink a bottle of wine (courtesy of Helo Ops) and talk some more and then pack up the rest of camp. I take down my trusty mountaineering tent, still in surprisingly good shape after a summer's worth of UV exposure, blasting by hurricane-force winds, and ablation by airborne gravel. A Coast Guard helicopter will be here in the morning to take us out to the ship at Beaufort Island, where we will meet up with David for another half day of chick banding and weighing, and then on to McMurdo after that. From McMurdo we will return to Cape Royds in a few days to complete the season's final chick condition check before the penguins (and all of us) leave the continent. Our work here at the colony is nearly done.

I walk down to the penguins at 1 a.m. for one last evening stroll under the midnight sun. When I hear the angry cry of the skua that nests below the ridge, it hits me that I really am leaving, and my heart feels like it might break. In my mind I bid farewell to the bird and its mate, wishing them well through the coming seasons. This is the pair that have occasionally followed me around, waiting for me to discard the dead penguin chicks I've collected for diet sampling; their chick is still half grown and scraggly-looking, pin feathers pushing through down, its ungainly small body on large, pale blue stilt-like legs making it look like it is wading across the gravelly ground.

In the morning the *Polar Star* lies enmeshed in pack ice off Beaufort Island in mirror-calm seas. This crew is more relaxed than the one on board their sister ship *Polar Sea*; two individual vessels have given rise to two crews with their own collective personalities. A couple of crew members come ashore on Beaufort to help us, and we band four hundred chicks, then weigh and measure the wings, tarsi, and bills of thirty of them as a condition check—all in two hours. It's a record-breaking time and the crew is ecstatic to help wrangle chicks, hold the weigh bag, and record data.

"This just made the entire season worthwhile!" exclaims Chris, the ship's science officer, bending over a data book wrinkled with water damage and stained with penguin guano. As we're packing up the remaining field gear, our two hand-held VHFs crackle to life.

"Shore party, this is *Polar Star.* You need to get out of there right now!" It's the urgent voice of an officer from the bridge. "Pack ice has started drifting in at five knots and you'll be cut off. I say again, you need to get out now." There's a pause while we all look at each other, and then quickly pick up our bags.

"Run!" comes the officer's voice over the airwaves, breaking with radio protocol. We literally sprint to the gap in the fast ice where we were dropped off by the landing craft, and pile aboard, panting.

"Two more minutes and we wouldn't have been able to get to you," says the boat operator laconically as we speed back to the ship and the pack visibly thickens along the shoreline behind us.

We arrive at McMurdo after staying for dinner on board the ship, then helicoptering back through a wall of wind north of Cape Royds that causes the helo to buck and dip and shudder like a wild pony. The first thing I do after ferrying our equipment from the helo hangar to Crary and a couple of duffels to my dorm room is take a very long shower. As I watch a grey scum of soap and exfoliated skin swirl muddily down the drain, I reflect on the mental liberty that time in the field provides, the freedom to cease thinking about appearances. There's the immersion in one's study environment that opens up unfettered time to explore ideas, but also, for women at least, there is the absence of a constant societal gaze, the unending social pressure to care about one's outward form. "I didn't recognize you; you clean up good," said one of my acquaintances when I ran into him in the hallway on a previous visit. I nodded my thanks to accept the intended compliment, but the cringeworthy comment served primarily to remind me of the perpetual nature of societal scrutiny, and its absence at Cape Royds.

After I've dried my hair I run into my old roomie Sarika in the hallway with her friend Jen, and am invited to Jen's place for martinis. On the way we come across a couple of Russians wearing green-and-black South Pole Station jackets, probably en route from the Russian mid-continent station Vostok, the place where the lowest temperature on Earth—nearly –90°C—has been recorded. From Jen's we head off to midrats at 12:30 a.m. and are joined by Rusty and James (of Cape Royds Christmas Day fame), Rusty's wife Regina, the head station physician, and a couple of others. I accuse Rusty of knowing everyone on station, which he denies, and then promptly greets each person who walks past our table. They'd been to Casino Night at Gallagher's Pub (named after a winter-over who died at McMurdo), and James had been to the Scott Base end-of-summer party. On the way back to our dorms, in the hallway near the bank machines, we run into a rather drunk trio of Coast Guard crew from the *Polar Sea*: the executive officer, the bosun, and someone I don't recognize. I guess by now I know a lot of people here too. When I mention that our penguin-banding stint went well this afternoon thanks to the *Polar Star*, they are rather venomous about it. The competition between those two vessels is intense.

In between packing field and research gear to be shipped north or to overwinter at McMurdo, Rachael and I do a half-day field trip to the aircraft skiway at Willy Field, catching a ride with the staff shuttle van and visiting the office of Kenn Borek Air Ltd. This turns out to be a dilapidated ATCO-type trailer on skis, painted orange. It's in a row of similar buildings, the only relief on the ice plain stretching around us, the horizon today obscured by blowing snow. The company is well known to residents of Canada's High Arctic as a provider of air services to remote communities, but in the northern winter Borek Air shuttles their fleet of ski-equipped Twin Otters down to Antarctica via South America, travelling south like a flock of swallows. (They are perhaps best known in the Antarctic for the 2013 crash into Antarctica's Mount Elizabeth that killed Inuvik-based pilot Bob Heath, along with a co-pilot and an engineer—and for their daring and successful midwinter rescue flight to retrieve two sick workers from the US South Pole station in 2016.) It's not just this building that is on skis; all the facilities out here are thus equipped, apparently so they can be towed into new formations as needed, given their location on the ever-moving ice shelf. On the door of the Willy Field office is a hand-painted sign reading "The Kenn Borek Flying Circus and Animal Act Pub"; the dispatcher snaps a photo of Rachael and me in front of it, huddled in all our clothing against today's bitter cold drifting down off the Polar Plateau.

When I awaken the next day, I realize it's the first of February. In less than a week I'll have been here three months. McMurdo is descending into an intense maelstrom of goodbye parties and overheard confabs of post-Antarctica plans, spiced with incoming military personnel for vessel offload and civilian winter-over crew for the station. I meet two of these at supper: Kim and Alisa are plump Midwesterners with similar upturned noses and self-satisfied demeanours, a very different sort of female from the friendly and athletic outdoorsy types that populate McMurdo and the field stations in the summer months.

After three months of relative isolation, seeing these newcomers feels a bit like observing an invasion of aliens. Suddenly McMurdo is no longer a self-contained and womblike little world.

As we leave the Galley we're invited to yet another party.

"What a surprise," says Rachael.

This time it's White Russians, gin martinis, crantinis, and shooting pool in Room 209's lounge, where we overlook the two Coast Guard vessels tied up at the ice pier. The ever-glittering sea ice shows pink and blue under the midnight sun. John the cook is there, providing fresh milk or garlic-stuffed olives, depending on your drink of choice, and promising fresh figs from tomorrow's plane. Rusty and Regina are doing bag drag—the pre-departure gear weigh—tomorrow night in prep for a Tuesday flight to New Zealand, and so this is a bit of a goodbye bash for them (except for tomorrow evening's get-together, of course). Rusty leaves the room for a pee and comes back with half a roll of toilet paper wrapped around his head, arms stretched straight in front of him while chanting incantations from the film *The Mummy*. Such is the genius of the scientific mind after three months of isolation. The days are starting to collapse into each other and very soon there will be too much to do and too little time to do it in, as if we are all reaching the ends of our lives.

"Take time to soak it all in" was all that my friend Tom wrote in an email from home. He's another Antarctican, a veteran of several seasons here; he knows what it means to leave.

On the fourth of February, Rachael and Viola and David and I do a final trip out to Royds for our last chick condition weighing of the season. We depart at 8:45 a.m. after a leisurely weigh-in down at the helo pad in our clean clothes. The last helicopter fly day here is this Saturday, three days from now, and the pilots all leave the continent on Monday.

Helo Ops has suddenly lost the air of frenetic activity that has defined it all summer.

The penguin colony too has lost that air. Most of the adults are now gone—heading north to where they'll spend the winter at the edge of the pack ice—and the chicks stand around in big groups, shedding fluffy plumules into the sunny air. We weigh and measure twenty-one of them, plump and healthy individuals; many are all but free of down and have lost their excess pre-fledging fat. Now they too are ready to head to the beach in preparation for going to sea. They roll their eyes nervously at us like miniature Holstein calves as I extract them gently from their weighing bag.

All too soon we are done, and we all walk down to the water one last time, staring out to sea to say our silent goodbyes to the penguins and Cape Royds. Each time I leave Antarctica I have no way of knowing if I'll ever be back. This is not a place that one visits on a whim. So much has to align for a scientist to return for another season: research grants, scientific permits, project approvals, lab and dorm space on station, our own health and that of our families. Each time I leave Antarctica I bid it farewell in my mind, and I suspect that my companions all do the same.

I try to imprint all this on my memory: the few sleek, wet adult birds still coming out of the sea, looking like they're suited up in neoprene; several nervous chicks hanging out at the water's edge in their new smoke-coloured plumage, waiting to build up the courage to take the first swim of their lives; the symmetrical shape of Mount Discovery, slate and white in the morning sun, and uncharacteristically not shrouded by clouds; mighty Erebus, emitting billows of smoke, its glaciers winking and gleaming in the diamond-hard light; and the distant Transantarctic Mountains across McMurdo Sound, as always looking impossibly high even though they're almost seventy kilometres away. Today the water is nearly ice-free, dotted here and there with small bergs, and a deep ultramarine that's ruffled by a quiet southerly wind.

In *The Heart of the Antarctic,* Shackleton wrote of their departure from McMurdo Sound: "On passing our winter quarters at Cape Royds we all turned out to give three cheers, and to take a last look at the place where, in spite of discomforts and hardships, we had spent so many happy days. We watched the little hut, which had been our home for a year that must always live in our memories, fade away in the distance with feelings almost of sadness, and there were few men aboard who did not cherish a hope that someday they might again live strenuous days under the shadow of mighty Erebus."[57]

As I stand and look out at the ocean, my sister comes to mind, unbidden. I think of her, my dad, others who are gone. Beloved pets, grandparents, my uncles. Perhaps one day we'll all be together again as the words of comfort would have us believe—but I don't believe this is true. I instead now find solace in thinking that we have all been fortunate to be here together in this beautiful world for a while.

27

THE PLANE IS full, a metal tube with all of us in four long fore-to-aft rows of red parkas on webbing benches, most of the seats occupied by people already eating the fresh bagged lunches we were given by the military flight crew as we stepped on board. I'm feeling numb, not from the cold, though my feet are cold enough on the metal floor of the LC-130, but because in a few minutes the door will close on Antarctica. Already all I can see of it is a patch of whiteness through the open door—snow or sky, I can't tell. But when I close my eyes, Mount Discovery remains vivid in front of me, frozen in time in its icy splendour. The door of the plane is slowly folded shut by the flight crew, but before it blocks out all the whiteness, I once again close my eyes. I sleep most of the way back to New Zealand while the mountains replay themselves in my head, a closed-circuit loop that's imprinted on my retinas, one that will always be there.

Getting off the plane in Christchurch, we're all stunned by trees and tarmac, by balmy air that smells of warm vegetation, and by walking past thousands of strangers. After sleeping through a night where the sun went down, a group of us go for brunch to a restaurant near our guesthouse, and we are all out in the street before we realize that we haven't paid.

Rachael and I decide to rent a car and tour around the South Island before heading back to our respective countries. David is going for a week of freshwater fishing before heading home to the United States and his wife and his little dog. At checkout time the next morning we wait for our taxis together in the old-fashioned guesthouse lobby, our bags resting on the floor beside well-worn armchairs upholstered in floral patterns. The tracks of our lives are diverging after three months of running in parallel.

When a cab pulls up outside, David and I regard each other for a few seconds from across the foyer, then simultaneously step forward into a hug.

"Well, uhhm . . . you take care of yourself," he says in his hoarse voice as we pull apart. "Don't put off that PhD."

"Thanks, David, I won't. It's been fantastic to work with you." We each give the other's arm a final squeeze, and then I turn to gather my bags and carry them to where Rachael is waiting with the cab.

After so much time together it is a physical wrench to say goodbye. In *The Worst Journey in the World,* Apsley Cherry-Garrard wrote that "in civilization men are taken at their own valuation because there are so many ways of concealment, and there is so little time, perhaps even so little understanding. Not so down South."[58] Like others who have cohabited in isolation in Antarctica, David and I concealed little, spent plenty of time together, and gained much understanding.

In Oamaru, Rachael and I pay money to go and see the fairy penguins at their managed colony. Unlike our Antarctic Adélies, these birds are nocturnal. We sit in the dusk on rows of bleachers with a handful of other late-season tourists, waiting for the penguins to come ashore. There's nothing, and then suddenly a tiny figure is standing on the beach where it has surfed ashore and been left behind by a receding wave. And another. Soon there's a small group of fairy penguins huddled there, blinking warily. Slowly they make their way up the shore toward their respective nest boxes, manufactured wooden shelters embedded in the ground. The birds are shy and creep around the edges of vegetation, frequently disappearing from sight as they skulk toward the boxes' entrance holes.

This is what we've reduced them to, I think: slinking ashore in the dead of night to hide from vandalizing humans and introduced predators. Once they would have been carefree under a daytime sun, waddling confidently ashore as I have watched their Antarctic cousins do, day after day in their rush to reproduce before the twenty-four-hour daylight begins to wane. These fairy penguins are like Adélies with some of the magic stripped away, lost to the modern world, to development and the fisheries that are outcompeting them for their prey in the sea.

Is this what we want for the future? Or do we want the world to be a place where all of its inhabitants can thrive? The choice is still ours to make. I close my eyes and think of Adélie penguins swimming northward through the Ross Sea, fleeing the freezing ocean and the setting sun until the spring sun rises and it is time for them to return to Cape Royds once again.

10 Things I'll Miss

A warm sleeping bag in a tent that's filled
with the light of a midnight sun.

Penguin music.

Cross-country skiing over the sea ice.

The bottomless silence of a calm summer day.

The fierce gaze of the skuas.

Nodding to the ghosts of Shackleton's men at their hut.

Coffee at the wanigan with the Kiwis.

The pale beauty of a monochromatic world.

The Transantarctic Mountains, taking up half the sky.

And the solitude . . . the purest of solitudes.

EPILOGUE

DAVID TALKED ABOUT Cape Crozier being one of the world's power spots, sites that, in certain spiritual traditions, are considered sacred and healing. Stonehenge and Uluru (Ayers Rock) are examples of these. To me, Crozier is a magical place, but Cape Royds is the more powerful one. Like most of the people who have been lucky enough to spend time there, I went home transformed: home to what was, for me, a subtly different world. After the stark simplicity of Ross Island, too much of life seemed superfluous—the trivialities of uncompleted chores, the banality of my job with government, clutter, possessions, crowds. With a renewed belief in the importance of science for conservation, I began and completed my PhD (in the end, on long-term changes in seabirds—gulls, this time—and their marine ecosystems in Pacific Canada).

In the years after my field season at Ross Island I went back there for another season—where I primarily worked at Cape Crozier—and also went back to the Antarctic Peninsula on a cruise ship as a visiting scientist, collecting data to monitor penguin populations. David's effort to protect the Ross Sea as the most pristine marine ecosystem on Earth gained momentum in the form of the Last Ocean campaign.

This campaign involved people such as New Zealand filmmaker Peter Young and American nature photographer John Weller (each of whom produced a separate award-winning project called *The Last Ocean*), and organizations like the Antarctic and Southern Ocean Coalition, World Wildlife Fund, Avaaz, and Greenpeace, and of course many dozens of the Antarctic scientists who work in the Ross Sea and elsewhere on the continent and its surrounding ocean. The intensity of my working relationship with David over that season naturally changed when we said our farewells in Christchurch, but we continued to collaborate on scientific publications related to Antarctic conservation and, more recently, on publishing seabird science in the peer-reviewed journal *Marine Ornithology*, where he is editor-in-chief and for several years I was managing editor. I continue to be inspired by his dogged determination to devote his time and intellect to conservation science and the protection of Antarctica and seabirds.

In 2016, after more than a decade of campaigning and immense public support from around the world, CCAMLR's voting parties unanimously supported the creation of the 1.55-million-square-kilometre Ross Sea Region Marine Protected Area (MPA)—the largest marine park on Earth—which came into force the following year, in 2017. It is to remain in place for thirty-five years from that date, and at the end of that time it can be continued, amended, or ended. The thirty-five-year timeframe was one of several compromises reached to allow for unanimous support (these compromises also included a 40 percent reduction in the original proposed size of the protected area). Clearly work remains to be done to ensure the MPA continues past the middle of this century and well into the future to protect the southern world of penguins and whales, toothfish and seals—some of the wild creatures with whom we share this planet, our collective home. Action on climate change is crucial to complement the physical protection provided by the MPA's boundaries, and indeed, our collective action to protect the world's wild places and their inhabitants everywhere is just as vital. We as human beings are diminished without our wild kin, and it is our responsibility to defend them. While it is difficult to know what we can do as individuals, there are many kinds of actions we can choose to take, from holding governments accountable to their environmental commitments and other types of advocacy, to consuming less and living life as if the planet we occupy were finite, as indeed it is.

The challenge of our times is to confront great change. In the same week that I read about the mass emperor penguin breeding failure reported in early 2024, I began reading American psychotherapist and author Francis Weller's remarkable book *The Wild Edge of Sorrow*. In it, he explores how to confront the impacts of these very sorts of changes, opening our hearts to the truth of loss: "No one goes in search of loss; rather, it finds us and reminds us of the temporary gift [of life] we have been given . . . The earth is a revelation, offering itself to us daily in an astonishing array of beauty and suffering. What is required of us is living with a level of openness and vulnerability to the joys and sorrows of the world . . . engaged in the ongoing conversation with all things . . . How well we do that will determine the fate of our communities and the planet."[59]

I hope that you, the reader, can close this book and proceed with an open heart through the world, in conversation with whatever it is that nature shares with you.

GLOSSARY

AFT: Antarctic Field Training, the New Zealand field safety program run by field training instructors and professional guides out of Scott Base.

Antarctic Heritage Trust: a New Zealand charity responsible for the conservation and care of the historic Ross Sea expedition bases.

ASPA: Antarctic Specially Protected Area. Areas protected under the Antarctic Treaty system for their outstanding natural or historical values.

Bag drag: Pre-flight luggage weigh-in and passenger *ECW* check.

Bergy bits: The larger bits of a broken *iceberg* floating between one and five metres above the waterline—about the size of a cottage (following Shackleton's description in his book *South*). Smaller pieces, up to the approximate size of a car, are called *growlers.*

BFC: Berg Field Center.

Biffy: Outhouse.

Boondoggle: A project or activity that is an enjoyable treat or perk for the participant(s), but of limited objective value to a wider program (known as a "jolly" to the Brits and Australians).

Brash ice: Dense floating accumulations of small pieces of ice wreckage, e.g., from a collapsing *iceberg* or colliding ice floes.

Crèche: In penguin colonies, a huddle of pre-fledge chicks.

ECW: Extreme cold weather gear, the insulating layers of clothing issued to all US Antarctic Program participants.

Fast ice: Sea ice frozen in situ and held fast to the shore.

Fingee: Military slang; pronunciation of FNG, fucking new guy.

FSTP: McMurdo's Field Safety Training Program, acronym pronounced F-STOP.

Graupel: Small, heavily rimed snow pellets formed when supercooled drops of water freeze on falling flakes.

Grease ice: An early stage of sea ice formation in which surface ice particles coagulate and form a viscous surface layer that is greasy in appearance.

Ground blizzard: A snowstorm of recently fallen snow picked up by high winds and blown along the surface, obscuring ground visibility; these often occur on an otherwise sunny day.

Growler: See *Bergy bits.*

Helo: Helicopter.

HF radio: Communications device using high-frequency radio waves in the band from 3 to 30 megahertz. Radio waves in this frequency are propagated via refraction from the ionosphere, meaning they can be used to communicate over very long distances between locations that are situated around the curve of the Earth from each other. This is in contrast to a *VHF radio*, which is primarily used for line-of-sight communications.

Iceberg: A massive chunk of ice broken away from a glacier (a non-tabular berg) or an ice shelf (a tabular berg), with the largest occasionally comparable in size to various small countries. Icebergs float five metres or more above sea level. *Ice floes,* in contrast, are broken pieces of *sea ice* (or freshwater ice) 20 metres or more across, and are low in profile. See also *Bergy bits.*

IGY: The International Geophysical Year, a global 18-month scientific project that ran from July 1957 to December 1958, modelled after the International Polar Years of 1882–83 and 1932–33. Its goal was to have scientists from around the world cooperate on observations of geophysical phenomena; ultimately, 67 countries were involved. Special attention was given to Antarctica in the IGY, which resulted in multiple advances, among which were the development and signing of the Antarctic Treaty, the construction of several permanent research stations, including Amundsen-Scott South Pole, and the initiation of modern climate-related Antarctic research. The lyrics of the 1982 jazz-pop song "I.G.Y. (What a Beautiful World)," by Donald Fagen of the group Steely Dan, are about the postwar era of futuristic optimism that gave birth to the IGY.

Lead (in the ice): A linear area of open water or new sea ice formed where the ice has cracked or separated.

Midrats: Navy slang for midnight rations, the late-night meal served from about 11 p.m. to 1 a.m. for crew on night watch. More generally, food served around midnight for night-shift workers.

Nilas: Flexible new ice formed in a thin and continuous crust on the sea surface.

NSF: United States National Science Foundation.

Overwinterer: A station crew member or researcher who remains on-station through the winter.

Pack ice or *drift ice*: The floating band of ice fragments of various shapes and sizes that surrounds Antarctica.

Pancake ice: Circular discs of *sea ice* with raised edges that form as the ocean's surface begins to freeze and small pieces of new ice jostle together.

Quonset hut: Prefabricated building made of corrugated steel and formed in a semi-cylindrical shape. Equivalent to the British Nissen hut.

Rebar: A Canadian and US term for steel reinforcing bar.

Retro: Short for "retrograde"—to return waste or unwanted gear back to station or off the continent: "We're going to retro this Human Waste Bucket when the *helo* comes tomorrow."

Sastrugi: Frozen ridges of blown snow that form on top of ice or land and resemble waves or sand dunes.

Sea ice: The frozen ocean in its various forms, often composed of *fast ice* or *pack ice*.

Seabee: A member of the US Navy's Construction Battalion (CB); Williams Field airstrip is named after a Seabee who drowned when his tractor went through the ice.

Sked (radio sked, radio schedule): One's scheduled (usually daily) check-in via radio to base.

Tarsus, tarsi (plural)*:* The lower leg bone in birds, formed from the fused second, third, and fourth metatarsals. Also called the tarsometatarsus. Tarsal length is a standard measurement for monitoring chick growth.

TDR: Time-depth recorder, a data-logging device for tracking the dive behaviour of marine birds and mammals.

VHF radio: Communications device using very high frequency radio airwaves. Radios employing this frequency range, from 30 to 300 megahertz, are generally used for local line-of-sight communications, via stations such as small hand-held marine radios, walkie-talkies, or larger mounted units. See also *HF radio.*

NOTES

1 Berger, John, "Why Look at Animals?" in *About Looking* (Pantheon Books, 1980), 1.

2 Shackleton, Ernest, *The Heart of the Antarctic: Being the Story of the British Antarctic Expedition 1907–1909,* popular edition (William Heinemann, 1911), 1.

3 *New York Times,* "William J. L. Sladen, Expert on Penguin Libidos, Is Dead at 96," 1 June 2017, https://www.nytimes.com/2017/06/17/science/william-jl-sladen-expert-on-penguin-libidos-is-dead-at-96.html.

4 de Beaulieu, Augustin, *Mémoires d'un voyage aux Indes orientales, 1619–1622 : Un marchand normand à Sumatra* (Maisonneuve & Larose, 1996), 47.

5 Murphy, Robert Cushman, *The Oceanic Birds of South America* (Macmillan, 1936), 387.

6 Ellsworth, Lincoln, "My Flight Across Antarctica," *National Geographic* 70, no. 1 (July 1936): 7.

7 Anthony, Jason, *Hoosh: Roast Penguin, Scurvy Day, and Other Stories of Antarctic Cuisine* (University of Nebraska Press, 2012), 122.

8 Shackleton, Ernest, *South: The Story of Shackleton's Last Expedition 1914–1917* (William Heinemann,1919), 72.

9 Keneally, Thomas, "Captain Scott's biscuit," *Granta 83: This Overheating World* (November 2003): 12.

10 Rykers, Ellen, "At the Mercy of the Ice," *New Zealand Geographic* 180 (March–April 2023), https://www.nzgeo.com/stories/at-the-mercy-of-the-ice/.

11 Mawson, Sir Douglas, *The Home of the Blizzard; Being the Story of the Australasian Antarctic Expedition, 1911–1914* (Lippincott, 1915), 239.

12 Ibid., 240.

13 Ibid., 243.

14 Cherry-Garrard, Apsley, *The Worst Journey in the World: With Scott in Antarctica 1910–1913* (United States: Dover, 2010), 183.

15 Ibid., 217

16 Béchervaise, John M., *Antarctica: The Last Horizon* (Cassell Australia, 1979), 19.

17 Murray, James, "Some Notes by James Murray, Biologist to the Expedition," appendix I in Shackleton, *South,* 346.

18 Ibid., 347.

19 Ainley, David G., "The Ross Sea, Antarctica, where all ecosystem processes still remain for study, but maybe not for long," *Marine Ornithology* 30 (2002): 55–62.

20 Spufford, Francis, *I May Be Some Time: Ice and the English Imagination* (Faber and Faber, 1996), 6.

21 Ibid.

22 Murray, "Some Notes," 347.

23 Shackleton, *The Heart of the Antarctic,* 81.

24 Young, Euan, *Skua and Penguin: Predator and Prey* (Cambridge University Press, 1994).

25 Fiennes, Ranulph, *Shackleton: A Biography* (Penguin Random House UK, 2021), 205.

26 Ibid.

27 Dunham, Will, "'Polar madness' grips many people working at poles," Reuters, 9 August 2007, https://www.reuters.com/article.

/us-polar-madness/polar-madness-grips-many-people-working -at-poles-idUSN2422650220070725/.

28 Palinkas, Lawrence A., and Peter Suedfeld, "Psychological effects of polar expeditions," *The Lancet* 371, no. 9607 (2008): 153–63.

29 Dunham, "'Polar madness.'"

30 Nash, Meredith, Hanne E. F. Nielsen, Justine Shaw, Matt King, Mary-Anne Lea, and Narissa Bax, "'Antarctica just has this hero factor...': Gendered barriers to Australian Antarctic research and remote fieldwork," *PLoS ONE* 14, no. 1 (2019): e0209983.

31 Mawson, *The Home of the Blizzard,* 258.

32 Pauly, Daniel, and Jay Maclean, *In a Perfect Ocean: The State of Fisheries and Ecosystems in the North Atlantic Ocean* (Island Press, 2003).

33 Pauly, Daniel, "Anecdotes and the shifting baseline syndrome of fisheries," *Trends in Ecology and Evolution* 10, no. 10 (1995): 430.

34 Pauly, Daniel, Villy Christensen, Johanne Dalsgaard, Rainer Froese, and Francisco Torres Jr., "Fishing Down Marine Food Webs," *Science* 279, no. 5352 (1998): 860–63.

35 Pauly, "Anecdotes and the shifting baseline syndrome," 430.

36 Elliott, Dave Sr., *Saltwater People: As Told by Dave Elliott Sr; A Resource Book for the Saanich Native Studies Program,* rev. ed., Janet Poth, ed. (Saanich: School District 63, 1990), 44.

37 "Fisheries," Commission for the Conservation of Antarctic Marine Living Resources, last modified 31 May 2017, https://www.ccamlr .org/en/fisheries/fisheries.

38 Ainley, David G., and Louise K. Blight, "Ecological repercussions of historical fish extraction from the Southern Ocean," *Fish and Fisheries* 10, no. 1 (2009): 13–38.

39 Shackleton, *South,* 112.

40 Ibid.

41 Mear, Roger, and Robert Swan, *In the Footsteps of Scott* (Grafton Books, 1987), 255.

42 Ibid.

43 Anthony, *Hoosh*, 107.

44 Priestley, Raymond E. *Antarctic Adventure: Scott's Northern Party* (E. P. Dutton, 1915), 279.

45 Murray, "Some Notes," 349.

46 Scott Polar Research Institute, "Scott's Last Expedition: The Diary of Captain Robert Falcon Scott, RN," https://www.spri.cam.ac.uk/museum/diaries/scottslastexpedition/page/7/.

47 Smith, Charmian, "Grahame Sydney's Antarctic splendors," *Otago Daily Times*, 18 October 2008, https://www.odt.co.nz/lifestyle/magazine/grahame-sydneys-antarctic-splendours.

48 Sydney, Grahame, *White Silence: Grahame Sydney's Antarctica* (Penguin New Zealand, 2008).

49 Johnson, Nicholas, *Big Dead Place: Inside the Strange and Menacing World of Antarctica* (Feral House, 2005), 130.

50 Scott Polar Research Institute, "Shackleton items from the Archives: Ernest Shackleton's diary of the Quest Expedition, 1921–22," https://www.spri.cam.ac.uk/archives/shackleton/articles/1537,3,9.html.

51 Macdonald, Helen, *H Is for Hawk* (Hamish Hamilton, 2014), 218.

52 Muir, John, *John of the Mountains: The Unpublished Journals of John Muir*, Linnie Marsh Wolfe, ed. (University of Wisconsin Press, 1979), 220, 99.

53 Priestley, *Antarctic Adventure*, 279.

54 Ibid., 235.

55 Ibid., 279.

56 Ibid., 190.

57 Shackleton, Ernest. *Shackleton in the Antarctic: Being the Story of the British Antarctic Expedition, 1907–1909*, adapted from *The Heart of the Antarctic* (William Heinemann, 1911), 340.

58 Cherry-Garrard, *The Worst Journey in the World*, 192.

59 Weller, Francis, *The Wild Edge of Sorrow: Rituals of Renewal and the Sacred Work of Grief* (North Atlantic Books, 2015), 1–2.

SELECTED BIBLIOGRAPHY

Abram, Nerilie J., Ariaan Purich, Matthew H. England, Felicity S. McCormack, Jan M. Strugnell, Dana M. Bergstrom, Tessa R. Vance, Tobias Stål, Barbara Wienecke, Petra Heil, et al. "Emerging evidence of abrupt changes in the Antarctic environment." *Nature* 644 (2025): 621–633.

Abrams, Peter A., David G. Ainley, Louise K. Blight, Paul K. Dayton, Joseph T. Eastman, and Jennifer L. Jacquet. "Necessary elements of precautionary management: Implications for the Antarctic toothfish." *Fish & Fisheries* 17 (2016): 1152–74.

Ainley, David G. *The Adélie Penguin: Bellwether of Climate Change.* Columbia University Press, 2002.

Ainley, David G. "A history of the exploitation of the Ross Sea, Antarctica." *Polar Record* 46 (2010): 233–43.

Ainley, David G. "Insights from study of the last intact neritic marine ecosystem." *Trends in Ecology & Evolution* 22 (2007): 444–45.

Ainley, David G., and Louise K. Blight. "Ecological repercussions of historical fish extraction from the Southern Ocean." *Fish and Fisheries* 10 (2009): 13–38.

Ainley, David G., Virginia Morandini, Kerry J. Barton, Phil O'B. Lyver, Megan Elrod, Michelle A. LaRue, and Jean Pennycook. "Varying population size of the Cape Royds Adélie penguin colony, 1955–2020: A synthesis." *Antarctic Science* 36 (2024): 127–40.

Ainley, David G., and Rory P. Wilson. *The Aquatic World of Penguins: Biology of Fish-Birds*. Springer, 2023.

Anthony, Jason. *Hoosh: Roast Penguin, Scurvy Day, and Other Stories of Antarctic Cuisine*. University of Nebraska Press, 2012.

Ballard, Grant, Viola Toniolo, David G. Ainley, Claire L. Parkinson, Kevin R. Arrigo, and Philip N. Trathan. "Responding to climate change: Adélie penguins confront astronomical and ocean boundaries." *Ecology* 91, no. 7 (2010): 2056–69.

Blight, Louise K., and David G. Ainley. "Southern Ocean not so pristine." *Science* 321 (2008): 1443.

Blight, Louise K., David G. Ainley, Stephen F. Ackley, Grant Ballard, Tosca Ballerini, Robert L. Brownell Jr., C.-H. Christina Cheng, Mariachiara Chiantore, Daniel Costa, Malcolm C. Coulter, et al. "Fishing for data in the Ross Sea." *Science* 330 (2010): 1316.

British Antarctic Monument Trust. "Those Who Died: List by Date." 2025. https://www.antarctic-monument.org/those-who-did-not-return/those-killed-in-british-antarctic-territory.

Cherry-Garrard, Apsley. *The Worst Journey in the World: Antarctic 1910–1913*. 1922. Dover, 2010.

Davis, Lloyd S. *A Polar Affair.* Pegasus Books, 2019.

De Roy, Tui, Mark Jones, and Julie Cornthwaite. *Penguins: The Ultimate Guide*, 2nd ed. Princeton University Press, 2022.

de Waal, Frans. *Are We Smart Enough to Know How Smart Animals Are?* Norton, 2016.

Dodds, Klaus. "In 30 years the Antarctic Treaty becomes modifiable, and the fate of a continent could hang in the balance." *The Conversation,* 12 July 2018. https://theconversation.com/in-30-years-the-antarctic-treaty-becomes-modifiable-and-the-fate-of-a-continent-could-hang-in-the-balance-98654.

Ellsworth, Lincoln. "My Flight Across Antarctica." *National Geographic* 50, no. 1 (July 1936): 7.

Emslie, Steven D. "Ancient Adélie penguin colony revealed by snowmelt at Cape Irizar, Ross Sea, Antarctica." *Geology* 49 (2021):145–49.

Fiennes, Ranulph. *Shackleton: A Biography.* Penguin Random House UK, 2021.

Fountain, Andrew G., W. Berry Lyons, Melody B. Burkins, Gayle L. Dana, Peter T. Doran, Karen J. Lewis, Diane M. McKnight, Daryl L. Moorhead, Andrew N. Parsons, John C. Priscu, et al. "Physical controls on the Taylor Valley ecosystem, Antarctica." *BioScience* 49, no. 12 (1999), 961–71.

Fretwell, Peter T., Connor C. G. Bamford, Aliaksandra Skachkova, Philip N. Trathan, and Jaume Forcada. "Regional emperor penguin population declines exceed modelled projections." *Communications Earth & Environment* 6 (2025): 436.

Fretwell, Peter, and Lisa Fretwell. *The Penguin Book of Penguins: An Expert's Guide to the World's Most Beloved Bird*. Viking, 2025.

Fretwell, Peter T., and Philip N. Trathan. "Discovery of new colonies by Sentinel2 reveals good and bad news for emperor penguins." *Remote Sensing in Ecology and Conservation* 7, no. 2 (2021): 139–53.

Jenouvrier, Stéphanie, Marika Holland, David Iles, Sara Labrousse, Laura Landrum, Jimmy Garnier, Hal Caswell, Henri Weimerskirch, Michelle LaRue, Rubao Ji, et al. "The Paris Agreement objectives will likely halt future declines of emperor penguins." *Global Change Biology* 26 (2020): 1170–84.

Jenouvrier, Stéphanie, Marika Holland, Julienne Stroeve, Mark Serreze, Christophe Barbraud, Henri Weimerskirch, and Hal Caswell. "Projected continent-wide declines of the emperor penguin under climate change." *Nature Climate Change* 4 (2014): 715–18.

Johnson, Nicholas. *Big Dead Place: Inside the Strange and Menacing World of Antarctica*. Feral House, 2005.

Kittinger, John N., Loren McClenachan, Keryn B. Gedan, and Louise K. Blight, eds. *Marine Historical Ecology in Conservation: Using the Past to Manage for the Future*. University of California Press, 2015.

Kooyman, Gerald L., and Jim Mastro. *Journeys with Emperors:*

Tracking the World's Most Extreme Penguin. University of Chicago Press, 2023.

Lanting, Frans. *Penguins.* Terra Editions, 2011.

Lauriano, Giancarlo, Enrico Pirotta, Trevor Joyce, Robert L. Pitman, Asunción Borrell, and Simone Panigada. "Movements, diving behaviour and diet of type-C killer whales (*Orcinus orca*) in the Ross Sea, Antarctica." *Aquatic Conservation: Marine and Freshwater Ecosystems* 30, no. 12 (2020): 2428–40.

Lyver, Phil O'B., Mandy Barron, Kerry J. Barton, David G. Ainley, Annie Pollard, Shulamit Gordon, Stephen McNeill, Grant Ballard, and Peter R. Wilson. "Trends in the breeding population of Adélie penguins in the Ross Sea, 1981–2012: A coincidence of climate and resource extraction effects." *PLOS One* 9, no. 3 (2014): e91188.

Macdonald, Helen. *H Is for Hawk.* Hamish Hamilton, 2014.

Mawson, Douglas. *The Home of the Blizzard: Being the Story of the Australasian Antarctic Expedition, 1911–1914.* Hodder and Stoughton, 1915.

Mear, Roger, and Robert Swan. *In the Footsteps of Scott.* Grafton Books, 1987.

Murphy, Robert Cushman. *Logbook for Grace.* Time, 1947.

Neider, Charles. *Edge of the World: Ross Island, Antarctica; A Personal and Historical Narrative.* Doubleday, 1974.

Pauly, Daniel. "Anecdotes and the shifting baseline syndrome of fisheries." *Trends in Ecology and Evolution* 10, no. 10 (1995): 430.

Ritter, Christiane. *A Woman in the Polar Night.* Jane Degras, trans. Pushkin Press Classics, 2024.

Rush, Elizabeth. *The Quickening: Creation and Community at the Ends of the Earth.* Milkweed Editions, 2023.

Rykers, Ellen. "The Ice Man." *New Zealand Geographic* 180 (March–April 2023). https://www.nzgeo.com/stories/the-ice-man/.

Sancton, Julian. *Madhouse at the End of the Earth: The Belgica's Journey into the Dark Antarctic Night.* Crown, 2021.

Secretariat of the Antarctic Treaty. The Antarctic Treaty. 2025. ttps://www.ats.aq/e/antarctictreaty.html.

Shackleton, Ernest. *The Heart of the Antarctic: Being the Story of the British Antarctic Expedition 1907–1909,* popular ed. William Heinemann, 1911.

Shackleton, Ernest. *South: The Story of Shackleton's Last Expedition 1914–1917.* William Heinemann, 1919.

Shirihai, Hadoram. *A Complete Guide to Antarctic Wildlife,* 2nd ed. Bloomsbury, 2007.

Stroud, Mike. *Shadows on the Wasteland: Crossing Antarctica with Ranulph Fiennes.* Overlook Press, 1993.

Trathan, Philip N., Peter T. Fretwell, and Bernard Stonehouse. "First recorded loss of an emperor penguin colony in the recent period of Antarctic regional warming: implications for other colonies." *PLoS ONE* 6 (2011): e14738.

Weller, Francis. *The Wild Edge of Sorrow: Rituals of Renewal and the Sacred Work of Grief.* North Atlantic Books, 2015.

Weller, John. *The Last Ocean: Antarctica's Ross Sea Project: Saving the Most Pristine Ecosystem on Earth.* Rizzoli, 2013.

Wheeler, Sara. *Terra Incognita: Travels in Antarctica.* Random House, 1996.

Wilson, David M. *The Lost Photographs of Captain Scott: Unseen Photographs from the Legendary Antarctic Expedition.* Little, Brown, 2011.

Young, Euan. *Skua and Penguin: Predator and Prey.* Cambridge University Press, 1994.

ACKNOWLEDGEMENTS

THIS BOOK TOOK a while to see the light of day. I'd like to thank those who believed in its potential while I conceived of it and encouraged me at key points to keep writing. These people include Peter Abrams, Fran Backhouse, Johnnie Christmas, Lisa Eccles, Janos Maté, Kathryn McCannell, Bryan Murray, Linda Nowlan, Andréa Olson, Nick Page, Janet Pelley, Jo Smith, and Richard Thompson. Particular thanks go to John for our conversations about the writing life and developing plot and story.

In October 2019, I participated in the Mountain and Wilderness Writers residency at the Banff Centre for the Arts and Creativity—along with Maria Coffey, Gloria Dickie, Martina Halik, Brian Hall, Michael Kennedy, Kate Rawles, Rhiannon Russell, Katherine Leonard, and faculty members Anthony Whittome, Marni Jackson, and Harley Rustad. There we all immediately formed a tight-knit group committed to supporting each other's projects. This support continued after the residency ended, with most of us reconvening in 2020 to form an international writing group that began meeting on Zoom in the early days of the COVID-19 pandemic, and we have carried on meeting to this day. I am grateful to every member of the group for the productive environment that it collectively fostered, and it has been a delight to see the many books and other publications that have emerged from it (and are still emerging).

Two earlier residencies at the Banff Centre were foundational, and I'd particularly like to acknowledge the motivation and encouragement provided by faculty members there, particularly Wayne Grady, Curtis Gillespie, and Sarah Musgrave. Thanks are also due to the Banff Centre's Literary Arts program itself, and to the funders who support its residents—especially the W. O. Mitchell Endowment. I am deeply grateful to my wonderful agent, Jackie Kaiser, for her warm support and wise guidance. I also thank Meg Wheeler, Bridgette Kam, Caroline Vassallo, and everyone else at Westwood Creative Artists. Nicole Maher at Pegasus Books is a delight to work with. Thanks go to Alexandra King and Talia Abramson for their excellent map-making and design skills, to Gillian Watts for her stellar indexing skills, and to Peter Norman, who elevates copy-editing to an art. The talented Pam Gregoriadis of Aiota Photography provided the author photo.

David Ainley, Michael Kennedy, Lora Morandin, Rachael Orben, Di Roberts, and Jo Anne Walton were early readers of the completed manuscript, and I thank each of them for their insightful comments and corrections. Any remaining errors are mine alone! Harley Rustad provided a quiet creative space at his Port Renfrew Writers Retreat, at a crucial point in the manuscript's development. I owe the deepest thanks to David Ainley, Doug Bertram, Alan Burger, Tony D. Williams, and Eric Woehler for being friends as well as mentors on my journey into the world of studying seabirds, and beyond.

On the family front, I would like to say thanks to Matt and Alex Champagne for being part of mine. And as always, I am deeply grateful to Iain Duncan for his unwavering love and moral and practical support in this, and in many other things in life. Finally, I send love to Tiger the cat for keeping my lap warm through the many stages of the writing process, until almost the end.

INDEX

Note: "New Zealand" is abbreviated to "NZ." Page numbers followed by "n" indicate a footnote.

ABOUT THE AUTHOR

LOUISE K. BLIGHT is a conservation scientist with a PhD in zoology from the University of British Columbia. An adjunct professor at the University of Victoria's School of Environmental Studies, she is also co-chair of the birds specialist group of the Committee on the Status of Endangered Wildlife in Canada, the expert national body that assesses threatened species. Louise lives on Salt Spring Island, British Columbia, with her partner, their dog, and two indoor cats.